THE ILLUSTRATED HARDWARE BOOK

Other books in the
HOMEOWNER'S LIBRARY SERIES

The ILLUSTRATED HARDWARE BOOK

TOM PHILBIN
and the Editors
of Consumer Reports Books

Line Drawings by Lynne Edler

CONSUMER REPORTS BOOKS
A DIVISION OF CONSUMERS UNION
YONKERS, NEW YORK

Library of Congress Cataloging-in-Publication Data

Philbin, Tom, 1934–
    The illustrated hardware book / Tom Philbin and the editors of
Consumer Reports Books ; line drawings by Lynne Edler.
        p.   cm.
    Rev. and expanded ed. of: The encyclopedia of hardware. c1978.
    Includes index.
    ISBN 0-89043-417-4 :
    1. Hardware.   I. Philbin, Tom, 1934-   Encyclopedia of hardware.
II. Consumer Reports Books.   III.   Title.

                                                                91-48159
                                                                CIP

Design by Ruth Kolbert

First printing, April 1992

Manufactured in the United States of America

To Hardware Lovers Everywhere . . .

ACKNOWLEDGMENTS

My thanks to John Trench, A&B Hardware in Huntington Station, Hugh and Mary Devaney at Centerport Hardware, and Don Klecher at Laurel Hardware in Northport.

My thanks also to those nameless folks I've met, across my years as a "how-to" writer, who furnished me with so many of the wonderful tips that I am now passing on to others.

Finally, and most important, my profound thanks to Dave Shannon, the chief consultant on this book, who delighted and enthralled me with his seemingly bottomless well of knowledge about hardware and how to use it. Though I've been writing in this field for 25 years, he made me feel like a student—one who looked forward to school every day.

CONTENTS

ELECTRICAL HARDWARE

PLUMBING HARDWARE

PREFACE

This book is designed to give the average person a comprehensive, detailed look at what is commonly available in hardware stores. At the same time it serves as a buying guide—information that will help determine what piece of hardware is best for a particular job. In other words, you are not only told what is there, but also what is best. In addition, there is abundant advice on how to use the items.

The book is not intended as a complete guide to how to use hardware yourself. Rather, the information is more along the lines, though not exclusively, of insider's tips—very handy hints rather than all the steps necessary to do the job. For example, an aluminum sheet can be cut with snips, but snips tend to bend it. A better technique is to score it and fold it back and forth at the score line—it will sever cleanly.

In many cases, detailed how-to instructions are on the package. There are also numerous how-to books available at the library, and dealers can help. We like to think, though, that much of what you will read in this book is not available on packages, or even in other books.

Four categories of hardware are covered: general, electrical, plumbing, and miscellaneous. This last category is a potpourri of things that may not be, in the strictest sense, hardware, but that cry out for inclusion.

Most of what is included here are standard, everyday things—nails, screws, bolts, and so forth—but there are a few truly amazing items, such as gimp tacks and lead wool.

The information on the items is organized as follows:

NAME OF ITEM
Description: What the item looks like
Buying information: What the item is used for, and how it may be better than comparable items for particular uses
How-to hints: Tips on working with the item

Of the items listed, 208 of the most common pieces of hardware are depicted in accurate, detailed line drawings. On your next trip to the hardware store, you'll find it helpful to know not only that you need pan-head sheet metal screws but that you know what they look like compared to regular sheet metal screws or machine screws or flathead screws, all of which may reside side-by-side in unmarked bins.

Before going to the items, we suggest that you read Appendix A on metals and finishes. Hardware items come in a wide variety of metals and finishes, and knowing the distinctions among them will affect your buying decision. For example, hot-dipped galvanized items endure weathering much longer than galvanized non-hot-dipped ones.

This book is only about hardware in its purest sense. Tools, which are sometimes thought of as hardware, are not covered. Normally, just simple tools are needed to use the hardware we describe. In some cases, though, special tools, such as a ''handle puller'' to take apart a balky faucet, can make the job much easier. Readers have been alerted to the proper tools as required.

In addition, we have provided Ratings of other hardware products (some tools are included) in Appendix C that have been culled from previous issues of *Consumer Reports* for your reference as you enter the world of hardware.

GENERAL

HARDWARE

BRACES

Braces is a term used to describe a variety of hardware items that differ in size and shape but have a common function: to strengthen joints on wood. Some braces are interchangeable; different ones can be used for the same job.

CORNER BRACE

Description: This is an L-shaped piece that looks like a bent bar. It has screw holes for mounting and comes in sizes from 1 inch long by ½ inch wide to 8 inches long by more than 1 inch wide.

Buying information: As the sizes get larger (over 5 inches), screw holes are normally staggered rather than being in one line. Corner braces are good for strengthening and supporting box corners and window and door frames.

How-to hint: Mount braces on inside corners, first drilling pilot holes for screws.

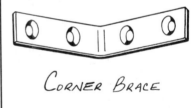

CORNER BRACE

T PLATE

Description: T plate, as the name implies, is the shape of the letter T, with both horizontal and vertical legs.

Buying information: It is good for strengthening screen-frame members and garage door sections.

How-to hints: If you have a particularly stressful job for a T plate (such as joining loose garage door parts), coat the screws with glue before installing them. A bar clamp is handy for holding the frame parts in position as you work on them.

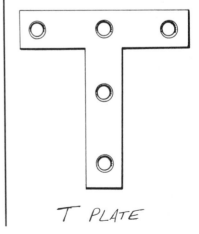

T PLATE

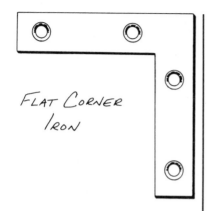

FLAT CORNER IRON

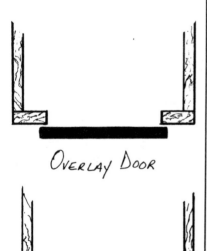

CHAIR BRACE

FLUSH DOOR (TOP VIEW)

OVERLAY DOOR

LIPPED DOOR

FLAT CORNER IRON
Description: This is shaped like the letter L, but is flat rather than bent like the corner brace. It is available in various sizes.
Buying information: It has a wide variety of uses. Typical is for strengthening boxes and screen doors, because the iron lies flat.
How-to hints: Use a 45-degree pressure clamp to hold frame parts in position as you secure the iron. Mount the iron on the face of the piece.

MENDING PLATE
Description: This is a flat piece of steel with staggered screw holes. It comes in sizes up to 8 inches long.
Buying information: A mending plate is versatile, probably used more than any other brace. It is particularly good for fastening boards end to end.

CHAIR BRACE
Description: This is an L-shaped piece with screw holes.
Buying information: Chair braces are shaped to fit easily into chairs at their joints. They come with screws, ready for use.

CABINET DOOR HARDWARE

There are a number of pieces of hardware designed to be used on cabinet doors, namely, hinges, catches, and knobs and pulls.

Cabinet hinges are made in a variety of styles, but design dictates upon which type of door they may be used.

There are three types of doors: flush, overlay, and lipped or recessed. The flush door fits within the cabinet frame, its face flush with the cabinet framework. The overlay door slightly overlaps the cabinet opening all around. The lipped door has a rabbet, or recess, cut in the edges.

Hinges come in a variety of finishes as well as metals, and though there are complicated formulas for installing them, the plain fact is that hinges are many times stronger than they need to be. Hence, the best way to get the correct size is by proportion: just pick a hinge size that seems in proper proportion to the door size—it is certain to be strong enough.

The tips above apply to new hinges. If the hinge is a replacement, simply bring the old one into the store so it can be easily identified.

Most hinges come "carded," a trade term meaning packaged, and most packages have instructions for installing the hinges. The package itself is sometimes used as a template for making the hinge holes.

You should, of course, match the pulls or knobs to the hinges used and cabinet style. This shouldn't be any problem because these items are available in a wide variety of styles and colors that harmonize with hinges.

Hinges

BUTTERFLY HINGE

Description: The hinge leaves look like wings on a butterfly. It usually comes in brass or brass plating; there are also some painted black wrought-iron versions.

Buying information: It is designed to be used on flush doors. Many people also use it on cabinet lids. There is a butterfly hinge variation with an offset that can be used on lipped doors.

BUTTERFLY HINGE

SELF-CLOSING HINGE

Description: This has two straight rectangular leaves with a nylon insert. It is available with various platings—chrome, brass, copper—and in black and white.

Buying information: This hinge can be used on all types of cabinet doors.

How-to hint: A door with this type of hinge is self-closing, as the name implies, so it tends to bang when closed. To reduce the noise and stress on the door, stick "dampers"—circles of felt or other material with a self-stick backing—on the top and bottom of the door to absorb the shock.

Since the hinges are self-closing, magnetic catches do not have to be used.

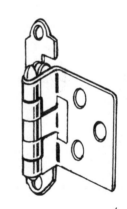

SELF-CLOSING HINGE

PIVOT HINGE

Description: This has bent-over leaves pinned together at the top. It commonly comes in chrome or is cadmium plated.

Buying information: This hinge is designed to be used on overlay and flush doors only, and is completely hidden when installed.

How-to hint: Pivot hinges are difficult to install and adjust unless you are familiar with the procedures.

PIVOT HINGE

Soss Hinge

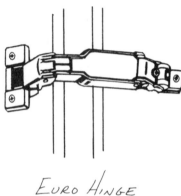

Euro Hinge

Soss Hinge

Description: This is a hinge for a flush door, designed to be completely hidden when the door is shut. It is usually brass-plated.

Buying information: For use on flush doors at least ¾ inch thick, this is a very strong hinge, available in five or six sizes, some large enough to be used on a standard-size door.

How-to hint: These are not simple to install: perfectly matching holes must be drilled into the cabinet frame and door edge to accept the barrellike hinge leaves. There is a jig (template) for making the holes in the right spots, and we strongly recommend that you use it.

Euro Hinge

Description: Nickel-plated, heavy, hooklike.

Buying information: This is a very popular hinge with contractors because, with the right equipment, it is easy to install.

How-to hint: You need a special drill bit and jig to hold it while you drill the holes for the hinge.

H or L Hinge

Description: This resembles the letters H or L; it has a black or copper-plated finish and comes with hammered (pyramid-style) screws.

Buying information: This hinge can be used on flush or inset doors. It is usually used on Colonial and Early American–style cabinets.

How-to hint: It is very easy to install. Lay the door flat and screw on the hinges.

Catches

A catch usually consists of two parts: a part that mounts on the door and another that mounts on the cabinet. Three kinds are common—magnetic, friction, and roller—and each can be used on any kind of door.

Magnetic Catch

Description: A rectangular portion mounts on the door and a right-angled, nonmagnetic piece mounts on the cabinet.

Buying information: Like all catches, it is designed for use only

Magnetic Catch

on lightweight doors. The magnetic catch is widely regarded as the best type of catch because it works on warped doors, where only part of it contacts the door.

There are variations of the magnetic catch that can handle heavier doors and doors of special design.

Friction Catch

Description: It has a female part that mounts on the cabinet and a male part on the door. The catch is spring-loaded.

Buying information: This is a good catch when you don't want the catch to show.

How-to hint: Friction catches are more difficult to install than magnetic catches.

Roller Catch

Description: This looks a bit like the friction catch, except the female part consists of rollers that engage the male portion.

Buying information: A roller catch is easier to open and close than other types, but wears out more quickly.

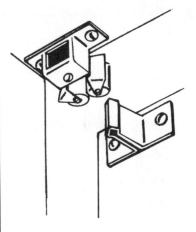

Roller Catch

Touch Latch Catch

Description: It looks like a friction catch.

Buying information: This is a very handy catch because it can be opened with a touch. When closed it cocks, ready to open.

Knobs and Pulls

Knobs and pulls are available in a vast variety of styles to match every conceivable decor.

Pull

Description: Pulls vary greatly, but they usually have two screw holes for mounting to the door.

How-to hint: Getting the screw holes in the right place on a door can be tricky, so a jig (template) is definitely suggested.

Knob

Description: Like pulls, knobs come in a huge array of styles.

Buying information: Knobs can be bought that attach with a screw through a hole in the door, or have a built-in screw.

How-to hint: Use a jig to make holes, particularly if you are installing knobs on many cabinets—for a good appearance, all knobs should be positioned uniformly.

CABLE

Braided cable is generally useful around the home, and it is usually much stronger than simple wire.

CABLE

Description: Braided cable consists of six or seven braided strands of wire wrapped around either a steel or fiber core. If six strands, the core is fiber; if seven, steel. Steel cable also comes twisted. The strands may be plain steel, galvanized, or stainless.

Cable may also be plastic-coated—usually the plastic is clear, but it may also be clear blue. Plastic-coated cable is much thinner than cable without plastic.

Buying information: Stainless steel cable is very expensive and is mostly used in marine applications. Plain steel is used indoors, such as in garage door mechanisms or with a turnbuckle for straightening a door. Galvanized cable is for outdoor applications, such as a tether on a garbage can or straightening an exterior door. Fiber-core cable is more flexible than steel-core cable, and is a good choice when greater flexibility—such as where cable must wrap around a pulley—is required. Clear plastic-coated cable is good wherever less visibility is desired; blue is good for high visibility. Many people use it for tethers on dog runs.

How-to hints: Braided cable is a tough material and should be cut with either aviation scissors or a cold chisel. It can also be cut with new, good-quality bolt cutters. Ends tend to unravel. To prevent this, first wrap electrical tape over the cut line, an inch or two to either side, then cut. Plastic-coated cable can be cut with tin snips. You can prevent cable rusting by applying dots of epoxy glue to the cut ends.

CASTERS

Casters are available with many features that should be linked to the job you have in mind.

One factor to consider is the weight of the item to which the casters will be attached. Casters for a heavy dresser would be different from those for a TV stand. Casters commonly come packaged, and the package usually lists the weight they can support and the types of items—beds, couches, refrigerators—that use them best.

Some casters swivel 360 degrees. While this may be a convenient feature on something like a dresser, it can be inconvenient on a refrigerator, making it move unpredictably.

There are also casters that lock. This feature is useful on a bed, particularly a child's bed. If the child flops on the bed, it won't take him or her for a ride.

Caster wheels may be hard or soft, rubber or plastic. Hard rubber wheels are good on concrete floors; soft rubber is good on resilient flooring (sheet or tile); plastic is good on carpet.

Some casters have metal wheels. One type is for heavy industrial uses, but another is the ball type that is used on furniture for esthetic purposes. They come in several colors and finishes, such as brass and chrome.

Caster wheels vary in size. Two-inch casters have wheels with a 2-inch diameter. The larger the wheel, the more easily the caster rolls.

BALL CASTER

STEM CASTER

Description: This has a metal tube or projection extending up from a metal frame in which the wheel rides.

Buying information: Stems vary in size; the bigger the wheel, the bigger the stem. Stem casters are made for mounting in legs that have corresponding sockets, either metal or simply holes drilled in the legs. They are particularly good on legs that are ragged or in otherwise poor condition.

How-to hints: Installation of stem casters may involve just inserting them into the leg sockets. In some cases, though, you'll have to drill new holes for sockets. If the sockets are too large for the stems, wrap the stems with masking tape or cellophane tape for a snug fit. You can also get a ridged nylon insert that can be forced into the socket hole; when the stem is inserted into this, it will hold solidly.

STEM CASTER

PLATE CASTER

Description: The caster wheel is attached to a frame on which is a flat metal plate with holes in it for screws.

PLATE CASTER

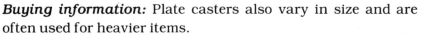

Buying information: Plate casters also vary in size and are often used for heavier items.

How-to hint: If the legs holding the caster are ragged, saw them off evenly, drill pilot holes for screws, then reattach casters using screws as long as is practical.

BALL BEARING CASTER

Description: This resembles an acorn with a metal ring on top with holes for attachment to the item, and part of the ball bearing exposed at the bottom.

Buying information: These wheels have rotating balls at the heart of the mechanism. They don't roll as well as casters with wheels, but have an advantage in that, when mounted, only about ½ inch of the caster projects; in other words, only ½ inch in height is added to the item, rather than the average 2 inches of wheel casters. Consequently, they may be a good choice where there is a shortage of headroom. On the negative side, all the weight is focused on one point on the ball, and this can lead to marks on floors if items are very heavy. Vinyl and wood floors are particularly vulnerable.

BALL BEARING CASTER

CHAIN

A great many types of chain are available, but the chain you can buy at hardware stores should be sufficient for most of your needs. Chain is commonly sold off 100-foot reels, and you can buy the exact footage needed; the dealer will cut it to order.

Chain can be divided into two groups: that which is used for decorative purposes and types whose primary function is strength. No matter what kind you buy, however, observe what is known in the trade as the working-load limit. All chain is tested for this, and it indicates the maximum amount of stress a chain can safely take under a steady pull.

Load limits vary greatly, depending on the metal the chain is made of and its diameter—the thickness of the wire. One-quarter-inch decorative brass jack chain, for example, has a working load limit of 10 pounds. But grade 30 proof coil chain has a working load limit of 1,250 pounds. Before you buy chain, make sure it is strong enough for your job. The dealer should be able to furnish you with these limits.

JACK CHAIN

Description: One style of jack chain has bow-shaped links and comes in various sizes with links up to ¼ inch in diameter. Another style looks like twisted S hooks that have been joined. It is available in solid brass or in galvanized, zinc-coated, or copper-plated steel.

Buying information: Jack chain can be used for both decoration and support.

How-to hint: Diagonal side-cutting pliers do a good job of cutting this chain in smaller sizes.

TWIST-LINK JACK CHAIN

SINGLE JACK CHAIN

MACHINE CHAIN

Description: This is a short-link welded chain; that is, the individual links are welded shut. It comes in straight-link and twisted-link styles; the former has links that are elliptical, the latter has links that are elliptical and twisted.

Buying information: Welded chain is the strongest type you can get. You will see machine chain used on overhead doors, tailgates, and agricultural implements.

How-to hint: It can be cut with bolt cutters or clamped in a vise and cut with a hacksaw.

STRAIGHT-LINK MACHINE CHAIN

GRADE 30 PROOF COIL CHAIN

Description: This resembles machine chain, but with heavier links. It comes in plain, galvanized, or zinc-coated steel.

Buying information: This type of chain is somewhat stronger than machine chain. It comes in various diameters. The ¼-inch size has a working load limit of 1,250 pounds; ⁵⁄₁₆-inch chain has a working load limit of 1,900 pounds. (If you need something stronger, get high-test grade 70 chain.) It is used for lifting engines and other jobs where great strength is required.

How-to hint: Links on this chain are shaped so that, when looped around something, the chain will grab and hold.

SASH CHAIN

Description: This has flat links either diamond- or oval-shaped. It comes copper-plated or sprayed with aluminum.

Buying information: Sash chain is used for double-hung windows. Since it is flat, it rides easily over pulleys. It is a good chain for replacing rope. (Rope is a better choice in areas close to the sea, where metal chain could deteriorate.)

How-to hint: Cut with the cutting jaws on slip-joint pliers.

SASH CHAIN

SAFETY CHAIN

DECORATIVE CHAIN

SAFETY CHAIN

Description: Also known as plumber's chain, this is a flat chain that closely resembles sash chain. It comes in closed and open S-hook-like links, in brass or in zinc-coated or stainless steel.

Buying information: This is a general utility chain and can be used for decorative purposes. Stainless safety chain is used in toilet tanks to raise and lower a flapper-type valve ball, and as a linkage on vertical blinds.

How-to hint: Cut with household scissors or side-cutting pliers.

DECORATIVE CHAIN

Description: This consists of large, thin, oval links, and comes in numerous colors as well as brass.

Buying information: Decorative chain is used to hang plants from the ceiling. Fancy toggle bolts or other hooks are usually secured to the ceiling from which the chain is hung.

How-to hint: Links on this chain can be pried apart with a pair of screwdrivers or inexpensive wedge pliers, which do the job with less likelihood of marring the finish.

BEAD CHAIN

Description: Bead chain may be hollow round beads (the balls are hollow, joined by dumbbell-shaped connectors) or a series of alternating round and elliptical beads. It comes chrome-plated, nickel-plated, and in stainless steel.

Buying information: Bead chain is sold by the foot in various sizes, and is also packaged for specific purposes, such as a pull cord for a lamp, but it is primarily used for decorative purposes around the home. It comes in "A" link (beads connected to one another) and "B" link (beads with an eyelet intended to be fastened to a wall with a screw). It is a good choice where a chain that won't twist or kink is required.

How-to hint: Bead chain can be cut with diagonal side-cutting pliers.

CHAIN ACCESSORIES

An assortment of accessories and attachments are available for chain. A common mistake is to select an undersized attachment. In essence, any connector or accessory used must be as strong as any link in the chain. Hardware store dealers can help you determine this.

S Hook

Description: As its name suggests, the hook is shaped like the letter S.

Buying information: S hooks come in various sizes and strengths and are for linking chain sections where safety is a prime concern, such as for backyard swings, play equipment, and the like. Any S hook should, as mentioned above, be as strong as any chain link under working load.

How-to hint: After attachment, use pliers to crimp the S hooks shut so that the chain links can't slip out.

Clevis Slip Hook

Description: This is shaped like a beefy fishhook.

Buying information: A clevis slip hook secured to the end of a chain works like a lasso. It can be looped around something, hooked to the chain, and tightened.

How-to hint: Attach the shank end of the hook to the chain; slip on the hook and slide it along the chain until all the slack is taken up; it will grip securely so you can pull on the other end of the chain without the "lasso" pulling off. For example, if you were pulling out a tree stump, you could get a tight hold before pulling the chain.

Clevis Grab Hook

Description: The clevis grab hook looks like the slip hook, but the curved portion is narrower.

Buying information: Since it's narrower, the grab hook will take better hold between links than the slip hook, making it good for applications where a fixed loop is desirable. The grab hook is more likely to get snagged, so use the slip hook when you want to be sure the chain will release.

Connecting Link (also called Mash Link)

Description: Picture a chain link laid flat and cut in half, and you have the essential shape of a connecting link.

Buying information: Connecting links are for permanently connecting lengths of chain and other attachments, and do the same job as individual links.

How-to hints: To form a connecting link, use a heavy hammer to pound the rivet on one half of the link into the opening on the other. Links can also be welded shut, but this is not essential for

CLEVIS SLIP HOOK

CLEVIS GRAB HOOK

CONNECTING LINK

strength. The connecting link should be the same size as the chain's links. If the chain has ⁵⁄₁₆-inch links, that's the size the connecting link should be.

SWIVEL SNAP

Description: This looks like a closed hook. It comes in many sizes and in stainless steel and bronze.

Buying information: Swivel snaps snap onto whatever you wish and rotate 360 degrees freely, also allowing the chain to rotate.

COLD SHUT

Description: This looks like an open link, one end of which is male, the other female. It comes zinc-plated and galvanized.

Buying information: Cold shuts are available in various sizes, and are used to connect chain lengths or hooks.

How-to hints: To close a cold shut, use a heavy hammer to pound the male end into the female end. For more strength, weld the connecting point.

COLD SHUT

LAP LINK

Description: This looks like an elongated link sliced in half at one end.

Buying information: Lap links are open at one end and are used where temporary fastening is required and safety is not a large factor—that is, where people would not be hurt or property damaged if they failed.

How-to hint: To close a lap link, simply squeeze the open end shut with a vise, or pound it with a hammer.

END OPEN LAP LINK

RING

Description: This is a circle of metal available in galvanized or brass-plated steel.

Buying information: Rings have a variety of uses; they may be used as a tether for rope, and are common components of saddle and bridle equipment.

CLAMPS

A variety of clamps are available. The most common is the worm-gear hose clamp, but there is another, used on cable, that is useful to know about.

WORM-GEAR HOSE CLAMP

Description: This is a perforated band of stainless steel with a barrellike worm-gear drive, one end of which is slotted to accept a screwdriver.

Buying information: Hose clamps come in many sizes characterized by number, generally ranging from 6 to 64. Number 6 is for a ⅜-inch diameter hose; number 64 is large enough to be used with a 3½- to 4-inch diameter material (such as smoke pipe). In the smaller sizes the clamps come already assembled, but in the larger sizes they come as flat strips that are put together by slipping the ends into the worm gear. For maximum resistance to corrosion, in outdoor or marine applications, be sure to get the all-stainless variety; on some brands the worm and housing are only zinc-plated.

How-to hint: Hose clamps can be linked together to form very large, individual-sized clamps for handling things up to a couple of feet in diameter.

Worm-Gear Hose Clamp

CABLE CLAMP

Description: This clamp consists of two flat pieces of metal with grooves inside, which, when assembled, form a sort of metal sandwich. It comes cadmium-plated and galvanized.

Buying information: This is used for making loops at the end of cable. The clamps have grooves in various sizes (commonly ⅛ inch, ³⁄₁₆ inch, and ¼ inch) into which you can lay the cable.

How-to hints: Make sure to select the correct size clamp: if it's too big, the cable could slip out. You can use an extra clamp below the first and also secure either or both of these with a plastic tie.

CLOSET DOOR HARDWARE

There are three kinds of hardware for closet doors: standard, sliding, and bifold. Standard is essentially door locks and handles (see pages 16–19). Sliding and bifold require specialized hardware, and these items are covered here.

SLIDING CLOSET DOOR HARDWARE

Description: Closet door hardware comes in kit form and usually consists of wheels, track, wheel brackets, and a floor guide.

Buying information: Different manufacturers make the hardware in different sizes and forms; thus, on a one-to-one replacement basis, there is no guarantee that one company's wheels, for example, can be used to replace another's. But in kit form the pieces are made to fit a particular door size (1⅜ inches or ¾ inch).

How-to hints: Sliding doors are easier to hang than bifold doors because they allow room for error. Sliding doors should overlap 1 inch, but a ½-inch overlap will work, and so will a 2-inch overlap.

Track comes in lengths of 4, 5, and 6 feet, but these can be easily cut down with a hacksaw. Also, wheel brackets—one straight and one bent—are made so they can be used on standard ¾-inch or 1⅜-inch doors.

Installation instructions come with the kit. These are written for replacing a door in an existing opening, but they can be adapted for new work.

BIFOLD CLOSET DOOR HARDWARE

Description: Several different pieces of hardware are used on a bifold door: track; a U-shaped bracket for aligning the doors at the bottom; an L-shaped socket that accepts a pivot on the door; hinges (mortise or butt style); and a "snubber," a spring device that helps keep the door closed.

Buying information: Closet door hardware comes in kit form containing all the parts necessary to install a door. Handles are usually not supplied. Hinges are usually brass-plated. Use butt rather than mortise (recessed) hinges if the door will be used frequently.

How-to hint: This is a very difficult door to hang. Installation instructions are normally supplied.

DOOR LOCKS

There are two kinds of door locks for the home: exterior and interior. For security, exterior locks are built more ruggedly than interior ones, and manufacturers also put greater care into their design and finish.

Door locks come in many different styles, with most of the

style variations occurring in exterior locks, which are available in everything from fancy filigree to brass-plated, the latter being the way most door locks are finished.

Prices can vary widely—up to hundreds of dollars—but paying a lot for a lock does not guarantee quality. What you pay for is style. However, if you pay a lot for a lock with a brass-plated finish, chances are you will get a top-quality lock; that is, the mechanism will be more durable and work better than less costly locks.

Interior and exterior door locks come with installation instructions. When shopping for a replacement, the key consideration is the ''backset''—the distance from the middle of the knob, or handle, to the edge of the door. Most locks have a 2⅜-inch backset and are installed in a 2⅛-inch diameter hole; some, however, are installed in a 1¾-inch hole. It's a good idea to stick with brand names when shopping for a lock. Many times there are subtle size differences among brands that can lead to installation difficulties.

Door lock selection is limited in hardware stores and lumberyards. To get a wider selection, ask to see lock catalogs or go to a wholesale outlet that sells to the trade and see what they have on hand.

Note that some locks, although they are called door locks, do not have a locking mechanism.

Interior Door Locks

PASSAGE LOCK
Description: This looks like any lock with a latch mechanism and two doorknobs.
Buying information: This lock has no locking mechanism and is designed for use on interior doors—bedroom, bathroom—where security is not a concern.
How-to hint: The hole for the center of the lock is normally made 37 inches from the floor.

PASSAGE LOCK

PRIVACY LOCK
Description: This looks like a passage lock but has a button inside and a small hole outside in which a small screwdriver can be inserted to open the door in case of an emergency.
Buying information: This type of lock is useful when some degree of security is wanted on, say, a bedroom door. Pushing

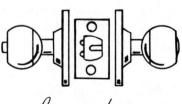

PRIVACY LOCK

the button locks the door. Many of these locks come with a special key or rod that enables them to be opened from the outside—handy if a child locks him- or herself inside a room. If there is no key or rod, sometimes a stiff bit of wire or a length of coat hanger will do.

BATHROOM LOCK

Description: This looks just like a privacy lock except that it's normally chrome-plated inside (brass-plated outside) to harmonize with other chrome items in the bath.

How-to hint: When a child gets locked in a room, it's usually the bath. Keep a rod or special key nearby, or drill a small hole in the top molding and store the key there.

Exterior Door Locks

Exterior locks furnish varying degrees of security. In a deadbolt lock, also called a deadlock, when the latch on the lock goes into the "strike" or slot on the door, it cannot be sprung free; a doorknob or latch has to be turned to open it.

The cylinder is the portion of the lock into which the key is inserted, and which turns to open or close the lock.

Most exterior locks are brass-plated steel, but some are solid brass. The latter are optimum in quality and very expensive.

When replacing any lock, try to get the same brand name. Some brands differ slightly in size, and this can create problems.

Incidentally, if you buy a prehung door, it will come with the lock hardware and the hole drilled for that hardware. There is no room for error.

SINGLE-CYLINDER DEADLOCK

Description: This lock is opened and closed with a key from the outside and opened and closed with a latch from the inside.

Buying information: This lock is easy for children to use.

How-to hint: Most locks are designed to fit a standard 1¾-inch door. If the door is a different size, you can buy adapters.

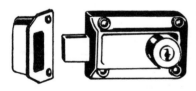

SINGLE-CYLINDER DEADLOCK

ENTRY LOCK

Description: This lock comes with a knob outside and inside the door. It has a keyway.

Buying information: This is a standard entry lock, opened with a key from the outside and with a knob from the inside.

How-to hint: For convenience, the lock should be 37 to 38 inches from the floor.

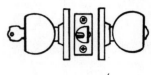

ENTRY LOCK

DOUBLE-CYLINDER DEADLOCK

Description: This lock opens and closes with a key from the outside and the inside.

Buying information: This is an excellent security lock. Even if the door has glass panels, a burglar can't break a pane of glass and then reach in to turn the lock; you can only open it by key.

Also, on a back door, such a lock can deter a burglar who has gained entry through the front of the house from staying too long if he has planned an exit from the back.

The lock can be hazardous, however, if you have to get out fast, as in a fire. Opening this lock from the inside may be very difficult in a smoky, high-stress environment.

DOUBLE-CYLINDER
DEADLOCK

MORTISE LOCK

Description: This is a squarish box.

Buying information: A mortise lock is expensive, but it is the ultimate in security. It is installed completely inside the door in a recess or mortise, and is very difficult to pick.

How-to hint: This is a difficult lock to install.

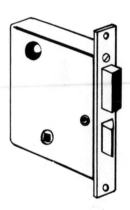

MORTISE LOCK

NIGHT LATCH (SLAM LOCK)

Description: This is a squarish lock with a prominent latch.

Buying information: This lock slams shut when you close it, a convenience. There is no key. It opens with a knob.

How-to hint: Mount on the surface of the door.

RIM LOCK

Description: This is a rectangular lock with one rounded end and rings through which the strike slips when closed. It also has a knob on the inside of the lock.

Buying information: A rim lock is similar to the night latch in that it has no key. It is considered jimmy-proof.

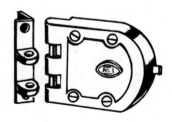

RIM LOCK

DOORSTOPS

SOLID DOORSTOP

Description: This is a slim, 3-inch-long, brass-plated casting with a plate at one end for mounting, and a rubber pad at the other, to prevent marring.

Buying information: This doorstop is designed to prevent the doorknob from banging into the wall when the door has opened too far.

How-to hint: If you have children, it's probably best to install the doorstop on the baseboard rather than on the door where children like to ride it—and eventually it breaks off.

SPRING-LOADED DOORSTOP

Description: This consists of a tight, rigid spring with a plate for mounting.

Buying information: It has the same purpose as a solid doorstop.

How-to hint: It can be installed on a door or wall. Since it will bend if stepped on, it discourages free rides.

ADJUSTABLE DOORSTOP

Description: This looks like a spring with a threaded end.

Buying information: When installed on a door hinge, it will stop the door from banging into a wall when it is not possible to install a stop in a regular position.

How-to hint: To install, just remove the hinge pin, drop the stop in place, and replace the pin.

DRAPERY HARDWARE

One overall tip for drapery hardware is not to use any nails to mount it, even if they are provided. Instead use small screws, first drilling pilot holes for them. If the molding that the hardware is mounted on is old and brittle, nails will split it, and so will screws that are used without first drilling pilot holes.

ROD

Description: This is a hollow, brass-plated tube in two lengths—28 to 48 inches and 48 to 86 inches, adjustable within those dimensions. It comes in brass, white, and walnut grained to simulate wood.

Buying information: Rings are slipped over the rod, and then fasteners are attached to these from which the draperies are hung.

How-to hint: If the rod required is close to 48 inches, say, 46 or 47 inches, purchase the next larger size rather than stretch out the rod close to its maximum capacity.

TRAVERSE ROD

Description: This is an adjustable horizontal bar usually 24 to 156 inches long, with eyes, manipulated by cords on the ends, that slide back and forth on it. Drapes on curtain folds are hooked into those eyes.

Buying information: Traverse rods serve the same purpose as standard rods, but come complete with hanging hardware in place. They come in center-pull and left- or right-pull versions for certain special installations.

How-to hint: Longer traverse rods come with a center bracket that should be used to ensure proper support.

CURTAIN ROD

Description: This is a two-piece rod with opposite ends turned at right angles to hook over brackets, with a top section that overlaps the second part. These rods come in adjustable widths: 28 to 48 inches and 48 to 62 inches. Tubular brass (brass-plated) Colonial and café rods are available in the same widths.

Buying information: The normal projection or distance from the wall of the curtain rod is 2⅝ inches. If a valance is desired with curtains, a rod that projects 3¾ inches can be used. There are also specially constructed double rods to use in this configuration.

DRAWER HARDWARE

ROLLERS

Description: These are small right-angle plates with plastic rollers on them.

Buying information: Rollers are normally used in the kitchen, or wherever there are heavy drawers, to make them slide more easily.

How-to hint: To install the rollers, ½ inch clearance is needed between the drawer and the drawer opening. Install with the small nails provided.

SLIDES

Description: These are small right-angled sections.

Buying information: Slides are used to make drawers slide easily, in any application where clearance is only ¼ inch. These don't last as long as rollers.

How-to hint: Secure with the small nails provided.

Side-Mount Tracks

SIDE-MOUNT TRACK

Description: This is an assemblage of metal interlocking track, part of which goes inside the cabinet and part on the sides of the drawer. The parts telescope together.

Buying information: It is available to support various weights.

How-to hint: To install this hardware, ½ inch clearance is needed.

CENTER-MOUNT TRACK

Description: There are two pieces of metal track, one of which mounts on the bottom of the drawer, the other on the bottom of the cabinet cavity.

Buying information: This type of hardware is best used when drawers are less than a foot wide.

How-to hint: A small level is very helpful in installing this hardware.

FRAMING FASTENERS

A number of companies make fasteners for framing that can be used in place of nails and screws. The devices, made of either 16- or 18-gauge zinc-coated metal, have predrilled holes. Essentially, you set the device between the two framing members and drive nails (or screws) through the holes to lock the members together. They make framing much quicker than it would be if just nails were used.

Framing fasteners also make connections stronger; indeed, a number are designed to join members so that they can resist hurricane-force winds. However, in most areas such strength is not required, so you should first determine whether the cost—and it is a lot more—justifies the extra strength.

Also, not all building codes accept these fasteners. Make sure yours does before using them.

Framing fasteners come in bulk—25 or 50 pieces to the carton. Buying in bulk can save you more than 50 percent over buying them individually. Check packages to make sure that the nails have been supplied; they are sometimes removed from their packages and sold separately.

Following are the most commonly used fasteners. There are others, covering a wide variety of framing needs.

Joist and Beam Hanger

Description: This is a squarish, U-shaped configuration.

Buying information: It is used to hang beams or joists of various sizes, everything from two-by-fours to four-by-fours.

How-to hints: These hangers can save a lot of time, in this case when installing beams or joists. In standard joist hanging, for example, the joists must be notched and then rested on and nailed to a ledger strip, which is nailed to the box or perimeter joist. The framing fastener is simply set in place on the box joist and nailed.

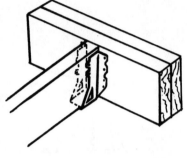

Joist and Beam Hanger

Post Holder

Description: This consists of a U-shaped configuration slipped over a bolt projecting from a concrete foundation. Drill a hole in the post, place on top of the bolt. The post is held in place by a U-shaped holder; once on the bolt, the post locks in.

Buying information: This device is for setting posts in place. It lets you adjust post placement and also allows the end of the post to ride on top of the U-shaped section rather than directly on the concrete.

How-to hint: To find the exact placement of the post holder, drop a plumb bob to locate the center of the concrete base.

Right-Angle Fastener

Description: This is a rectangular piece bent at a right angle. It is available in various sizes.

Buying information: This fastener is particularly good for do-it-yourselfers who are inexperienced at installing studs. It ensures that the studs are true when installed.

How-to hint: If you install a stud and find that you've cut it a little short, use a piece of cedar shingle under the stud for a tight fit.

FENCE BRACKET

Description: This looks like a narrow, four-sided box.

Buying information: These brackets allow you to install fence permanently or temporarily, so that entire fence sections may be removed for such tasks as cutting the lawn, painting, or shoveling snow; the sections can also be permanently fastened in place.

The brackets can also be used for nailing privacy screens onto the porch, patio, or carpet; they have indoor applications as well.

How-to hint: Nail or screw the brackets to the posts and slide the ends of the fence sections into the brackets.

POST AND BEAM CONNECTOR

Description: This is a T-shaped connector.

Buying information: It is good for installing horizontal beams on posts.

How-to hint: To use this connector, nail the fastener to the post and then flip the horizontal members into it and nail in place, eliminating toenailing.

TRUSS FASTENER

Description: This is a flat metal plate with holes for nailing, or with built-in barbs.

Buying information: As the name implies, it is good for assembly of trusses, where it eliminates the need for plywood gussets; it is also useful in connecting horizontal and vertical framing members.

How-to hints: To use the nailing type, position the plate so that it overlaps the members to be joined and then simply nail it on, using the nails provided. The same thing is done with the barbed type, except a special tool is sometimes needed. To create a smooth surface for Sheetrock or the like later, cut a shallow channel for the fastener so it is flush with the surface.

TRUSS FASTENER

GARAGE DOOR HARDWARE

To many people, fixing a garage door seems like a difficult proposition, perhaps one best left to a professional. But, in fact, the average do-it-yourselfer can fix a garage door. It is usually just a matter of replacing broken or worn parts.

Parts should be replaced as soon as there is any sign of trouble. Left alone, the breakdown of one part, say, a spring, can lead to the breakdown of another. More than this, though, once a door is broken it is usually in the down position—and garage doors are heavy, weighing 100 pounds and more. It is always much easier to fix when the door is still working well enough to be in the up position.

Following are the parts—in the order they normally wear out—that can be replaced on a typical garage door.

SPRING

Description: This is a thick coiled black spring 24 to 30 inches long.

Buying information: Springs come in three different "weights": 110, 150, and 210. The 110 is designed for a standard garage door, the 150 for a heavy-duty garage door, and the 210 for a 16-foot double garage door. For older people, a good choice is the 150-weight spring, which makes the door much easier to raise than the 110-weight spring.

How-to hint: As mentioned, it's best to remove parts when the door is in the raised position. To hold it in position, two pairs of locking pliers come in handy. Use one pair to keep the cable stationary, the other on the roller.

PULLEY

Description: This is a stamped galvanized metal wheel.

Buying information: Pulleys come in standard sizes. Just show the existing pulley to the hardware store dealer to get a replacement.

How-to hints: Again, use locking pliers to hold the door up as you remove the pulley (it's held on by a nut and bolt). If both pulleys need replacing, do the entire operation first on one side, then on the other.

CABLE

Description: This is either ⅛- or ³⁄₁₆-inch stranded cable.

Buying information: Kits are available for replacing cable. They come with two cables and instructions.

LOCKING HANDLE

Description: This is a narrow handle that is turned to open and close the door.

Buying information: Replacement handles come in universal sizes: The same handle will fit a wide variety of doors.

How-to hint: Replacing the handle is mainly a matter of using pliers to remove cotter pins.

Night Latch Assembly

Description: This is the standard lock on a garage door.
Buying information: Most night latches fit in all garage doors, no matter what make. Some have three screw holes and some have four.

GUTTER

Gutters that are properly installed will carry away thousands of gallons of water every year. But if they are not installed correctly, or if they leak, water can spill over (especially when the gutters ice up), saturate the foundation, and seep into the house. It's safe to say that incorrectly installed or leaky gutters are the number-one cause of damp and wet basements.

Gutter may have a half-round or "K" shape (sort of squarish) and be 4 to 5 inches across at the top. The 5-inch size is necessary for most areas.

Gutter is made of many materials, and each type requires fittings—downspout tube, leaders, and hangers. Fittings vary slightly from one manufacturer to the other, but the same store that carries, say, Brand A gutter will also carry Brand A fittings. Hangers may be the concealed type (you can't see them when you look at the gutter); the type that wraps around the gutter and fastens to the roof (rather than the fascia board, the way the concealed type does); or those designed to fit around the molding on the house. Aluminum spikes and ferrules may also be used. These are driven through the gutter into the fascia and, preferably, into the ends of the rafters. Lifting up the ends of the shingles on the house (if you can) ordinarily shows where rafter ends are located. To transport gutter, tie it to an extension ladder that is tied to the roof of your car.

Wood Gutter

Description: This is standard gutter shape, but since it's made of wood (usually fir), the material is thicker than other types.
Buying information: Wood gutter is good-looking and can be used on most homes, but it is very expensive—and heavy (five or six times the weight of metal gutter). It comes in 50-foot

lengths. Every couple of years it must be coated to protect the wood from rotting and, of course, it must be regularly painted.
How-to hint: Wood gutter is very difficult for the average person to install.

COPPER GUTTER

Description: This is a standard gutter shape, made of copper.
Buying information: It is available in 10-foot-long sections and is very expensive. After it weathers, verdigris may run down and stain exterior surfaces.
How-to hint: Because the joints must be soldered, copper gutter is very difficult for the do-it-yourselfer to install.

VINYL GUTTER

Description: Available in standard gutter shapes but in a limited range of colors, this is made of polyvinyl chloride and comes in various lengths: 10, 16, 21, and 32 feet.
Buying information: Vinyl can be used just like any other gutter, and is not susceptible to rust, corrosion, rotting, or peeling, but in very cold weather it can crack from expansion and contraction.
How-to hint: This is installed like any other gutter but is connected with sleeve connectors in which the ends of sections fit into the sleeves.

GALVANIZED STEEL GUTTER

Description: This is available in standard gutter profiles and in various baked-enamel finishes as well as unpainted. Standard length is 10 feet, but you can also get it 20 feet long.
Buying information: Galvanized steel can be used anywhere other gutter is used. It stands up well, but if the enamel finish is scratched, it can eventually rust after the galvanizing corrodes.

STANDARD ALUMINUM GUTTER

Description: This is available in various configurations and in 10-foot lengths, and up to 32 feet long at factories that specialize in making gutter. Ten-foot lengths are .027 inch thick, while the longer lengths are a beefier .032 inch. Available in various colors.
Buying information: Aluminum gutter is used like any other gutter, but if the lengths are only 10 feet, connections will have

to be made at the joints. Longer lengths can be unwieldy to transport and handle. Some companies sell gutter that is thinner than .027 inch. This is known in the trade as "Reynolds Wrap" and should be avoided.

How-to hints: Install aluminum gutter using a blind rivet gun. It allows you to assemble sections and install end caps much more easily than by using screws. Assembled gutters should be pitched slightly downward toward the downspouts; to make sure pitch is correct, the gutter should be pitched off a level line, never the house. Houses look level, but almost all are tilted slightly.

CUSTOM-CUT (SEAMLESS) GUTTER

Description: This is standard except it is thicker—.032 inch—and is available in many more colors: white, brown, gold, black, and green.

Buying information: Seamless gutter can be used just like standard. It is cut on site to the exact length needed.

How-to hint: Custom-cut is easier to install than standard gutter because there are no sections to join.

HANDLES

Chests, trapdoors, and boxes occasionally need handles to open and close them. A wide variety of types are available. In general, they have a zinc finish, but also are available in brass and brass plate.

TRAPDOOR RING

Description: This is a squarish metal plate with a recessed bail handle.

Buying information: For use on trapdoors, toolboxes, or wherever a handle that doesn't protrude from the surface is needed.

How-to hint: The bail on a trapdoor handle is recessed into the surface to ensure that no one trips over it. So, too, when installing, make sure the ring lies flush with the trapdoor.

CHEST HANDLE

Description: This is a flat metal plate.

Buying information: These handles turn only up to 90 degrees from the surface so fingers don't get jammed.

HARDWARE CLOTH

Description: This looks like rugged metal screening. It comes in various gauges and "meshes," or number of squares to the inch—commonly 2x2, 2x4, and 8x8. For example, in 2x2 mesh there are four squares per square inch. As the number of squares per square inch increases, the gauge or diameter of the wire gets smaller. It comes in rolls 2 and 4 feet wide, and is sold by the foot.

Buying information: One of the main uses of hardware cloth is in sifting sand, topsoil, cement, and the like. Another good use is for pet cages. Yet another is for screening where you want extra security to keep birds, bats, or squirrels out of house or barn sections.

How-to hint: Hardware cloth can easily be cut with snips and bent to shape.

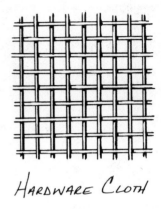

HARDWARE CLOTH

HASPS

STANDARD HASP

Description: A standard hasp has two flat hinged pieces of metal that fold together, both of which have screw holes for mounting; one has a slot for the staple, a ringed portion that the slotted part fits over. It may be plain or decorative, with the slotted part ranging from about 2 to 6 inches long and the entire hasp 1 to 1½ inches wide.

Buying information: The hasp is the section mounted on a door or chest that accepts a padlock so the door or chest can be made secure.

SAFETY HASP

Description: This looks something like the standard hasp, but the hinged piece conceals the hasp screw holes.

Buying information: For use in securing valuables.

How-to hints: To keep someone from being able to unscrew the hasp, use carriage bolts. But they can only be used on rather large hasps because of the size of the bolts themselves: typically they are ¼ inch in diameter and larger, which would require ⁵⁄₁₆- or ⅜-inch mounting holes in the hasp. Carriage bolts are not always available in ⁵⁄₁₆-inch diameter.

SAFETY HASP

ADJUSTABLE-LEVEL
HASP

ADJUSTABLE-LEVEL HASP

Description: This looks like a regular hasp except the slotted end is jointed.

Buying information: This is an excellent hasp when a door and its frame are not level with each other.

How-to hint: It is installed like any other hasp.

TURN HASP

Description: This is a regular hasp, but with a bail handle that turns.

Buying information: A turn hasp allows you to turn the staple to keep the hasp closed while there is no lock in place.

HINGES

There is a seemingly endless variety of hinges, but the following facts should eliminate some of the confusion.

Many companies specify that hinges are "handed"—that is, designed to go either on the left-hand or the right-hand side of the door. In some cases the left is from the perspective of viewing the door opening from the outside of the house; in others it is from the inside. This can get very complicated; the simple fact is that unless you're involved in a very special situation, you don't need to know the hands, because hinges are interchangeable. Turn them over, then put the pin in, and they become left-handed or right-handed, as required.

Hinges come in different sizes; the very small sizes would be used on cabinet doors. In selecting a hinge, you should know door thickness, weight, and clearance. But a long-time engineering trick (as suggested for cabinet doors) makes it simpler: If the hinge seems to be in proportion to the door, use it. For example, if you are hanging an exterior door, you wouldn't use tiny hinges, nor would you use extra-large ones. We are all generally familiar with hinge size, and your own judgment should suffice.

Generally, if the size of the hinge looks right, it is right, simply because hinges are considerably stronger than is usually necessary for the job they are required to do.

BUTT HINGE

Description: This has two rectangular leaves with screw holes joined by a pin or rod.

Buying information: As mentioned above, if a hinge looks strong enough to support a door, it likely is. But as a rule of thumb, for a normal-weight interior sash door 1⅜ inches thick or a hollow-core flush (flat and smooth) door, use a pair of 3½-by-3½-inch butt hinges; for a solid door 1⅜ inches thick, use 1½ pairs (3 hinges) of 3½-by-3½-inch hinges; for a door 1¾ inches thick, use 1½ pairs of 4-by-4-inch hinges; and for louvered closet doors 1⅛ inches thick, use one pair of 3-by-3-inch hinges.

Note that butt hinges can be obtained with "loose" or "fast" pins. Loose pins can be removed and the door taken down; fast pins cannot be removed and the door cannot be taken down, a security plus.

How-to hints: Butt hinges are mortised into the door and frame: one leaf goes into a recess in the frame and the other into the side of the door. To facilitate placement, there is a handy device called a butt marker, which comes in the shape of a standard butt hinge but has turned-over, sharpened edges. Place the butt marker on the door or frame, rap with a hammer, then clean out the scored area with a chisel and hammer.

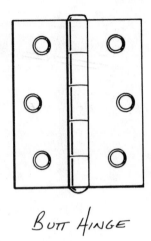

BUTT HINGE

GATE HINGE

Description: This hinge has two parts: an L-shaped lag screw that screws into the fence post and a leaf with a knurled nut that fits over the L of the first part and is screwed to the gate. It is available in various sizes, but usually 5 or 6 inches. Gate hinges are usually painted black or galvanized.

Buying information: Gate hinges were designed to be mounted on round posts, but they can also be used on square ones.

How-to hint: Sinking the hinge screws is much easier if you first drill pilot holes.

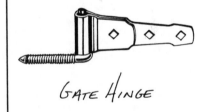

GATE HINGE

DOUBLE-ACTING HINGE

Description: This comes in a couple of forms. The common type has two leaves and knuckles and is loosely jointed to allow both leaves to open at once. It is brass-plated.

Buying information: This is a good hinge if you want to fold dividers or sectional screens in both directions or fold flat for storage. It is also good for shutters.

How-to hint: Only an experienced handyperson should attempt installation. The double-acting hinge is tricky to install.

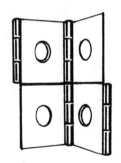

DOUBLE-ACTING HINGE

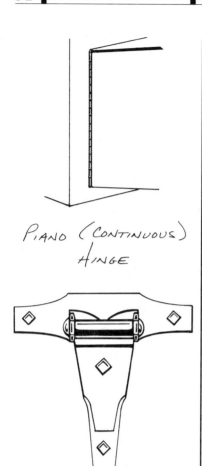

PIANO (CONTINUOUS) HINGE

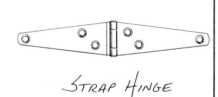

T HINGE

STRAP HINGE

PIANO (CONTINUOUS) HINGE

Description: This is a long, narrow hinge with narrow leaves and many screw holes. It commonly comes in 1- to 3-foot lengths, brass-plated or aluminum, as well as stainless steel. Widths vary.

Buying information: As the name suggests, this is the hinge used on a piano because it combines great strength with an attractive appearance. It is often used on lids of specially crafted boxes.

T HINGE

Description: This hinge is shaped like the letter T. It is available plain and in ornamental styles, copper, brass-plated, and painted black.

Buying information: This hinge is flush mounted—not recessed into the door. You'd use the plain one where you care more about function than esthetics. T hinges are commonly used on garage doors, chest lids, and for other utility jobs.

STRAP HINGE

Description: This hinge has long, identical leaves tapered down in width from the pivot to the ends. It comes in various sizes and in plain steel as well as some finishes.

Buying information: The length of the leaves militates against this type of hinge being mounted on a normal doorjamb. Rather, it is appropriate where you have a lid of some sort hinged in the center. In marine use, for example, you find strap hinges on fish box lids. When small fish are caught, either side of the lid can be lifted and the fish tossed in the box. Around the home you might use a strap hinge on an outdoor storage box or a shed door.

METALS

There are two basic kinds of metals that the do-it-yourselfer can use to repair and create things around the home: aluminum and steel. A number of forms are available.

Aluminum

ALUMINUM SHEET

Description: This comes in thin panels, either solid or perforated, and may or may not be decorative. It comes in two sizes:

2 by 3 feet and 3 by 3 feet. It comes plain, embossed, and gold-anodized.

Buying information: Perforated aluminum sheets are popular as coverings for cabinets and radiators.

How-to hints: Cut with snips or, even better, score it on both sides and bend it back and forth until it breaks. This produces a clean, straight edge; snips tend to bend it.

ALUMINUM ROD

Description: This product comes in various diameters and lengths, the most common being 6 and 8 feet.

Buying information: One popular use is as a flag holder.

How-to hints: It can be cut with a hacksaw and bent. To make soft bends, hold the rod in a vise and bend by hand. To make a sharp bend, use a propane torch to soften the rod at the point where you want to bend it. Take care when using a propane torch not to contact flammable materials.

ALUMINUM BAR

Description: This is flat, 1½ by ¾ inches or ¼ by 1 inch. It comes in 6- and 8-foot lengths.

Buying information: Bars are used as shelf supports or as a protective edging on wood, among other things.

How-to hints: It is very easy to use. Cut it with a hacksaw and connect with sheet metal screws. It can be bent by hand.

ALUMINUM ANGLE

Description: This is like bar stock bent in half lengthwise. It comes ¾ by ¾ inch and 1 by 1 inch, in 6-foot and 8-foot lengths.

Buying information: Angles are good for protecting shelf edging and thresholds, or as corner beading.

How-to hints: Cut with a hacksaw and connect with sheet metal screws. If drilled, a good trick for this (and any other thicker metal) is first to push the drill bit into vegetable shortening. This keeps it from binding.

ALUMINUM TUBING/FITTINGS

Description: Tubing is square or round, with an outside diameter of ¾ inch to 1¼ inches, and in lengths of 6 or 8 feet. Various fittings, which resemble plumbing fittings, are available for connecting the material; these are made of cast aluminum.

Buying information: Use for tent poles, backyard chair frames, frame for a boat cover.

How-to hints: Cuts with a hacksaw. Use ordinary hammer-to-hammer connectors between pieces, which friction-fit inside tubing.

ALUMINUM TRACK

Description: This is a narrow length of metal with a ⅛-inch or ¼-inch groove, and it comes in 6-foot and 8-foot lengths.

Buying information: It is used mainly as a runner for small sliding doors in cabinets.

How-to hint: Cut with a fine-toothed hacksaw.

STORM WINDOW/SCREEN FRAMING

Description: This consists of two parts: flat lengths of aluminum with or without weatherstrip, and L-shaped corner connectors. It comes in 6-foot and 8-foot lengths and in plain aluminum or anodized white.

Buying information: One good use is to make storm window frames for cellar windows.

Steel

STEEL ROD

Description: This is cold rolled steel in 3-foot and 6-foot lengths, and in diameters ranging from 3/16 inch up to ¾ inch. Ends are painted in various colors to identify diameters.

Buying information: Rods have various uses, such as for axles.

How-to hints: Cut with a hacksaw. Bend in a vise to make a soft bend, or heat with a propane torch for a sharp bend.

STEEL BAR STOCK

Description: This is a flat bar, available in 12-foot lengths, 3/16 inch to ½ inch thick.

Buying information: Typical uses are for fence and railing repair, and lawn and garden equipment.

How-to hint: It is easy to work with, but on thinner diameter stock it has to be bent with heat from a propane torch.

STEEL ANGLE IRON

Description: This is an L-shaped, cadmium-plated bar folded lengthwise down the middle and bent at a 90-degree angle. It comes ⅛ inch thick, 1½ by 1½ inches wide, in lengths of 2, 3, and 4 feet.

Buying information: Angle irons are often used in constructing basketball hoops, reinforcing fencing, making frames for carts, or making hanging storage units in a garage.

How-to hints: Cut with a hacksaw and connect with nuts and bolts, or weld.

SLOTTED ANGLE

Description: This is a steel angle with holes and elliptical slots at close-together intervals. It is typically 4 feet or 6 feet long and 1½ by 1½ inches.

Buying information: A slotted angle is useful for building a framework, such as for a storage unit in a garage. Ready-made holes make it easy to fasten the material without having to drill holes.

How-to hint: Handle like angle iron.

SLOTTED FLAT BAR

Description: This is a 1⅜-inch-wide flat bar with holes at regular intervals, and it comes in 3-, 4-, or 6-foot lengths.

Buying information: It has the same advantage as slotted angles—handy holes—and it can be bent.

How-to hints: Handle like angle iron. Use straight for diagonal bracing of angle iron framing.

HANGER IRON

Description: This is a metal strap with equally spaced holes.

Buying information: Use for hanging pipes and all manner of things. Its flexibility makes it quite versatile.

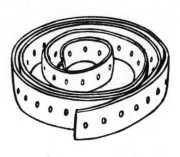

HANGER IRON

NAILS

Nails are generally available in lengths that range from 1 to 6 inches; as the nail gets longer, the diameter gets correspondingly thicker. When speaking of size, nails are commonly referred to by weight and number. Weight is expressed by the letter *d*, which stands for "pennyweight" (the way nails used to be sold), with sizes running from 2d (1 inch long by ⅛ inch thick) to 60d (6 inches long by ⅜ inch thick).

There are many different kinds of nails available; some can serve a variety of purposes while others, such as roofing nails, are designed to do just one task.

Nails are packaged in various ways, the most common being 1- and 5-pound boxes. The less packaging there is, the less you usually pay. The cheapest way to buy nails is in large quantities—25- and 50-pound boxes.

COMMON NAIL

COMMON NAIL

Description: This comes in various lengths and has a large, round, flat head. It is available in plain steel and galvanized finishes.

Buying information: The common nail is used for a variety of jobs, but mostly general construction work, such as framing. Galvanized nails are rough-surfaced, grip better, and resist rusting, so they're the best type for exterior work. They're also more expensive than plain steel.

How-to hints: The key to driving in any nail is your wrist action: snap it like a whip. When fastening two boards together, the nail should be long enough to penetrate through the first board and about three quarters of the way through the rearmost board. In some cases there is danger of splitting a hard wood with a thick nail. To avoid this, drill a slightly undersized pilot hole in the wood to accept the nail without undue stress, or use two thinner nails instead. In addition to minimizing splitting, the connection will be stronger.

BOX NAIL

Description: This is a very thin nail that comes rosin-coated.

Buying information: Use where a common nail might split the wood. Very good for wood flooring and subflooring, these work particularly well for securing oak and pine.

How-to hints: Box nails, which are thinner than common nails, bend more easily, so take particular care to drive them in straight. As the nail is driven into the wood, the rosin heats up; when it cools it grips tenaciously, an important consideration when fastening wood flooring or plywood.

Finishing Nail

Description: This is a slender nail with a small, cupped head. It comes in various lengths; most are 1½ inches. Plain and galvanized types are available.

Buying information: Finishing nails are designed to be used where you don't want nailheads to show. The small heads may be left flush with the surface, but usually they are countersunk; the heads are driven slightly beneath the surface and then the holes above are filled with wood putty and sanded so that the nail is completely hidden.

How-to hints: When countersinking nails, use a countersink that is the same size as the head of the nail. If you are working with very expensive wood and want to lessen the risk of hitting the wood with a hammer blow, use a magnetic spinner. This tool holds the nail and actually spins it into the wood up to the point where it can be countersunk. The spinner can be used on 4d and 3d nails.

FINISHING NAIL

Brad

Description: A brad is a finishing nail that is shorter than 1½ inches. It is available in lengths of ¼ inch to ½ inch, and is very thin (19 gauge).

Buying information: It is very good for making picture frames.

How-to hints: To work with these nails more easily, since they are so small, hold them in place with needlenose pliers as you drive them, or use a brad driver (basically a hollow metal tool that has a spring and a magnet in it). Brads (up to 1¼ inch) are dropped into the tube and then can be pushed in place rather than hammered.

Casing Nail

Description: This is a variation on the finishing nail. It is slightly thicker and has a flat head rather than a cupped one. It gets its name from the fact that it was once primarily used on case molding. It comes in plain and galvanized finishes.

Buying information: Casing nails can be used for securing trim where sinking nailheads beneath the surface doesn't matter. Drive the heads flush with the surface and paint over.

CASING NAIL

Roofing Nail

Description: This has an enlarged head and a smooth shank. It comes in various lengths, ¾ inch, 1¼ inch, 1½ inches (most popular), and 2 inches.

Buying information: A roofing nail is used to secure roofing shingles and felt. The size of the nail used depends on the thickness of the material being driven through.

How-to hints: To grip properly, the nail must be long enough to penetrate the roofing, felt, and deck; when it punches through the back side of the deck, it creates splinters, and it is these splinters that help prevent it from working loose.

DRYWALL NAIL

Drywall Nail

Description: This comes in two forms: one is blued and threaded, and the other is plain steel. The plain steel type has a smaller head. Standard lengths are 1⅛ inches and 1¼ inches.

Buying information: This nail is used to secure drywall, also known as plasterboard and Sheetrock.

How-to hints: Drywall nails are meant to be driven so that they "dimple" the surface. Then joint compound is laid on top of the heads. In practice, because of the way the heads are designed, the plain steel nail is better. Blued drywall nails tend to cut the paper surface of the drywall, which can lead to the nails' loosening, and they are more difficult to cover with joint compound during finishing).

SPIRAL NAIL

Spiral Nail

Description: There are two types. One has annular spiral threads and comes in 1-inch and 1¼-inch lengths. The other is fluted and has a spiral head and is longer, 2½ or 3 inches.

Buying information: These nails have tenacious gripping power—they turn as they are driven. They cost half as much as screws and are twice as fast to use. The first type is used to secure hardboard underlayment, and the other is used when the underlayment is waferboard, which is thicker and therefore requires a longer nail. It is also used for textured hardboard siding.

How-to hint: Use a hammer, not an electric drill.

MASONRY NAIL

Description: This looks like a common nail but is thicker and fluted.

Buying information: It is used to secure wood or other materials to masonry.

How-to hints: To drive these nails, use a 2-pound sledge hammer and wear goggles to protect eyes against flying chips—and heads of nails that may fly off. The best procedure for safety and ease of use is to select a nail that is long enough to penetrate through the item and no more than 1 inch into the masonry. It will be difficult for the nail to penetrate more deeply than this, and once it stalls, the chances of knocking the head off are that much greater. Screws—which work better—are also available for masonry.

CUT NAIL

Description: This nail is tapered, with a flat top and a flat tip.
Buying information: It is used to secure tongue-and-groove flooring, and can also be used to secure wood to concrete.
How-to hints: The only practical way to use these nails is to load them into a nailing machine that sets up and drives each nail. Driving cut nails freehand is very difficult. The dealer should give you the necessary information on using the tool.

Cut Nail

3D FINE NAIL

Description: This is a thin nail, 1⅛ inches long, with a small head, always hot-dipped galvanized.
Buying information: This very strong nail is waterproof and is commonly used in assembling lobster pots and lattice.

GUTTER SPIKE

Description: This comes 6 inches long and either in galvanized steel or aluminum with ferrules (tubes that slip over the nails). The steel spikes are thinner.
Buying information: It is used to secure metal gutter.
How-to hints: If the fascia wood is old, use the galvanized nail. As mentioned, it's thinner and there is less chance of the wood splitting than if you use the thicker aluminum type. A good trick with spikes is to hammer one into the fascia at one end of the house and another in at the other end to support the loose gutter as you drive in the rest of the spikes. Since you will be using a ladder, take care that it is firmly set on the ground.

PANEL NAIL

Description: This is a small-headed thin nail available in various colors—tan, gray, green, and black, to name a few. It comes in various lengths.

Buying information: These are used to secure paneling. The nails are color-matched to the paneling, and when in place the heads are not noticeable. They are also good for securing pre-stained molding.

How-to hints: For mounting paneling on drywall with the nails going into the studs, use 1⅝-inch nails; for driving through paneling alone, 1 inch is sufficient.

ORNAMENTAL NAIL

ORNAMENTAL NAIL

Description: This has a short shank and a large, fancy oval head. Some are forged and are extra tough.

Buying information: Standard ornamental nails are used to fasten upholstery. The forged kind can be used to hang fireplace implements on masonry. Another type, called pyramid nails, can be used to fasten fine flooring.

How-to hints: To use forged nails to hang fireplace implements, first drill pilot holes in the masonry (holes should be slightly smaller than nail diameter) and drive them in with a small lump hammer or heavy claw hammer or framing hammer. Wear safety glasses or goggles.

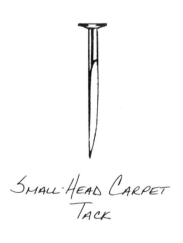

SMALL-HEAD CARPET TACK

TACK

Description: This is a large-headed nail available in copper, aluminum, or blued steel. Small-headed tacks, called gimp tacks, are also available. The sizes range from $\frac{7}{16}$ inch to $\frac{9}{16}$ inch, but tacks over 1 inch long can be found.

Buying information: Tacks are mostly used for securing upholstery, but they have other uses. Copper tacks can be used to secure webbing on outdoor furniture, for example, and in marine applications. Aluminum tacks, usually $\frac{7}{16}$ inch or $\frac{1}{2}$ inch, can be used for securing screening to wood frames. Gimp tacks are good for securing carpet.

How-to hints: To secure carpeting with gimp tacks, drive them in along the edge. The heads will grip the base of the carpet but will not be visible beneath the pile.

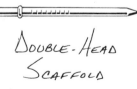

DOUBLE-HEAD SCAFFOLD

DOUBLE-HEAD SCAFFOLD NAIL

Description: This is a common nail with a standard head and a neck or rim of metal a little lower than the standard head. It is normally 2½ inches or 3 inches, but a 12d size (3¼ inches) is also available.

Buying information: Use this nail for temporary assembly of scaffolding. The 12d nail is bigger and stronger than the others and is excellent for house framing. Smaller sizes are good for other tasks. Drive the nail only up to the rim of metal. The portion still projecting allows for easier pulling.

STAPLE

Description: This has a U-shaped configuration with two sharpened points. Common sizes are ⅜ inch to 1¼ inch, though larger sizes are available. Also available are square-topped staples, which are blued.

Buying information: Steel staples are used for fencing, holding wire to a fencepost, or anchoring armored cable (BX). Square-topped staples are good for securing screen wire.

How-to hint: Drive staples with a hammer.

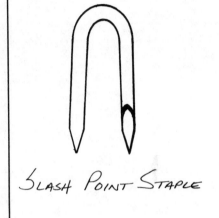

SLASH POINT STAPLE

CORRUGATED FASTENER

Description: This looks like a small piece of corrugated metal with one edge sharpened. It comes in plain steel, in various sizes.

Buying information: A good choice when you want to join wood edge-to-edge and nails won't do. For example, if you wanted to create a board 24 inches wide by joining two 12-inch boards, you could do this with corrugated fasteners. It is also good for assembling parts of large picture frames.

How-to hint: Use only in soft wood, such as fir and pine.

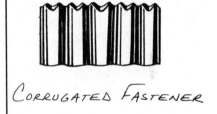

CORRUGATED FASTENER

CHEVRON (SCOTCH JOINER)

Description: This is sort of an L-shaped piece with four sharp points. It is available galvanized.

Buying information: Like corrugated fasteners, chevrons are used to assemble boards end-to-end and to join the corners of picture frames. They are also excellent for preventing big boards from splitting.

How-to hints: Unlike corrugated fasteners, you can use these in hard wood as well as soft. Some boards are split at the ends and are in danger of splitting along the length. To stop this, just drive a chevron or two over the split so it can't pull apart.

NUTS AND BOLTS

Nuts and bolts are for fastening things when you need strength greater than nails and screws can provide. Nuts and bolts come black with an oil finish as well as galvanized. Nuts and bolts for marine use are available in stainless steel and brass.

LAG SCREW (LAG BOLT)

LAG SCREW

Description: This looks like a thick wood screw with a hexagonal top. It comes in various lengths, usually from 1 to 6 inches, and either cadmium-plated or galvanized.

Buying information: Lag screws are for fastening wood when regular screws aren't strong enough. They are usually used in the smaller sizes because they have to be turned with a wrench. They are cheaper than machine and carriage bolts described below, so if you have a choice, use them.

How-to hints: Since lag screws are so thick, it is necessary to drill pilot holes for them so that they can be turned more easily. An impact wrench makes turning them even easier.

CARRIAGE BOLT

CARRIAGE BOLT

Description: This looks like a machine screw. It has a square end and is partially threaded, but also has a rounded head with no slot; directly beneath the head is a square shoulder.

Buying information: Carriage bolts are good for use in wood-to-wood connections. They come with either rolled or cut thread. The cut-thread type has the threads cut right into the bolt; the rolled kind has the threads pressed into the bolt shaft that results in the threaded section being a little thicker than the bare shank.

How-to hints: The cut-thread kind is generally preferred. In the smaller bolt sizes, rolled thread works okay, but in the large sizes the shank or smooth part of the bolt may be a bit loose in a hole large enough to pass the threaded end. The cut thread will be uniform.

To use a carriage bolt, drill a hole the diameter of the shank. Drop the bolt into the hole, then use a hammer to drive it in the rest of the way to seat the square neck in the hole. You then place a washer and screw a nut on the end of the bolt that protrudes. Since the head is locked into the wood it does not have to be restrained while the nut is turned home.

MACHINE BOLT

Description: This is partially threaded and has a square head.

Buying information: Machine bolts are used mainly to fasten metal to metal, but they can also be used to fasten wood and metal together.

How-to hints: Machine bolts are used with washers and nuts. The nuts are slipped on the protruding end and tightened by holding a wrench on the head. Because of this technique, the bolt can be made quite tight. Machine bolts, like carriage bolts, also come with cut and rolled threads; the cut-thread type is better for the reason cited above.

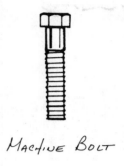

MACHINE BOLT

STOVE BOLT

Description: This bolt is threaded all along its length and comes with a nut. The head is slotted.

Buying information: Stove bolts are usually used to assemble metal items, but they work on wood as well. A very handy fastener.

HEX CAP SCREW

Description: This is essentially a machine bolt with a hexagonal head.

Buying information: These are often used in prethreaded metal items, but can be used with nuts like machine bolts. The screws come in various sizes: the diameter is described first, followed by the number of threads per inch. In a ¼x20 cap screw, for example, the fastener is ¼ inch in diameter and has 20 threads per inch. Cap screws come in various "codes"; dash markings on head indicate strength rating—the more marks, the stronger the bolt.

HANGER BOLT

Description: This is a metal shaft threaded on one end like a lag screw and having machine threads on the other end.

Buying information: Hanger bolts are ordinarily used to secure legs to furniture, but they are excellent for hanging things, typically in the garage. The lag-screw portion may be turned into a beam, and the machine-screw part threaded into the matching threads on the fixture or used with a nut and washer to retain anything with a mounting hole.

How-to hint: For easiest use, first drill a pilot hole.

HANGER BOLT

Eyebolt

Eyebolt

Description: This is a metal loop and shaft on which are either machine-screw or lag-screw threads. If it has machine-screw threads, it is used with a nut.

Buying information: Eyebolts are excellent as a base from which to hang other things—the eyes make a handy place to secure wire, strap iron, or rods.

Dowel Screw

Description: This is a metal shaft with lag-screw threads on both sides.

Buying information: Dowel screws are excellent for hanging things on wood.

How-to hint: As with other large-diameter items, first drill pilot holes to make driving easier.

Standard Nut

Description: This is a hexagonal stamping with a threaded hole.

Buying information: Two nuts—it's called double nutting— are good to use with carriage or machine bolts to reduce the chance of something loosening.

How-to hint: Double nutting is often used when assembling workbenches, which are subject to a great deal of vibration.

Elastic Stop Nut

Description: This is an ordinary nut with a nylon insert.

Buying information: It is excellent for use on power tools, machinery, or wherever there is great vibration; the nylon insert holds the nut from loosening in spite of shock.

Acorn Nut

Acorn Nut

Description: It looks like an acorn; available in steel and brass.

Buying information: Acorn nuts are decorative, but they do have holding strength. They are commonly used on children's toys, to cap various bolt ends to eliminate the hazard of sharp ends.

Lock Washer

Lock Washer

Description: This looks like a regular washer except it's split, with the ends slightly askew from each other. It comes in steel in various sizes: ¼, ⁵⁄₁₆, ⅜, and ½ inch.

Buying information: When you need reasonable assurance that something won't vibrate loose, a lock washer is the best thing to use. It works nearly as well as double nutting.

Wing Nut

Description: This has two projections on it that look like wings, and a threaded hole between them. It comes in cadmium-plated steel and brass, and in various sizes: from smaller machine screw threads, up through ³⁄₁₆, ¼, ⁵⁄₁₆, and ⅜ inch.

Buying information: A wing nut is good wherever something needs to be assembled and disassembled easily on a regular basis without the need for tools, since it can be tightened and loosened with your fingers.

How-to hint: You can make wing nuts extra tight by gripping them with pliers.

WING NUT

PERFORATED HARDBOARD FITTINGS

For years, there was only one type of fitting for use with perforated hardboard, but in recent years slot hangers have become available.

Perforated Hardboard Fittings

Description: These come in a wide variety of shapes, made from hard wire.

Buying information: These fittings are hung in holes in the hardboard, and then things are secured to them—everything from tools to shelves. It is best to get hardboard that has been enameled (or paint it yourself) to guard against warping. If you prefer to paint it yourself, starting with the bare board, be sure to do both sides.

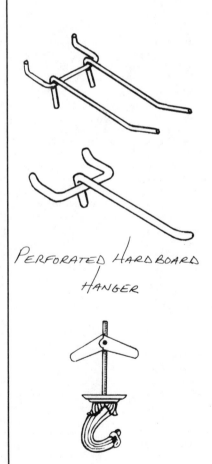

PERFORATED HARDBOARD HANGER

PLANT HANGER

PLANT HANGERS

Plants may be hung from walls or ceilings. If you are hanging a plant from a ceiling, the weight of it (plant plus water) should not exceed 15 pounds. Ceiling hooks are usually affixed with a toggle bolt (see page 66). If you intend to use a chain, see page 10. See also wire, page 72.

BRACKET

Description: This has various appearances, but it is universally fancy looking and has holes for mounting.

Buying information: When you want to hang a plant on a wall, use a bracket.

How-to hint: When mounting a bracket, use whatever fasteners are best for the wall material being penetrated.

PULLEY

Description: This is simply a pulley and rope arrangement.

Buying information: When you want to keep plants on display, but need to water them frequently use a pulley. Pulleys work like venetian blinds, allowing you to raise and lower the plants.

SWIVEL HANGER

Description: This consists of a fancy hook and, secured at the bottom, another hook that swivels.

Buying information: Use a swivel hanger when you want to be able to turn a hanging plant so that different sides can face the sun.

TRACK

Description: This is a grooved length of metal with holes for mounting it to the ceiling.

Buying information: Track is designed to accept hanging hardware that rides along the groove and to which other hanging hardware may be connected.

RIVETS

About 20 years ago the blind rivet gun was introduced and, unlike new products, it has not only survived, but thrived. Indeed, it deserves a place in any toolbox.

There are a number of other types of rivets that are useful as well.

BLIND RIVET

Description: This is an aluminum nail with an elongated head.

Buying information: Blind rivets come in a variety of lengths:

as the nail shank gets longer, so does the head. They can be used to fasten leather, cloth, toys, and light metal of all kinds—they're popular for assembling gutters—from one side only, hence the term "blind": the rivet doesn't necessarily show on the other side.

How-to hints: A rivet gun is essential for using blind rivets. Make a hole in the material (unless one already exists), then insert the rivet, shank first, in the tip of the rivet gun, which grips it. Insert the head of the rivet in the hole and squeeze the tool handles; it compresses the head, pulling the parts together. The bigger the head, the thicker the material the rivet can fasten.

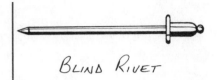

BLIND RIVET

SPEEDY RIVET

Description: This is a small, naillike device with mating part.

Buying information: Rivets are used for fastening soft materials, like canvas to leather, or canvas to canvas.

How-to hint: Squeeze the parts of the rivet with special pliers or hammer together.

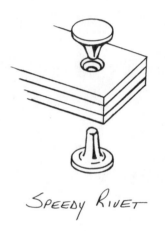

SPEEDY RIVET

PIN RIVET

Description: This is a solid cylinder of metal with a narrow head. It is usually ¹⁄₁₆ inch or ⅛ inch in diameter and comes in various lengths.

Buying information: Use this for the quick connecting of two pieces of metal.

How-to hint: Install with a setting tool that is placed on the rivet and then hammered to expand the rivet and lock the pieces together.

SPLIT RIVET

Description: This has two tinelike legs and a cone-shaped top. It is usually ¼ inch to ½ inch long, with a copper finish.

Buying information: A split rivet is used to join canvas, leather, and other soft materials.

How-to hint: Insert in hole and then peen with a hammer.

ROPE AND CORD

The main difference between rope and cord is size: anything ⅛ inch in diameter or smaller is cord; anything above that size is rope. Rope is more common. Both materials are sold packaged, but mostly they are available cut from reels by the foot. Rope also comes packaged for particular uses such as clothesline, winches, and tie-downs.

When buying rope, pay attention to the SWL or safe working load, which means the maximum pressure, measured in weight, that should be applied to the rope when it is brand new and used in situations where failure may be injurious to life, limb, or property. ST refers to breaking strength and is the theoretical strength of the rope in noncritical situations—no danger to life, limb, or property. Check with your dealer to make sure the rope is strong enough for your purposes. Bear in mind, however, that knots weaken a rope, perhaps by as much as 50 percent.

MANILA ROPE

Description: This is braided rope, usually tan, in various diameters.

Buying information: Years ago, manila rope was made of hemp, but today it is almost all plastic, made to simulate real manila. (Manila made of hemp is still available at marine supply stores, but is very expensive.) Still, it has real manila characteristics: it won't melt in sunlight (as nylon will), it ties and knots well, and it doesn't stretch much.

How-to hints: It is most easily cut with pruning shears. To prevent the ends from unraveling, apply electrical tape over the cut line. The tape will hold the strands together at the ends when the rope is cut. In lieu of taping, you can dip the severed ends into rubber or contact cement.

SISAL ROPE

Description: This is straw-colored, stranded fiber rope.

Buying information: This is another "natural" rope, but it has less strength than manila. It is excellent for package tying. If an item is expected to be tied and untied a lot, however, manila is better.

How-to hint: An ordinary sharp knife cuts sisal easily.

NYLON ROPE

Description: This comes in woven and braided forms; the woven type has eight strands while the braided type has three. It comes in white only.

Buying information: Nylon is strong and stretches well. It is good for applications such as outboard motor starter cords, playground swings, and as a tow rope; it absorbs shock as it stretches. On the negative side, it has a low burning point. The braided form tends to unravel at the ends when cut.

How-to hint: To prevent the cut ends of braided rope from unraveling, melt the ends with a flame to form solid nubs.

POLYPROPYLENE ROPE

Description: This stranded material is usually bright yellow, but also comes in red and orange.

Buying information: The main asset of this rope is that it floats, therefore it is used to mark the dropoff point to the deep end of a swimming pool. It is good in any situation where you want a rope with high visibility.

How-to hint: The best tool to cut this material is an electric knife. The heat keeps the ends from unraveling by sealing them.

POLYPROPYLENE ROPE

CLOTHESLINE

Description: This is made of various materials. Commonly it is ¼-inch or 5⁄16-inch white cotton braid (also known as number 7 sash cord); another type is wire covered with a thin sheath of plastic; yet another is braided polyethelene. It comes in 50- and 100-foot hanks.

Buying information: Cotton clothesline holds clothespins better than plastic, but soils more easily.

How-to hint: Cut with ordinary scissors or a sharp knife.

TWINE

Description: Twine comes in various stranded forms. Jute twine has a fuzzy surface. Masonry line is a three-strand thin— but strong—cord made of cotton or a synthetic material, and comes in a ball. Sisal twine is two-ply.

Buying information: Sisal is inexpensive; masonry line is very strong; jute is good for package tying.

BUTCHER'S TWINE

Description: This is thin white cotton cord.

Buying information: Butcher's twine is a very strong cord that can be used for a variety of wrapping purposes, and also in food preparation, since it is sterilized. A classic use is tying a beef roast.

ROPE ACCESSORIES

A variety of hardware can be used with rope and cord, but three pieces predominate: the snap, the swivel eye snap, and the pulley.

SNAP

Description: This is a teardrop-shaped device with an eye on one end and a snap mechanism on the other.

Buying information: In use, a rope is tied to the eye end of the snap. Snaps are good for a wide variety of jobs where it is necessary to fasten a line to a ring, including flagpole lines, dog runs, and water skis.

How-to hints: In tying the snap to the rope, be sure your knot will hold. A rope clip can be used and the knot reinforced by tying it with a plastic tie-down.

SWIVEL-EYE SNAP

Description: This looks like the regular snap, except the snap rotates 360 degrees.

Buying information: Because it swivels, it is popular for dog runs.

How-to hint: Tie securely, as suggested above.

PULLEY

Description: This has grooved metal wheels, usually capable of accommodating ⅛-inch, ³⁄₁₆-inch, and ¼-inch rope. It is available with single and double wheels.

Buying information: A pulley is mostly used for clothesline, but is used for other things as well. For example, you can rig a winch that would enable you to lift heavy materials to a second floor. The double pulley is good for awnings.

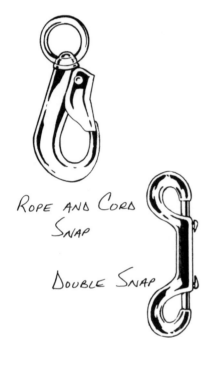

ROPE AND CORD SNAP

DOUBLE SNAP

SWIVEL-EYE SNAP

SCREENING

Screening is available in a variety of finishes and materials: aluminum (plain and anodized charcoal), bronze, and fiberglass. It also comes in several colors.

ALUMINUM SCREENING

Description: This is bright metal screening in virtually endless lengths (100-foot rolls) and in widths of 24 to 48 inches.

Buying information: Aluminum screening is strong and easy to see through. It also reflects light better than any other screening, making it relatively opaque from the outside in daylight. It is available in a couple of gauges. For most uses the finer-gauge wire (called 18x16) works fine. If children are in the area and you want the screening to be able to take extra punishment, install the heavier screening (18x14). In addition to being available by the foot, screening also comes in precut rolls, but this is more expensive. A typical length for packaged material is 6 feet, and it comes in various widths up to 48 inches.

How-to hints: With the right tools, installing aluminum screening is a good job for the beginning do-it-yourselfer. The main tool is a screening tool with a convex metal wheel on one end and a concave wheel on the other. One wheel presses the screening into the groove on the screen frame and the other presses the spline, which holds the screen in place. Spline comes in various diameters (you must get the diameter that fits the grooves in the screen frame you're working on) and in smooth or ridged form. Smooth is faster to use (good if you have a lot of screens to do) but ridged is less likely to slip out of the groove in the frame.

To make the job easier, use small C clamps; they hold the screening down on one side while you work on the other. Use a sharp utility knife to cut screening, changing blades as needed, and wear gloves to protect your fingers against cut screening edges.

You may be able to use the old spline that holds the screening in place at the edges by first washing it in warm, soapy water to clean and soften it. Otherwise you can buy new spline in five different diameters; take a piece of the existing spline with you to the store to get the proper size.

Old-fashioned screens with wooden frames are also simple to rescreen. Fold over the screen at the edges and staple it in place. It's usually better to use new molding strips.

If you are right-handed, it's easier if you do the right side and top first. If left-handed, do the left side and top first.

To keep the screening taut so it won't "belly" in or out, warp or bow the screen and staple the screen at the top, stretching it across the inside of the bow; staple it at the bottom as well. When the clamps are released, the tension of the frame will pull the material taut. It can then be stapled at the sides and the moulding strips can be attached.

ANODIZED CHARCOAL SCREENING

Description: This is black aluminum screening, the most transparent of all. It is available in the same sizes as aluminum.
How-to hint: Same as for aluminum screening.

BRONZE SCREENING

Description: This is bronze-colored metal screening.
Buying information: Bronze screening is very expensive, but it is the only metal screening that will last a lifetime in communities close to salt water.
How-to hint: Same as for aluminum screening.

FIBERGLASS SCREENING

Description: This looks like any other screening. It is available in gray and black.
Buying information: Fiberglass is inexpensive, and lasts for years—even in saltwater areas. Its only drawback is that it can be cut easily. An object that will bounce off aluminum will tear fiberglass.
How-to hints: Install this type like other screening, but in metal-screened frames it is advisable to use spline that is one size larger in diameter than you would use for comparable metal screen. Otherwise the fiberglass can work its way free.

SCREW EYES AND SCREW HOOKS

Screw eyes and screw hooks are handy devices with a variety of purposes, mainly to hang things and hook them together.

Screw eyes are classified according to eye size: the larger the eye, the longer the shank. Screw eyes and hooks range from a tiny ½ inch long up to 3 inches.

To get the right screw eye or hook, you don't need to know the numbering system that is used; knowing the job at hand and what's available is enough. In some cases the items are carded together, but you can also buy them loose.

Screw Eye

Description: This is a closed hook with a straight shank, part of which may be threaded like a lag screw, or with a blunt end and fine threads like a machine screw.

Buying information: It is commonly used to hang things. For example, the screw eye with the lag-screw end can be turned into wood and the item hung from the eye. Or the screw eye may be used in combination with a hook (see below). The screw eye with machine-screw threads would pass all the way through the wood and have a nut and washer.

How-to hints: In some cases, a screw eye may be installed a little out of alignment with the mating hook. Rather than removing it and reinstalling it, you can bend it into alignment with pliers.

For maximum strength when hanging things, use the screw eye with machine-screw threads rather than the lag-screw type.

Screw Eye

Screw Hook

Description: This is an open hook with a shank, having lag or machine-screw threads.

Buying information: A screw hook is usually used in wood, but it works on other materials where the hook can bite securely. It is commonly used to hang clothesline and to pull cable taut.

How-to hints: To drive the screw in more easily, drill a pilot hole for it. If the hook is extra large, apply soap to the threads to make it easier to drive.

Screw Hook

Square Bend Hook

Description: This looks like a screw eye except the hooked part is an L shape. Ninety percent of these are brass-plated, but cadmium-plated ones can be ordered.

Buying information: It is good for supporting things like drapery rods.

Square Bend Hook

Gate Hook

Description: This is a combination of screw eye and screw hook. A closed loop at the butt end of the hook's shank passes through a screw eye; a separate screw eye receives the hook. It

Gate Hook

commonly comes with a screw hook 6 or 8 inches long.

Buying information: As the name suggests, gate hooks are for gates. You can also get them with self-closing latches.

How-to hint: When mounting the parts of a gate hook, try to ensure that they are aligned accurately. This will make the gate that much easier to open.

CUP HOOK

Description: This looks like a screw hook except that it has a plate or shoulder between the shank and the hook. It commonly comes in a ½-inch size (the diameter of the hooked part), but can be purchased in 1⅜-inch and 1½-inch sizes. It is almost always made of brass.

Buying information: Cup hooks are for hanging cups (under shelves). They can also be used for hanging keys and Christmas tree lights. The plate or shoulder prevents the hook from being driven in too far.

How-to hint: Since cup hooks are made of soft brass, they are easier to install if you first make a pilot hole with an awl.

SHOULDER HOOK

Description: This is just like the cup hook except it has an L-shaped end rather than a hook.

Buying information: It can be used to hang a variety of items including cups, plaques, and fishing rods.

CLOTHESLINE HOOK

Description: This comes in two forms: one is a simple hook with lag-screw threads, the other is a hook mounted on a plate with four screw holes. Such hardware is normally electroplated.

How-to hints: The lag-screw type can be driven into a wooden post, while the plate type is better for siding, where you want the stronger connection made possible by using four screws.

HAMMOCK HOOK

Description: Two kinds predominate: one is a screw hook with a swiveling plate that has holes in it for screws; the other is simply a hefty screw eye.

How-to hints: If you are screwing into wood, the screw eye should work fine; if you are screwing into siding, use the plate type, which allows the use of small screws that collectively get a stronger bite in the siding than would a single lag screw.

ROUND CUP HOOK

TV Cable Hook

Description: This looks like a hammock hook with a plate.

Buying information: This is used for mounting TV wire, and the plate handily hides the hole made for the cable.

How-to hint: Since this is ordinarily mounted on the roof, a good idea is to swab the underside of the plate with roofing cement before mounting, to prevent water from getting under it.

Flat Hook

Description: This has a decorative look and is machined so that it can lie flat. It mates with a corresponding pin, and comes in various sizes.

Buying information: A flat hook is commonly used on chest and cabinet lids.

How-to hint: An alternative way to attach a flat hook is to drive a wood screw into place and use this instead of the pin.

Turnbuckle

Description: This is a barrel-shaped device with holes at the ends—one threaded right-handed, the other left-handed. A threaded rod with an eye at the other end is threaded into each hole. It commonly comes in a 42-inch length. Most turnbuckles are zinc-plated, but galvanized ones are available in the larger sizes.

Buying information: Turning the turnbuckle tightens the rods. An eye-and-eye turnbuckle is good for securing to screens or other doors to take the sag out by pulling the door square.

How-to hints: The turnbuckle may be screwed directly to the door, or wires may be looped into the eye ends of the rods and secured. You first turn a turnbuckle by hand, and then insert a rod (screwdriver, etc.) through the turnbuckle and use it as a handle to tighten it the rest of the way. Don't tighten it any more than necessary to support or align the door.

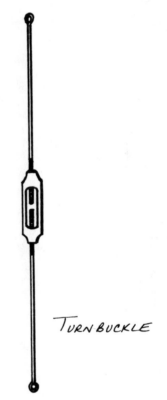

TURNBUCKLE

Hook-and-Eye Turnbuckle

Description: This is a standard turnbuckle, except one of the rods has a hook rather than an eye on one end.

Buying information: Use wherever an eye and hook works best, particularly on wood-framed screen doors.

Hook-and-Hook Turnbuckle

Description: This is a standard turnbuckle, but with a hook on each rod.

Buying information: A hook-and-hook turnbuckle can be used with strap iron for pulling something tight. Just insert the hooks in appropriate holes on the iron and turn the turnbuckle until the strap iron is taut.

SCREWS

Screws have greater holding power than nails and can be removed when desired; in other words, you can disassemble the job at will.

There are four things to consider when selecting a screw for the job: finish, length, gauge, and head.

Screws can be plain steel, blued, or dipped—the latter two types are partially resistant to moisture—galvanized, brass, or chrome-plated. Screws range in length up to about 4 inches.

Screws are also classifed according to the diameter or gauge, commonly ranging from No. 5 to No. 14, though larger sizes are available. The gauge refers to the diameter under the head. If the screw is a type that tapers, the diameter is smaller at its tip than nearer its head. Screws of the same gauge are available in different lengths.

Screws are designed to operate best in certain materials, though there are some that have multiple uses.

If you have many screws to drive in wood, or a few large ones, drilling pilot holes is the first thing you should do. Special profiled bits are available for drilling slightly smaller diameter holes than the tapering screw diameters and makes them much easier to drive.

If you have many screws to drive, or large screws, use some sort of power tool, such as a cordless screwdriver. This, too, will make the job much easier.

FLATHEAD
SCREW

Wood Screw

Description: This has a tapered, partially threaded shank that comes to a point. There are three types of heads: flathead, roundhead, and ovalhead.

Flathead screws have a countersunk head, meaning that they are tapered to be recessed or sunk flush into the wood, and then the space above filled with a wood plug or putty to hide the head.

The head of a roundhead screw forms a half-circle in profile.

Ovalhead screws are partially recessed.

ROUNDHEAD
SCREW

OVALHEAD
SCREW

Heads may be straight-slot or Phillips. The straight-slotted head has just that—a slot across the head of the screw. The Phillips has crisscross slots and is turned with a Phillips screwdriver. A Phillips screwdriver is less likely to slip out of its slots than a conventional driver, which is why this type of screw is commonly used on finished surfaces.

Buying information: As the name suggests, wood screws are designed to be used in assembling wood components. They are usually available in brass or steel. The roundhead is easiest to grip and turn. Ovalhead screws are often used when the screw head will be visible and must look good.

How-to hints: Wood screws can be recessed—countersunk beneath the surface of the wood. The best way to do this is with a countersink bit. These come in various sizes to match screw sizes and are designed to drill the exact holes needed with a minimum of difficulty.

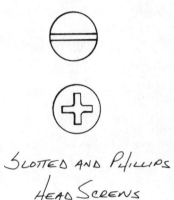

Slotted and Phillips Head Screws

MACHINE SCREW

Description: Unlike the wood screw, the machine screw is threaded the entire length of its shank. Ends are flat rather than pointed, and the heads are either round or flat. The finish may be plain steel, cadmium-plated, or chrome-plated; screws may also be brass.

Threads may be "coarse" or "fine" for a given diameter or gauge. The screws come in lengths from ½ inch to 4 inches.

Buying information: Machine screws are used to assemble metal components, such as slotted metal shelving. These screws are bought by gauge and thread number. An 8x24 screw, for example, means a No. 8 gauge screw with 24 threads per inch, which is one of the "coarse" series. A "fine" No. 8 screw has 32 threads per inch.

Machine Screw

SHEET METAL SCREW

Description: This screw is tapered all along its length and has a pointed end, and the threads are spiraled loosely, like those of a wood screw, rather than tightly, like those of a machine screw. It comes with either a Phillips head or a slotted pan head.

Buying information: Sheet metal screws are designed to cut their own threads in thin gauge metal. Drill an undersized pilot hole first. These screws are used for holding parts on aluminum storm doors or assembling aluminum gutters. They are also commonly used to attach panels to home appliances.

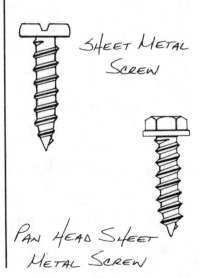

Sheet Metal Screw

Pan Head Sheet Metal Screw

TECS Screw

Description: This is a fully threaded screw with a tip shaped like a drill bit and a head that is either Phillips or hex. It comes zinc-plated, in various sizes.

Buying information: These screws can be used to drill and fasten heavy sheet metal in one operation. They are great for securing track on closet doors.

How-to hint: Use an electric screwdriver with a magnetic bit. The cordless type works well.

Contek Screw

Contek Screw

Description: This is double-pitched (threads go at different diagonal directions) with a recessed Phillips or $\frac{5}{16}$ hex head. They are zinc chromate-plated.

Buying information: Contek screws are excellent for securing boards to concrete, and are much safer than masonry nails.

How-to hint: These screws must be installed with a masonry drill bit and cordless drill. They screw into the cement.

Drywall Screw

Drywall Screw

Description: Made of blued steel, with a bugle-shaped head, this screw is threaded all the way to the Phillips-type head and has a very sharp point. It comes in lengths of 1¼ to 3 inches, and in various gauges.

Buying information: A drywall screw can be used on wood or metal studs for securing drywall. Because of the thread design, there is little chance of wood splitting, as can happen with drywall nails.

SHELF SUPPORTS

Utility Bracket

Description: This is an L-shaped metal support with holes for mounting.

Buying information: Utility brackets are, as the name suggests, for utility. They are mounted on the walls and shelving laid across them. They are usually gray, but also come in gold and black.

How-to hints: For strength, try to find wall studs and mount brackets on them with screws. In newer homes, studs are 16 inches apart, while in older homes they are usually 24 inches

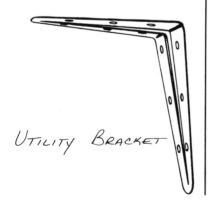

Utility Bracket

apart. If the studs are not located where you need them to be, use hollow-wall fasteners or another appropriate type, making sure they can support the weight of the shelf and its contents.

Standard and Bracket

Description: This consists of two pieces of hardware, a slotted vertical section that mounts on the wall and brackets in various shapes that mount, by means of hooked ends, onto the standard.

Buying information: Standards and brackets come in various sizes, characterized by bracket width, which can range from 4 to 18 inches, in 2-inch increments. They come in various configurations for every decor.

The big plus of this hardware is that the brackets can be moved up and down along the standard, increasing or decreasing shelf height as required.

Sometimes the standards and brackets of different manufacturers are interchangeable, but in most instances you must use the same brand.

How-to hint: See utility bracket, above. If you are using standards and brackets to support something very heavy, such as a TV, don't use other fasteners: find the studs and drive screws into them.

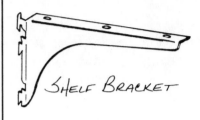

Shelf Bracket

Pilaster

Description: This consists of a flat metal slotted standard and clips that fit into the standard.

Buying information: Pilasters are used inside cabinets.

How-to hint: Screw two standards to each side of the cabinet and then insert the clips in the standards and rest the shelves on them. The arrangement allows you to raise or lower shelf height as required.

Pilaster Clip

Shelf Support

Description: This is an L-shaped piece with a small round projection coming from the back of the top part of the L.

Buying information: Shelf supports may be plastic or metal. They are mounted in the drilled holes made in kitchen cabinets, and when the shelves are laid on top, the weight locks them in place.

How-to hints: Proper installation of shelf supports depends on

Shelf Support

drilling holes ¼ inch apart in an absolutely straight line, something that is not very easy to do. It is best to use a jig (template) with previously drilled holes for proper hole location and alignment. This can easily be made from a one-by-two board: Just mark the holes needed and use an ordinary electric drill to drill them, or, better, use a drill press.

Shelf supports are not especially good for supporting heavy weights, such as bookshelves. Plastic supports will break, and metal ones, if set into anything but hardwood, may sag within their holes, enlarging the holes so that the supports pull out.

SLIDING DOOR HARDWARE

SLIDING (PATIO) DOOR HARDWARE
Description: A variety of parts are available, such as wheels, locks, and track.
Buying information: The only reliable way to replace any of the hardware on a sliding door is to bring the old part into the hardware store and get a matching piece. Parts from different manufacturers can't be mixed. Also take note of the door manufacturer's name. It will help you in selecting the exact replacement part.

SPRINGS

There are three categories of springs: compression, extension, and torsion. The first two kinds are widely used, while torsion springs are not.

Springs come in a vast number of gauges and lengths. Some are hot-dipped galvanized for use outdoors; others are painted with black enamel and are for interior use only. Chrome-plated springs are also sometimes available, and can be used outside.

The quickest way to get a replacement spring, since they come in so many sizes, is to bring the existing one into the store and match it up with samples (many dealers have boards displaying a variety of springs).

You can also buy assortments of springs, but this is probably for the rare individual. Springs are not used that much in average do-it-yourself projects.

Springs are made of tough metal and are difficult to cut and handle. If you want to cut one, nick it with a cold chisel or old pair of pliers at the desired spot. Work it back and forth until it snaps. If you want to open or close a spring, locking pliers work well.

COMPRESSION SPRING

Description: This is the type that almost everyone thinks of when the word *spring* is mentioned. It has spaced coils and either flat or slightly extended ends.

Buying information: These springs keep things pushed apart. They are often enclosed within a cylinder or wrapped around a shaft.

COMPRESSION SPRING

EXTENSION SPRING

Description: Coils are usually close-wound, i.e., shoulder-to-shoulder, and the ends, unlike those of the compression spring, usually have either a closed loop or a hook.

Buying information: This spring has a variety of uses, and the more coils it has the longer it expands. You can either hook the spring onto something, or hook something onto the spring.

EXTENSION SPRING

One extension spring has hooked ends 3 inches long, which is useful in getting into tight places, such as oven doors. Instead of having to snake in your hand and attach a spring with a short hook, you can fish in the long hook until it can grab on.

Another useful extension spring is the one used on screen doors. The end of this spring has a cap with a threaded eyebolt and nut. By rotating the bolt you can increase or relax the tension in order to make the door close more quickly or slowly.

TORSION SPRING

Description: This is a standard spring with a U-shaped extension piece on each side. The extensions act as levers to twist the spring, rather than elongate or compress it.

Buying information: The torsion spring is good for a quick fix on a self-closing screen door or to make a self-closing gate or to give spring action to a door that doesn't have it.

TORSION SPRING

STORM DOOR AND SCREEN DOOR HARDWARE

Over the last twenty years or so, the American public has been reminded of the value of energy-saving products and devices, and one of the most important of these is the storm door. The glass or plastic outside entry door makes it more difficult for hot air to get out—a boon in the winter—and also helps to keep cooled air in the house during the summer.

Most storm doors, of course, double as screen doors.

LOCK MECHANISM

Description: This varies, but it normally consists of a knob on the outside and a lever-type handle inside. It usually comes in black or white to match the colors of most storm doors, but some are of plain aluminum.

Buying information: It's best to remove the existing lock mechanism and take it to the store to get a replacement; screw holes vary from brand to brand, and you have to get what fits in your door, whether the door is of metal or wood.

It is possible to increase the security that the lock mechanism provides. Some don't lock, but you can get replacements that have a lever you flip to lock. This allows you to keep the entry door open and yet have the storm door locked.

For even greater security, you can get a lock mechanism that operates with a key.

If the lock mechanism you buy does not come out far enough to engage the old striker, you can get nylon shims to insert under the strike plate to bring it out as far as necessary.

PNEUMATIC CLOSER

Description: Storm door closers also vary, but most are of the bicycle-pump variety: a long cylinder with a plunger mechanism attached.

Buying information: Again, take the old one to the store to get a suitable replacement.

How-to hints: Pay careful attention to installation instructions, because they are crucial for the closer to work properly. In particular, separate closer from mounting bracket. Snap it in under tension when door is closed.

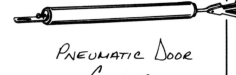

PNEUMATIC DOOR CLOSER

ROTARY DOOR CLOSER

Description: This is a double-hinged arm connected to a pneumatic cylinder with a plate for attaching the cylinder to the door and the arm. It comes with an aluminum finish.

Buying information: This does the same job as a closer, except that it is installed near the top of the door. It comes in various styles and sizes, so it is best to take the existing closer to the store to get the proper replacement.

SPRING

Description: Standard spring.

Buying information: Show the old one to the dealer.

How-to hint: Opening and closing the door puts a lot of stress on a spring and the screws holding it in place. When installing the new spring, use beefy screws instead of the flimsy ones that are usually provided.

STORM/SASH HANGER

Description: This is a rectangular plate with a squarish hook and screw holes for mounting. It mates with a corresponding hook part, also with screw holes for mounting.

Buying information: It is used to hang screen/storm windows.

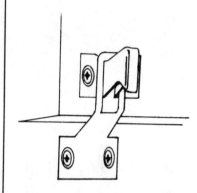

SCREEN OR STORM
SASH 3/8-INCH INSET

SCREEN CORNER

Description: This is an L-shaped metal brace with screw holes and raised edges.

Buying information: It is used to reinforce screen door corners.

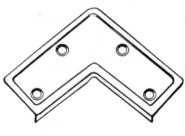

SCREEN CORNER

SCREEN PATCH

Description: This is a small square of aluminum screening with hooked edges.

Buying information: Patches usually come five to a package, and are used to patch holes in screens. They are noticeable, but they work.

How-to hints: To use a patch, thread the hooked edges through the screen, then press down to lock the patch over the hole. You could easily make a similar patch from scrap screening, but the process would not be as fast. Screening can also be replaced relatively easily (see pages 51–52).

DOOR CLIP WITH SCREWS

Description: This is a fancy knurled screw and an L-shaped door clip.

Buying information: These come in packages of eight, and are used to hold screens and storm windows in place.

TURNBUTTON

TURNBUTTON
Description: This is an aluminum stamping that resembles a bow tie and comes with a mounting screw upon which it swivels.
Buying information: This, too, is used to hold screens or storm windows in place.

THREADED ROD

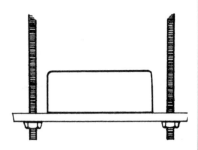

THREADED ROD

THREADED ROD
Description: This is a continuous metal rod with threads.
Buying information: Threaded rod can be used with nuts and washers to do a variety of bracing, fastening, and mounting jobs; it can also be used to support hanging shelves. In some situations, bolts are not suitable because of limited thread portions (for example, a 6-inch bolt may have only 1 inch or 1½ inches of threads); threaded rod can serve such problems well.

It comes in a variety of lengths and diameters. Hardware stores commonly carry it in 2- and 3-foot lengths, with diameters ranging from ³⁄₁₆ to ½ inch in small increments. However, it is also available in diameters all the way up to 1¼ inches and in lengths of 6, 10, and 12 feet. To obtain these sizes you may have to special-order them—or visit a number of hardware stores. Rod sizes are identified by a dot of color on the end of the rod. Finish on threaded rod is either electroplating or plain steel. In addition, it comes in various precut shapes such as U's and J's, and with eyebolts.
How-to hints: Threaded rod may be cut with a hacksaw or, if narrow enough, with a bolt cutter.

Threads on the rod run at a slight angle, so it is easy to create burrs when cutting with a hacksaw. To avoid this, run nuts down from each end of the rod until they flank the points where you want to cut. Make the cut, then run the nuts off the cut ends; they will dress the ends, removing any burrs.

Threaded rod can be cold-bent—no heat required.

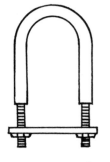

THREADED ROD
IN U-BOLT SHAPE

WALL FASTENERS

Wall fasteners are useful where there is no solid surface, such as a stud, in which to drive a nail or screw. They can also be used on ceilings.

There are three basic kinds of fasteners: expansion shields for masonry, toggle bolts, and hollow-wall anchors for hollow-wall construction. They come in various sizes: the bigger they are, the more weight they can support.

LEAD SHIELD

Description: This consists of a lead shield or cylinder in various sizes.

Buying information: Lead shields are good for hanging things on concrete. Any of a variety of items can be hung, but the weight of the item must not exceed the capacity of the fastener or it will pull out of the wall. Lead shields are used in conjunction with wood screws or lag screws—not machine screws.

How-to hints: To use a lead shield, drill a hole in the wall that is the diameter of the sleeve. Insert the sleeve through the item and into the hole, and tighten. As the screw is turned, the sleeve expands and locks in place.

The screw used should be ¼ inch deeper than the sleeve.

See also information on lead wool in this section.

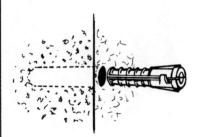

LAG SCREW ANCHOR SHIELD

FIBER SLEEVE

Description: This is a jute cylinder with a lead interior. It comes in various sizes.

Buying information: It is used with wood screws only to hang things on concrete.

How-to hint: Fiber sleeves break easily, and the holes to receive them must be drilled to an exact size.

PLASTIC SLEEVE

Description: This is a plastic cylinder that comes in various sizes.

Buying information: These fasteners are good for hanging things on concrete, plaster, drywall, and even ceramic tile. They are durable and easy to install, and they hold very well.

How-to hints: Drill a hole and insert the sleeve. Align the hole on the item and drive in a wood screw. As with other sleeves, these expand as a screw is driven into them.

PLASTIC SLEEVE

MACHINE SCREW ANCHOR

Description: This is a cylindrical anchor with a machine screw at one end.

Buying information: When you want to hang something with

machine screw threads on concrete, use machine screw anchors.

How-to hints: A setting tool must be used with this. Drill proper hole in concrete, insert machine screw anchor with large base in first, then use setting tool to center, and drive lead sleeve over insert to tighten it in the hole. Put machine screw through item to be hung, and tighten.

Toggle Bolt

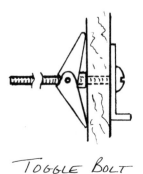

Toggle Bolt

Description: This is a machine screw on which are threaded collapsible "wings" that may or may not be spring-actuated.

Buying information: Toggle bolts are used in hollow-wall construction, that is, construction where studs are covered with wall material and there are cavities within the walls. They can also be used on ceilings.

They are very strong, and are good for hanging things on plaster, drywall, and hollow cement blocks.

Toggle bolts come in long sizes. Make sure that the one you use will not be too long for the cavity and thus will contact the adjacent wall. Observe weight limits.

How-to hints: Drill a hole in the wall, fold the wings of the toggle, and slip the toggle through the hole in the item to be hung. Then tighten the screw at the same time as you are pulling the bolt toward you. Otherwise, it may never tighten; the toggle will just keep spinning as the bolt turns. If you are doing it right, the wings, which have opened, will push against the back side of the wall.

Hollow-Wall Anchor

Description: This is a cylinderlike device with expandable wings.

Buying information: Hollow-wall anchors (commonly called Molly bolts after one trade name) are for hanging things in drywall. They come in a variety of sizes so that they can be used on walls up to 1⅛ inches thick.

How-to hints: It works like a toggle; however, unlike a toggle, you can remove the mounting screw without losing the hardware behind the wall. Drill a hole, slip the anchor through, and then tighten the screw so the wings in back expand. Withdraw the screw, position the item to be hung, then reinsert and tighten the screw.

Three tips: (1) The flange or smooth part of the anchor

should be the same thickness as the wall material. (2) Make sure the hole in the wall is clean and solid. There are little teeth under the head of the anchor, and they must be able to bite into solid material in order for the anchor to stay stationary and the screw to turn. (3) If the anchor starts to turn, you can get a thin forked tool (two-prong collar holder) to hold it stationary.

JACK NUT

Description: This is a small hollow-wall anchor.

Buying information: Jack nuts are designed to hang things on hollow-core doors—ones consisting of a sandwich of wood with a filler such as corrugated cardboard. Not for solid wood doors; 6x32 machine screws are used on those. Jack nuts can only be used on surfaces that do not exceed ⅛ inch in thickness.

PICTURE HOOK

Description: This is a hook with a downward-angled nail hole on top.

Buying information: Picture hooks are widely used for hanging pictures, mirrors, and the like. They come in single- and double-nail forms: both types can hang pictures up to 40 pounds. Just read the package label. Picture hangers also come in decorative styles.

How-to hint: When driving nails in plaster or plasterboard, first stick on a small piece of transparent tape to ensure that the wall surface does not crumble.

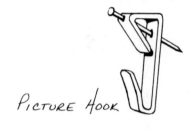

PICTURE HOOK

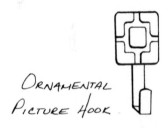

ORNAMENTAL
PICTURE HOOK

MIRROR HANGER

Description: This is a small clip with screw holes.

Buying information: It is used to secure a heavy mirror to the back of a door. The clips are screwed to the door and grip the mirror by the edges.

LEAD WOOL

Description: Lead wool resembles very coarse steel wool.

Buying information: This is available in 1-pound clumps. It is used as a hole filler, and works like a plastic sleeve for anchoring screws into holes made in concrete walls or floors.

How-to hints: Use lead wool when a hole for a screw is fractionally out of position. Just fill the hole with lead wool, tamp it

MIRROR HANGER

down a bit, then drive in the screw. The screw will grip firmly, as it might not if a standard sleeve that was slightly misaligned were used. Lead wool can also be used for fastening a door threshold to a concrete floor. Be sure to pack lead wool lightly in the hole—it will grip the screw threads better.

WEATHER STRIPPING

Of all the things you can do to make a home energy-efficient, the one that gives the greatest return on your investment is weather stripping: using some sort of material to seal gaps around doors and windows. A properly caulked and weather-stripped house can reduce your fuel bills significantly.

Weather stripping works simply. In the winter it helps keep warmed air inside the home and cold air out; in the summer, cooled air is blocked from getting out and hot air from getting in. The result is that the heating system doesn't work as hard to maintain temperature in the room—and fuel savings are achieved.

There is a wide variety of weather stripping, most of it simple to install.

SPRING BRONZE
Description: These are narrow strips, slightly bent, with nail holes along the edges.
Buying information: This material is used around a door. When the door is closed it seals tightly. It is difficult to find in stores.
How-to hint: Spring bronze is hard to install, since it involves planing down the door so it can fit in place.

STEEL-INTERLOCKING WEATHER STRIP
Description: These are two U-shaped metal strips with lips meant to interlock when installed.
Buying information: One strip is installed on the door, the other on the frame. When the door is closed the strips interlock, providing protection against the weather and burglars.
How-to hint: This is very difficult to install properly: special tools are required.

SERRATED FELT/METAL WEATHER STRIP
Description: These are strips of felt encased in metal.
Buying information: This seals gaps around windows and

doors. It is not pretty, but it does the job—and it's cheap.

How-to hint: Nail in place using very small nails that come with it. To ease the job, use a brad driver, a device that allows you to push the nails in place rather than having to hammer them.

TUBULAR VINYL GASKET

Description: This consists of a flat lip of vinyl with one edge tubular in cross-section.

Buying information: It is used to seal doors or windows. It can be used for sealing or to replace factory-installed weather stripping on windows.

How-to hint: To ease the job, use staples.

TUBULAR VINYL GASKET
WEATHER STRIPPING

ALUMINUM-VINYL DOOR BOTTOM

Description: This is a molded vinyl section that is mounted on the front of the door, and a mating aluminum section mounted on the floor.

Buying information: Use this for sealing a gap beneath the door. This type of weather stripping is very sturdy and will last a long time.

How-to hint: It can be cut with a hacksaw. Take care when using a hacksaw that the weatherstrip is solidly held so the tool doesn't slip.

ALUMINUM SADDLE WITH VINYL GASKET

Description: This consists of a rounded aluminum strip that is mounted on the bottom of the door and a corresponding rounded vinyl section mounted on the threshold beneath the closed door.

Buying information: It seals the gap between the bottom of the door and floor: When the door is closed, the vinyl and aluminum sections interlock.

How-to hint: Installation is difficult because the door must be planed exactly so that the parts mate.

STRIPPING FOR GARAGE

ALUMINUM SADDLE WITH INTERLOCKING DOOR BOTTOM

Description: This is a formed aluminum saddle that is installed on the floor and mates with a flat vinyl strip installed on the bottom of the door.

Buying information: This seals the gap under a door.

How-to hint: It is easier to install than the aluminum saddle with vinyl gasket, but the interlock can catch on rugs as the door is closed.

ALUMINUM AND VINYL STRIP

Description: This is a strip of aluminum with vinyl facing.

Buying information: Install it on the doorstop so that the door closes against it. It is expensive.

How-to hint: Easy to install.

RUBBER GARAGE-DOOR STRIPPING

Description: This is a molded, double-lipped rubber strip.

Buying information: It is used to seal the space beneath the garage door; the strip also acts as a shock absorber when the door is closed.

How-to hint: It is simple to install with 1¼-inch roofing nails, but stagger the nails to avoid tearing.

WOOD

Description: These are thin moldings, edged with a narrow strip of foam or vinyl. They come in thicknesses of ⅜ and 3⁄16 inch.

Buying information: The thick material is designed to replace the stop molding on a door. The thinner material can be installed on the doorstop molding (frame).

How-to hint: You can use a brad driver to drive home the tiny nails used for attaching this material.

ALUMINUM LOW RUG THRESHOLD

Description: This is a 36-inch-long aluminum casting with a vinyl insert.

Buying information: In place, this threshold can be adjusted from ¾ inch to 1¼ inches, allowing a lot of room for error in installation and when the floor isn't true.

How-to hints: To level this threshold, run a bead of caulk under it as needed. You can also use self-stick foam rubber.

WINDOW HARDWARE

There is a tremendous variety of window hardware available; indeed, thousands of parts exist for different windows. Nonetheless, the range of hardware can be broken down into manageable bites, as follows, for casement as well as double-hung windows.

Casement Windows

Roto Handle
Description: This comes in various shapes, but always with a small handle for turning.

Buying information: Such handles are used to open and close casement windows. Sizes vary, so take the existing handle with you when you shop for a new one. You'll likely have better luck finding the piece you need at a home center than at a hardware store.

How-to hint: In some cases a handle that was welded on has broken off. If so, it may be possible to reattach it with a pair of sheet-metal screws driven into the holes where the existing screws were. Get the Phillips-head type so that you can turn them in well.

Locking Handle
Description: This is roughly an upside-down L with a hook on the end of the L.

Buying information: Again, take the existing piece with you when shopping for a new one.

How-to hint: Use sheet metal screws to attach it.

Double-Hung Windows

Cam Sash Lock
Description: This is a curved piece for gripping that engages a hooked-over piece with screw holes. It is available in brass, brass-plated, and chrome-plated.

Buying information: Screw holes might match or be slightly off on the new lock. Show it to the dealer.

How-to hint: When installing the lock, first drill pilot holes and take great care; the pieces must mesh perfectly.

Window Control Spring
Description: This is a short piece of wavy stainless steel.

Buying information: It is excellent when regular double-hung sash-control hardware, such as cords and weights, fails. You don't need to remove any hardware.

How-to hint: One of these pieces goes on each side of the window. Just raise the sash and push the piece up between the track and side of the window. The hardware will keep the sash tight in the track so that it can be lowered or raised as required.

Window Control Spring

SAFETY SASH LOCK
Description: These locks vary. Your best bet is to go into the hardware store and see which one you like and is the easiest to install. All work pretty well.

SASH HANDLE/PULL
Description: Some are handles, while others are just turned-over metal pieces for gripping with a couple of fingers. Both handles and pulls, however, have screw holes for mounting. They come in different materials and finishes, including brass.

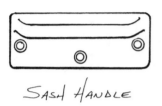

SASH HANDLE

WIRE

Like electrical wire, wire for standard uses is available in various gauges, stranded and solid. Stranded wire consists of individual strands wound together; solid is one wire. The lower the gauge number, the thicker the wire. Wire that is flexible works best with plants, because it can be formed to the shape of the pots.

GALVANIZED WIRE
Description: This material comes in various gauges—20, 12, 9—and hot-dipped galvanized as well as plastic-coated.
Buying information: The gauge of the wire determines its flexibility and use, everything from guy wires to clothesline (the plastic-coated variety). It is available in 1- and 5-pound coils and on reels.

COPPER WIRE
Description: This is 24-gauge soft copper in coils.
Buying information: Copper wire has many uses, from tying ends of rope so they won't unravel to hanging pictures.

GREEN ENAMELED WIRE
Description: This is thin-gauge wire painted green.
Buying information: It is easy to form, used in flower arranging.

WIRE FENCING

BED GUARD

Description: This is 14-inch-high galvanized open-pattern wire fencing in rolls of 25 feet.

Buying information: This material keeps small animals, such as rabbits, out of flower beds. Normally available galvanized, it sometimes can be found in colors—white, green, and yellow—and add a decorative accent.

How-to hint: Using bed guard is simple. Cut it with snips and push the sharpened ends into the earth.

BED GUARD

POULTRY FENCING

Description: This is large-mesh (1 or 2 feet) material available up to 6 feet high and in 50-foot rolls. It is galvanized.

Buying information: Though its principal use is to keep small animals off a property, it can be nailed to a ranch-style fence to create an inexpensive pen for a dog.

MISCELLANEOUS HARDWARE

Some hardware items do not belong to a family of similar-function products, but stand alone.

THREADED INSERT

Description: This looks like a short piece of tubing with coarse threads on the outside and fine threads on the inside.

Buying information: Inserted in wood, it serves as the female portion for furniture assembly.

COTTER PIN

Description: This looks like a beefy hairpin.

Buying information: Cotter pins are slipped through holes in rods and the like. Often used to hold a wheel on an axle, they are made of brass, copper, and plain or stainless steel.

How-to hints: To lock a cotter pin in place, just bend back the ends so that it can't slip back through the hole in the rod or axle. One leg of the pin is longer than the other to facilitate separation of the legs.

COTTER PIN

CABLE TIE

Description: This is a slim piece of nylon with a loop at one end.
Buying information: Once tied, cable ties don't release. They are used for tying bundles of wire, even as temporary hinges.
How-to hints: To make a hinge, drill holes and tie the ties in place.

Safety is the watchword with these. Since the ties, once pulled taut, don't release, children can choke or otherwise hurt themselves. By the same token, be sure you have set things up the way you want them before you pull the tie up tight.

SOFFIT VENT

SOFFIT VENT

Description: Small, barrellike plastic device with one louvered end, this comes in various lengths and diameters.
Buying information: Soffit vents bleed hot air from a house.
How-to hint: They can even be used on cedar siding, though they're white. Paint them bronze so they blend in.

SHANTY CAP

Description: This is a galvanized metal piece that looks like a coolie hat (in fact, this is one name for it), consisting of a length of pipe topped by a wavy conical cap 3 to 12 inches in diameter.
Buying information: Caps are used to shield the top of a stack vent or other pipe from rain and snow. They are used only on small shacks and the like. A standard house usually has a chimney whose design prevents water getting in.

GLAZIER'S POINT

GLAZIER'S POINT

Description: This is either a flat triangle of metal or a V shape with a raised portion.
Buying information: They come in small boxes, and are used to secure glass in wooden window frames.
How-to hint: The kind with the raised portion is easier to use. Just push it in place with a putty knife.

T-NUT FASTENER

T-NUT FASTENER

Description: This consists of a circular pronged portion with a threaded core.
Buying information: It is used to provide a threaded core for mounting a machine screw, such as to join boards.
How-to hint: To use the T-nut, drill a hole and hammer it in place over the hole so that the threaded part is inside the hole.

ELECTRICAL
HARDWARE

SOME PRELIMINARY NOTES

To have a better understanding of electrical products, it's a good idea to have at least a rudimentary understanding of how electricity works.

In essence, it must travel in a loop. The loop starts at the power source where electricity is generated, then pushed along wires (the "push" is called volts or voltage) in a quantity called amps or amperage, and then through the wires in your house, where it is divided into circuits at the fuse box or circuit breaker box. The electricity travels along circuit(s) inside the house, passing through the receptacle or plugged-in electrical devices, then heads back to the power station to complete the loop. If the circuit isn't completed, nothing works. How many volts and amps are used depends on the particular device. A toaster, say, might use 6 amps, a dishwasher, 12.

For safety, most major electrical items in the house are grounded. This is a separate circuit to the ground. If there is an electrical malfunction, the errant electricity will follow the metal path established to take the current harmlessly into the ground rather than into your body.

All devices you buy will have the voltage and the wattage or amperage stamped on them.

Wattage, or watts, measures power usage, which may often be calculated by multiplying amps used by voltage used. For example, if a device is 6 amps and 110 volts, then it uses 660 watts.

Finally, all electrical products should have the UL stamp on them. UL stands for Underwriters Laboratory, an independent testing organization that tests products for safeness. The UL label doesn't mean that a product is high quality, just that it has passed minimum, that is, reasonable safety standards. Then it is considered "listed."

BOXES

Wherever wires are stripped of insulation and hooked onto terminal screws, such as on a receptacle or switch or joined to a fixture, or where they are joined for the purpose of rerouting the direction of the current, they must be housed in a metal or plastic box for safety. No raw wires should be left exposed, not only because of the possiblility of fire from electrical malfunctions, but also to protect anyone working on the wires in the future.

The same applies outside: any switch, receptacle, or lamp must have its electrical mechanism protected by a box, in this case a weatherproof box.

Boxes are available in various shapes and sizes. The National Electric Code—which many municipalities follow—puts restrictions on how many wires may be in a box of a given size, because crowding of wires can be a safety hazard.

All localities allow metal boxes, but some don't allow plastic. Boxes are for "new" work or new construction, where framing members are exposed, or "old" work, where framing is not exposed. Metal boxes are designed to be used on both old and new work, whereas plastic, except for one box noted below, is strictly for new work.

For new work inside the house, use boxes that have nailing brackets on them. Simply locate the box where you want it on the framing, and nail it in place to studs or other framing members. The brackets are notched or otherwise constructed so that they tie in well with wall or ceiling material—they will bring the housed electrical device flush with the material. If you are installing a box in old work, first cut a hole the size of the box. Then slip the box into the hole. The plaster ears on it—brackets at top and bottom—stop it flush with the wall. To keep the box from falling out, it may have clamps that can be opened, somewhat like a Molly bolt, to grip the back side of the wall. Or there may be built-on screws, devices called Madison clips to grip it, or, if the wall is plaster, the plaster can be chipped away so that screws can be run through screw holes on the box and into the

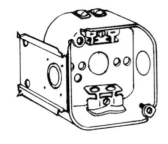

BOX AND BRACKET
WITH BX CONNECTORS

lath. Boxes with clamps or Madison clips can be used for any kind of installation—plaster or drywall—but drywall is not solid enough to accept screws.

All boxes have screw-hole tappings in front to accept 6x32 machine screws to secure switches and receptacles, and all have "knockouts," which are holes plugged with either metal or plastic disks. To get the cable through on metal, pry out the disks with a screwdriver and feed the cable through. (If you make a mistake and take out the wrong disk, you can get toothed replacements to plug up the holes again.)

On plastic, the disks are pushed open and remain in place, "hinged" at the top and pushed up when the cable is passed through.

Cable or conduit (the other ways wires can come to a box) is secured to the box in a variety of ways, as detailed below. The main idea, though, is to prevent the cable from moving, which can lead to loose connections and electrical hazards. Indeed, unwanted movement is the bane of any electrical installation.

Weatherproof boxes are made of cast aluminum or an alloy and have either plates—on alloy types—inside with screw-hole tappings to screw switches or outlets to, or, on cast aluminum, built-in screw threads. Use stainless steel screws on aluminum boxes. Regular steel screws do not react well to aluminum and the reaction can lead to the screws' corroding. A dab of silicone paste on the screws helps too.

WEATHERPROOF BOX AND COVER

There are also covers for boxes. You can get metal or plastic covers with knockout slots for receptacles or switches, blank covers that screw on for a rarely used receptacle, or covers for junction boxes where wires terminate and are connected to one another.

Screw-on covers are made for weatherproof boxes. Sometimes the covers are solid—when the box is not used for a long time—and sometimes the covers have knockouts for switch toggles and receptacles and flip covers for them—or you unscrew the entire cover to get at the receptacle. The covers are weatherproof not only in the material they're made of, but also in their gasketed edges, which provide a watertight seal between them and the box.

BOX COVER

Sometimes, too, covers have ½-inch threads to accept fixtures (lampholders). These come prewired, ready for hookup inside the box.

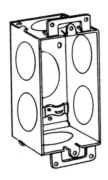

GEM BOX

GEM BOX

Description: This is a metal box 2 inches wide, 3 inches high, and 2½ inches deep, with or without plaster "ears."

Buying information: This is the standard box for switches and receptacles. A single gem box (or gang box) has room for one receptacle or switch. If necessary, the sides of gem boxes can be removed and the boxes linked up—ganged—to form a larger box, a two- or three-gang box. Gem boxes also come deeper than 2½ inches.

How-to hints: Gem boxes can be used on old or new work. For new work, get the kind without plaster ears—just nail through holes in the box into the framing member. On old work, plaster ears and Madison clips should do the job. Gem boxes also come with expandable brackets that can take the place of Madison clips.

PLASTIC ONE-GANG BOX

Description: This is blue or gray plastic and looks like a gem box with expandable brackets.

Buying information: This is the only plastic box available for old work, and it will accept either a switch or a receptacle. It is—like all plastic boxes—cheaper than metal.

How-to hint: Cut a hole and insert the box. The ears expand and hold it flush with the wall.

FOUR-INCH-SQUARE BOX

Description: As its name implies, this is a box 4 inches on a side, usually only 1½ inches deep, but also found in a 2⅛-inch depth.

Buying information: When the wall cavity is too shallow to accept a 2½-inch-deep gem box, use a 4-inch square box. While shallow enough to fit into the wall, it has the same cubic capacity as a gem box.

HANDY BOX

Description: This is a small box with rounded corners.

Buying information: The corners of this surface-mounted box are rounded so that if someone bumps into it, he or she will not be hurt. It is usually in the basement.

How-to hint: This box, like others, has screw holes in the back so it can be screwed to the wall.

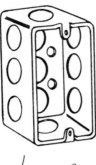

HANDY BOX

STUD BOX
Description: This is a metal or plastic box, in various sizes, with a bracket on one side.
Buying information: It is used for new work. The bracket enables it to be nailed to a stud.

JUNCTION (CEILING) BOX
Description: This is a 4-inch-wide octagonal or round box, either 1½ inches or 2⅛ inches deep. It may have extendable arms.
Buying information: As the name suggests, this is for use on a ceiling. It may house a light fixture or be a point where a number of wires meet, a branch-off. Use it for new work.
How-to hint: Extend the arms on the box until they contact the framing members and then drive the nails through the holes into the framing members.

CIRCUIT BREAKERS

Circuit breakers are the modern equivalent of the fuse (see below). Indeed, they are much more popular, though many electricians feel that fuses are safer.

The reason for the popularity of the breaker is convenience: a flip or push of a switch can get a circuit going again, rather than having to unscrew a fuse and screw in a new one.

A circuit breaker senses overload and trips out to avoid overheating a wire and possibly causing a fire. At the heart of its construction is a bimetallic strip linked to a couple of springs and contact points. When a circuit becomes overloaded or a short occurs, this strip bends and pulls away from the contact points, breaking the circuit. The electrical flow shuts down. When the breaker lever is reset, the strip is pushed against the contact points and electrical flow starts again.

Two types of circuit breakers are common: those that snap in place and those that screw in place.

If you want to replace a breaker, you sometimes must get a direct replacement unit from the same manufacturer. To find out the name, look on the box door or on the box itself. In many cases, however, circuit breakers are interchangeable. To ensure that you get the right size, take the old circuit breaker to the store.

It should be emphasized that only the experienced do-it-yourselfer should replace a circuit breaker.

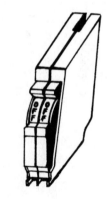

Circuit Breaker

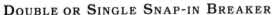

DOUBLE OR SINGLE SNAP-IN BREAKER
Description: This is a black rectangular box (or boxes) with toggle switches.
Buying information: It comes with various electrical capacities, described in terms of amperage, from 15 to 100 amps. For 220-volt appliances, two 110-volt breakers may be fitted side-by-side, and gauged together by a bracket that straddles both toggle levers.

PLUG-TYPE BREAKER
Description: This looks like a fuse with a button.
Buying information: It is used with a motor or the like. When the circuit trips, the button pops; reset by pushing it in.

CONDUIT

In general, conduit is a hollow tube or pipe that comes in various forms and materials and through which insulated electrical wire is run.

There are limits to how many wires may be pulled through conduit, depending on the diameter of the pipe and the wire sizes. The thicker the wire, the fewer wires are allowed. Check with your local building department to find out how many wires are permitted in a given size of conduit.

EMT

THIN-WALL (EMT) CONDUIT
Description: This thin-walled pipe, also called EMT (for electric metallic tubing), comes in an internal diameter of ½ inch to 4 inches and even larger, and in 10-foot lengths. The ½-inch diameter is most commonly used.
Buying information: EMT is normally used inside the house, such as along a garage wall or in basement workshop wiring. It is not practical to install the material inside existing walls, because they must be opened up to do so. It is secured to boxes with EMT connectors—formed metal pieces held together by pairs of screws.
How-to hints: EMT should not be buried in the ground or exposed where it can be struck, such as by a lawn mower. Thin-wall is often used outside, but we do not feel it is made for this (its walls are only ¹⁄₁₆ inch thick).

Thin-wall can be bent easily with a device called a hickey

and cut with a hacksaw. It can be mounted on walls securely with straps (see below).

A variety of fittings are available that allow EMT to make turns without having to bend it, and they are secured with EMT connectors.

HEAVY-WALL CONDUIT

Description: Heavy-wall, or rigid, conduit comes in the same diameters as thin-wall, but is made of galvanized metal. Walls are also twice as thick, and it is threaded at the ends.

Buying information: Heavy-wall can be installed where it is exposed to the elements, in danger of physical abuse, and underground. For example, it could be buried in a lawn. Another possible use is to carry wire between the main house and an addition or garage.

It can also be used inside walls on new construction. Once in place, and assuming there is space, new wires can be pulled in easily to increase electrical capacity.

Rigid conduit is secured to boxes with pairs of nuts.

How-to hints: Rigid conduit should be cut with a pipe cutter—it is too laborious a job with a hacksaw. To bend it, use an electrical bender. A variety of fittings are available for rigid conduit to allow it to make turns.

Rigid conduit is difficult to work with because it must be cut to fit precisely between boxes—just long enough to screw into the boxes. This takes great accuracy and experience and should be left to a professional.

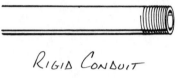

RIGID CONDUIT

GREENFIELD CONDUIT

Description: This flexible conduit looks like BX armored cable (see pages 107–108), having a hollow, beaded metal jacket. It comes in various diameters.

Buying information: Thin-wall and rigid conduit are not normally used inside the house walls on old work. Greenfield can be, but usually in a limited way—in lengths under 6 feet. For example, it is a good material to use between a junction box and an electrical fixture.

The reason for using limited lengths is conductivity. As mentioned, all electrical devices must be grounded—provided with a path to ground for errant electricity—and Greenfield is not considered a good enough electrical conductor to provide this necessary path.

GREENFIELD

There are special connectors for securing Greenfield to boxes.

How-to hints: Greenfield can be cut with a hacksaw. To simplify this, cut it on an angle of about 30 degrees, which will result in your cutting just one bead of the jacketing, rather than the two you would cut if you cut straight up and down.

PLASTIC CONDUIT

Description: This is rigid, usually gray, and it comes in rigid pipe sizes.

Buying information: It can be used underground, but will not take a damaging blow the way metal will. It is cheaper than metal conduit.

How-to hints: If you want to change direction with conduit, you can obtain fittings for the job just as you can for EMT and rigid pipe. Plastic pipe is secured to boxes with its own fittings, or if the boxes are plastic, it can be glued in place. A separate grounding wire must be used since the plastic is nonconductive.

CABLE/CONDUIT STRAPS AND STAPLES

Description: These come in various shapes: Two-hole straps are U-shaped with extending parts at the ends of the legs of the U and holes for fastening; one-hole straps are U-shaped with one extending part that has a hole in it for fastening. Staples are also U-shaped with the legs of the U sharpened.

Buying information: Cable normally runs inside house walls and ceilings, and to a lesser degree so does EMT and plastic conduit. But when any of these is in the open, it needs to be held secure—a job for cable/conduit fasteners.

The most popular fastener is the staple. It is available in various sizes and will accommodate cable up to No. 10 wire. Staples are driven in place with a hammer, but some people find this awkward and instead use the one-hole or two-hole metal cable strap that is placed over the cable, and then drive in nails to secure it. Straps make a neater job than staples, and can be shaped to fit more easily than can staples. One-hole straps cost less than the two-hole type.

You shouldn't use staples for conduit, EMT, or plastic conduit; use only straps.

Straps are available in various sizes. Select the same size as the conduit or cable. If you are using a ½-inch conduit, get a ½-inch strap, and so on.

How-to hints: Install staples over cable every 4 feet; also install one within 1 foot of a junction box to guard against the conduit pulling free.

For fastening thin-wall, heavy-wall, or plastic conduit, straps, as mentioned, are best. Use these every 5 feet, and one within 1 foot of a junction box.

To make fastening greenfield and heavy-wall conduit, EMT, or plastic conduit easier to install and more secure on various types of siding, follow these tips:

- *Brick and other masonry:* A plastic or fiber plug with a No. 10 sheet metal screw works well. Plastic is preferred by many electricians: it's cheaper than fiber and grips the screw better. To use a fiber or lead plug, use a ³⁄₁₆-inch carbide bit to drill a 1¼-inch-deep hole. Insert the plug, lay the conduit in place, then the strap, and turn the screw through the strap hole (or holes, if you use the two-hole type) into the plug.
- *Cedar or asbestos cement:* Use No. 10 sheet metal screws; they grip much better than regular wood screws because their threads go all the way up to the head.
- *Aluminum and metal siding:* Punch a hole with an awl, then use a sheet metal screw. The method works on up to ³⁄₁₆-inch gauge siding.
- *Wood:* Use a sheet metal screw. It will hold better than a regular wood screw.

CORD SETS

Wire is, of course, the basic stuff of electrical work, and you can buy it for permanent installation in various lengths and off rolls by the foot. But wire comes in another form, commonly referred to as "cord set," which means cords in specified lengths with plugs, terminals, or bare wire leads ready to be attached and for use on small and large appliances.

Extension cords are also considered cord sets.

SMALL/LARGE APPLIANCE CORD SETS

Description: These vary, from wires with a female plug on one end that plugs into the device (such as on a waffle iron) and with a male plug on the other, to wires with a heavy-duty three-prong plug on one end and spade lugs on the other.

SMALL APPLIANCE CORD

Buying information: The best way to buy this cord set is to ask for it by specific use: If you need a cord for a toaster or an air conditioner, ask for it. If you have difficulty locating the cord set at a hardware store, try an electrical supply or an appliance-repair store.

How-to hints: Installation of a cord set is straightforward and simple. Just make sure the connections you make are tight. Also, you can make your own cord sets using appropriate wire and plugs, but in higher amperages the wire and plugs are available only in black and don't win high marks for appearance.

EXTENSION CORD

Description: This comes flat or round and in various colors—white, brown, yellow, orange, and blue—with two or three wires and with a two- or three-prong plug at one end and a tap at the other. It is available from 6 feet to 100 feet long.

Buying information: Here, again, match the amperage of the device to the cord; the cord should be heavy enough to take the current drawn by the device. If grounding is required, the cord should be grounded (three-wire type).

Colors are standard throughout the industry and indicate the strength of the cord. Flat brown and white extension cords are used in the household for lamps and other light uses. Flat yellow can be used for outdoor power tools and the like, but the wire is not as well protected or insulated as the round orange ones made of rubber. The orange (so the cord can be seen) is the best choice for hedge clippers and the like, or for using safely outdoors, because of its durability and visibility.

You can also get extension cords in blue—this is the Cadillac of the breed, in that it is able to withstand extremes in temperature and is the most heavy duty. Most people reserve these for marine use. Whatever the color, be sure the cord you choose is UL approved.

Cords can be found that stay flexible down to 58 degrees below zero Fahrenheit. Cords are also available that will resist oil and acid.

EXTENSION CORD PLUGS
(MALE AND FEMALE)

FUSES

Fuses, like circuit breakers, work on a simple principle. Each is designed to handle a specified amount of current. When the current exceeds that amount, a metal linkage in the fuse melts: The current stops flowing before the overloaded wires can heat up. A fuse, then, is a safety device, and you should never try to circumvent it.

PLUG-IN FUSE

Description: This consists of a housing with a threaded end, the linkage inside, and a tiny glass window through which you can see if the fuse has blown; that is, if the linkage has melted because of an overload (too much current) or a short circuit, which amounts to the same thing. These fuses actually screw in like a light bulb.

Buying information: Plug-in fuses can be bought singly or in small packages, but dealers will commonly open a package to sell you one. Fuses are sized by the amperage, or current they can take; they come in 5-amp increments ranging from 5 to 30 amps. Fifteen amps is normally used for the lighting circuits in the house. Large appliances such as air conditioners use 20-, 25-, and 30-amp fuses. In each circuit, the wires are designed to handle just so much amperage. If the wires are carrying too much amperage, the fuse blows. Never use a fuse of higher rating than originally intended for the circuit or the protection will be lost.

How-to hints: When changing a fuse, make sure the floor you're standing on is dry. In case of errant electricity, you won't be grounded and in danger of getting a serious shock.

TIME-DELAY FUSE

Description: This looks like a standard plug-in fuse. It is available in a variety of amperages: 3¾, 6¼, 7½, 10, and 15.

Buying information: When a motor starts up, it draws a lot of current briefly, which might blow an ordinary fuse. A time-delay fuse will ignore a momentary current surge, which makes it a good fuse for motors.

How-to hints: Select an amperage rating that is above the minimal amperage draw of the motor, but as close as possible. This way there is not such a large tolerance that the motor might burn out before the fuse blew.

TIME-DELAY FUSE

TYPE S FUSE

THREADED ADAPTER
FOR TYPE S FUSE

CARTRIDGE FUSE

RENEWABLE FUSE

Description: This, too, looks like a standard fuse, except it has a little pushbutton at the top.

Buying information: Unlike a standard fuse, where the linkage is destroyed when too much current is passed through the fuse, a renewable fuse has a heating element: when the current is too great the element separates, stopping electrical flow. Although this reset feature is convenient, some electricians say that the fuse is subject to malfunction. The interior mechanism can short itself and won't blow when overloaded. Other electricians, however, say it is fine when you want the push-pull convenience of a circuit breaker in a fuse-box panel.

Renewable fuses come in the same sizes as standard plug-in fuses but cost around 50 percent more.

How-to hint: Select the minimum amperage required in the situation.

TYPE S PLUG-IN FUSE

Description: This consists of two parts: one looks like a standard plug-in fuse; the other is a threaded adapter.

Buying information: The advantage of this type of fuse is that it is tamperproof. While other plug-in fuses are interchangeable because they have the same size screw-in bases—and therefore a higher amperage can be used than is advisable—a type S fuse cannot be compromised. For example, if an adapter for a type S 15-amp fuse is screwed in place, it will accept only a 15-amp fuse—none other. Amperages are stamped on the tops of the fuses, which are also color coded.

These fuses make sense for people who own rental property, because someone unfamiliar with the electrical system cannot inadvertently use a replacement fuse of the wrong capacity and compromise protection.

STANDARD CARTRIDGE FUSE

Description: This fuse has a shotgun-shell shape, with metal caps on the ends.

Buying information: Cartridge fuses are used less in the home than are the plug-in types. They are designed for handling large power demands—above 30 amps and 220 volts—for such things as appliances and air-conditioning equipment, where a separate fuse is required to control a particular appliance circuit. There are two range sizes: 10 amps to 30 amps and 35 amps to 60 amps.

How-to hints: The cartridge fuse is installed between clips on the fuse box and works like any other fuse: inside is a linkage that will melt if the current is too high.

To remove the fuse safely, obtain a cartridge fuse puller. This is a pliers-like tool made of hard plastic with which the barrel of the fuse can be grasped and the fuse pulled easily.

LAMP PARTS

There are many individual lamp parts available, as well as complete carded kits that provide all the hardware necessary for making a lamp, except the lamp body, which can be created by drilling a hole into a bottle or some other container.

Various outlets carry lamp parts, including electrical supply stores, discount houses, and hardware stores.

THREADED TUBING

Description: This is hollow, threaded tube commonly available with an internal diameter of ³⁄₁₆ inch, the external diameter being ⅜ inch. It comes in 3-foot lengths and brass-plated or plain steel.

Buying information: Threaded tube is used exclusively for lamps, and forms the spine of the lamp, running through it and secured at top and bottom with locknuts.

How-to hint: Tubing can be cut with a hacksaw (see page 64).

THREADED TUBE

LAMP WIRE (ZIP CORD)

Description: This is flat wire in various colors that is segmented or grooved in the center for easier splitting (hence the name "zip cord") when preparing the wire for attaching to a lamp. It used to be 18 gauge but now must be 16 gauge.

Buying information: Lamp wire can be bought off a reel in whatever length you wish, or in set lengths (9, 12, and 15 feet) and with plugs already attached.

How-to hint: Lamp wire is polarized, meaning one wire is meant to be attached to the neutral side of the socket and the other to the "hot" side—the one with the voltage. To identify this polarity, the hot wire is smooth, the neutral wire striated.

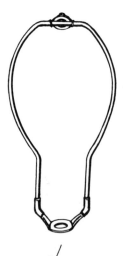

Harp

Finial

Pull-Chain Socket

HARP

Description: This item comes in one-piece or two-piece form. The one-piece harp consists of a bulb-shaped wire with a threaded nut at the base. The two-piece also has a bulb-shaped wire, but it is designed to fit on the lamp and to be held there by retaining sleeves. Harps are available in sizes up to 2 feet high and are usually brass-plated.

Buying information: The harp is the device that supports the shade and keeps it from contacting the bulb.

FINIAL

Description: This is a decorative cap with internal threads. It comes in a wide variety of sizes, designs, and finishes.

Buying information: The finial screws onto the top of the threaded tube in a lamp. It keeps on the shade.

How-to hint: When a finial is lost, many people try to screw something else onto the top of the lamp, not realizing that the internal threads are an odd size, designed to accept only finials, which are specifically threaded to mate with them.

LOCKOUT

Description: This is a round washer available in a variety of sizes: ⅛ inch, ¼ inch, ⅜ inch, and ½ inch.

Buying information: Lockouts serve as a base for the nuts that hold the threaded tube to the lamp at the top and bottom.

SOCKET SHELL

Description: The socket shell consists of a cylindrical, usually brass or silver-colored device, and an insulating sleeve. Inside is the electrical mechanism.

Buying information: Sockets come with various on/off actions. Some have a pull chain, others a push-pull switch, still others a turnbutton that can provide three levels of light with the appropriate bulb.

How-to hints: When securing wire to the two terminal screws inside a socket, wrap the bare wire clockwise around the screw shank. This ensures that as you tighten the screw, the wire gets tighter. The hot wire should go to the brass screw, and the neutral wire to the silver screw. For safety, make sure the screws are tight.

To remove a socket from the base, look for the words PRESS HERE on the socket. Use your thumb or a small screwdriver to apply pressure, and the socket will usually come apart easily.

SOCKET BODY

Description: This is the guts of the socket, the actual mechanism that contains the terminals and the on/off switch that controls the lamp's light.

Buying information: When a socket body goes bad, you can save money by buying just that part and using the old socket shell.

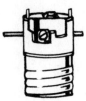

SOCKET INTERIOR MECHANISM

KEYLESS BODY

Description: This is like any socket body with the necessary connections, but without a switch.

COUPLING

Description: This looks like a pipe fitting, a sleeve with internal threads on both ends. It usually has an internal diameter of ⅛ inch or ¼ inch.

Buying information: Couplings are used to join lengths of threaded tubing.

REDUCING BUSHING

Description: This is a short, cylindrical fitting with different internal diameters at each end.

Buying information: It lets you reduce the inside diameter of the threaded tube from ½ inch to ⅜ inch.

How-to hints: These are sometimes used to build lamps by plugging one size threaded rod into another. They are also used in hanging light fixtures, plugging one diameter rod into a smaller one.

SOCKET REDUCER

SOCKET REDUCER

Description: This is the threaded part of a socket.

Buying information: It is used to reduce the size of a socket to accept a smaller device with a smaller socket, such as a candleabra or chandelier bulb.

Coupling Nut

Coupling Nut

Description: Similar to a coupling with internal threads at each end, except that it has a hexagonal shape.

Buying information: It is used to join lengths of threaded tube. It is hexagonal so that you can tighten it with a wrench.

LIGHT FIXTURES

Ceiling Fixture

Description: This can have many different shapes, but it usually comes with three wires.

Buying information: In this case there is simply no substitute for taking a look at what's in the store.

How-to hints: Mounting ceiling fixtures is usually done one of two ways. If there is an existing joist, the box can be screwed in place; then add a shaped, holed device called a hickey, which screws onto the joist. Screw the fixture to it. If there is no joist at the desired location, fit a crossbar piece as a bridge between the nearest joists and screw the fixture to that. If you come up against a particular hanging problem, go to an electrical supplies dealer and ask for help. If you have to improvise, make sure that whatever you use, it is strong enough to hold up the fixture. Some weigh 60 or 70 pounds.

Wall Fixture

Description: These are as varied as ceiling fixtures.

Buying information: Follow the advice given for ceiling fixtures—visit stores to find out what's available.

How-to hints: The same essential methods and materials are used as for hanging a ceiling fixture.

Porcelain Fixture

Description: This is an old-fashioned round ceramic disk with a socket.

Buying information: Some porcelain fixtures are a plain light socket, while others also have a plug receptacle or other available options. Maximum wattages range from 250 to 600. Get the higher wattage if you think you might need the capacity.

How-to hints: Porcelain fixtures come with screw terminals, prewired leads, or two leads ready for connecting. The lead type is easiest to install. If necessary, the sockets on porcelain fixtures can be replaced—you needn't buy the entire fixture.

Fluorescent Fixture

Description: This is a rectangular box with end caps (sockets) for housing fluorescent tubes.

Buying information: Fluorescents, or course, use much less energy than incandescent lamps for a given amount of light, but you should give some thought to getting a tube whose color best serves the application. For utility areas, a workshop, etc., get "cool white" tubes for most efficient lighting. This may be a bit too blue for living areas; we'd suggest one of the "warm white" colors for a closer match to incandescent lighting. Any part of a flourescent is replaceable, including the sockets (lampholders) that hold the lamp and the starters and ballasts that give it the electrical surge it needs to start. Fluorescents can be installed by anyone, but you should use THHN wire, as suggested on page 108. Handle tubes carefully—they are fragile and can break easily.

Incandescent Lamp Holder

Fluorescent Fixture Starter

Weatherproof Fixture

Description: This is usually a cap-shaped lamp with a threaded section for screwing into a weatherproof box.

Buying information: These are standard sizes, usually with ½-inch pipe threads.

PLUGS

Electrical devices occasionally require plug replacement. There are two types available: male and female. The male plugs have prongs; the female plugs have slots. The male plug may have two or three prongs: two flat ones and one U-shaped grounding plug. The latter is for protection. If there is an electrical malfunction involving errant current, it will take the path of least resistance—through the ground prong and following the wire linked to the ground, rather than through your body.

Plugs, like other electrical items, are rated to handle the current of a particular device. This appears on the nameplate in terms of amperage, usually where the wires disappear into the housing. Always get one to match. For example, the plug on an extension cord is almost always 15 amps and of a three-wire type. Replacement plugs for major appliance cords may be 20, 30, or 50 amps. Dryer plugs are rated for 30 amps, range plugs for 50 amps. This means that these plugs are designed to handle that current, but as a practical matter, the appliances will normally draw less current than those ratings. If the current exceeds the plug amperage, a fuse will blow or a circuit breaker will trip.

OPEN-CONSTRUCTION PLUG

Description: The shape of this plug varies, usually round or flat. Colors are normally black, white, or brown. Inside the plug there are screw terminals covered with an insulating panel that is slipped down over the prongs.

Buying information: This type of plug can be used on lamps, tools, and much more. However, the fiber panel that covers the terminal tends to come off, exposing the terminals.

How-to hints: The wires that are wrapped around the screw terminal may be solid or consist of individual strands. If strands, they can be "tinned" after being bent to the shape desired by heating solder on them. Tinning keeps the fibers together better, so there is less chance of a short circuit. In any event, the wires should be wrapped clockwise; as the screws are tightened, this tends to pull the wires tighter.

OPEN-CONSTRUCTION CLAMP PLUG

Description: This is an open-construction plug with a pair of screws on the neck.

Buying information: It is particularly good for items that are frequently plugged and unplugged, such as vacuum cleaners. The wires are attached to the screws as in a regular open-construction plug, but tightening the clamping screws on the neck keeps the strain off the connections, when the cord is pulled from the outlet, and helps ensure that the wires won't pull off the screw terminals.

SPEC-GRADE PLUG

Description: This comes in various forms but with a "dead front," i.e., the wire connections are safely inaccessible from the front; they are rated for 20 amps.

Buying information: These plugs are for use where the plug takes a lot of stress. The interior parts are more substantial than an ordinary plug; it is simply better made and should last longer.

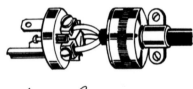

OPEN-CONSTRUCTION
CLAMP PLUG

SAFETY PLUG

Description: Made entirely of plastic, this somewhat resembles an ordinary plug without any mechanism.

Buying information: This is good for protecting outlets against foreign objects being inserted by youngsters.

SAFETY PLUG

DEAD-FRONT PLUG

Description: This is a heavy plastic cylinder consisting of two parts that are screwed together.

Buying information: This plug has come to replace the open-construction plug because it is safer; the wires are much less likely to come loose.

How-to hints: This contains screw terminals to wrap bare wires around or to accept stripped wires. If the latter, proper stripping depth is very important. Plugs come with instructions that explain this.

CLAMP-ON PLUG

Description: This comes in various forms, but essentially looks like a regular small lamp plug with two prongs.

Buying information: Use this plug for a quick way to replace a bad lamp-cord plug. Clamp-on plugs may be rated to handle higher amperages, but the consensus among electricians is that these may be dangerous for a current load greater than a bulb or two.

How-to hints: To install a clamp-on plug, cut off the old plug, than insert the line cord end into the clamp-on plug, with the clamp part opened up. Press down the clamp part; its teeth then pierce the insulation on the cord and contact the wires.

CLAMP-ON PLUG

ADAPTER

Description: This is a three-prong plug.

Buying information: It is good for converting a standard outlet into a grounded one.

ADAPTER

RANGE PLUG

Description: The prongs on this plug are arranged in "crow's foot" configuration.

Buying information: The range plug is designed to handle up to 50 amps of power draw and to be used with a 220-volt line.

RANGE PLUG

How-to hints: Some of these plugs come with a pigtail, a short lead wire for connection to the socket. A common mistake is to use it as a ground wire when it should be used as a neutral wire.

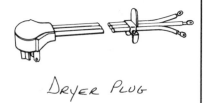

DRYER PLUG

DRYER PLUG
Description: This has two angled blades and one L-shaped blade.
Buying information: Dryer plugs are designed to handle up to 30 amps of draw and to be used with a 220-volt line.

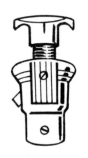

FEMALE APPLIANCE PLUG

FEMALE APPLIANCE PLUG
Description: This is a flat rectangular receptacle plug with slots for prongs.
Buying information: This plug is used on small appliances: It plugs into prongs on the appliance.
How-to hints: To replace the plug, remove the screws holding the two halves together and unfasten the line cord wires. As a rule, however, this type of plug ''burns up'' and is not repairable.

RECEPTACLES

Receptacles, also called outlets or sockets, are devices with slots for plugs. They are made in some colors, but are mostly found in brown, ivory, and white. Intended for tapping off power where needed in the house, they are always on. When you plug in an item, the circuit is completed and power is available.

Receptacles are available in single or duplex style (two outlets in one device). They have terminal screws: The line, or hot-side, screw is copper- or brass-colored; the neutral side is silver. Receptacles may also have a green grounding screw on one corner of the frame. The bare ground wire on the cable gets attached to this.

Most of today's receptacles also have holes in the back into which bared ends of wires are pushed. The holes are identified according to electrical function, which makes for a faster connection than the screw type. These are also handy in wiring a device when there is not enough room on the screw terminals for the wires, or the clamp holes allow for more convenient routing of wires within the box.

Like other electrical devices, receptacles are rated in terms of voltage and amperage capacity, and the device plugged into it must not exceed this capacity.

Standard receptacles are for 15 amps, but they are available in 20 amps that are "spec" or specification grade. These are better made than ordinary receptacles and are a good choice in a kitchen, bath, or wherever the receptacle gets a lot of wear.

Most receptacles have three slots—two flat slots for the plug prongs and a D-shaped one for the ground prong on the plug. All receptacles are—or should be—grounded. One type is automatically grounded when it is attached to the box. On other types a wire must be fastened from the screws to the box. In cases where there is no easy way to hook grounding wires, you can attach a U-shaped device called a grounding clip to the box, or install a green 8x32 grounding screw in one of the tappings in the back of every metal box and link the wire to this.

Receptacles may or may not have metal ears that bear on the plaster or wallboard for the purpose of location. These brackets are on top and bottom and keep the receptacle flush with the wall. If you wish, depending on the situation, the ears can be snapped off with pliers.

If you are housing more than one receptacle in a box, wrap electrical tape around each after making the connections. The tape should cover the terminal screws. This ensures that a short circuit won't occur due to exposed wires contacting one another.

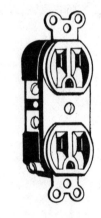

Duplex Receptacle

Duplex Receptacle
Description: This is a single rectangular device that accommodates two plugs.

Single Receptacle
Description: This receptacle is characterized by two slots with a ground slot for accommodating a single plug.
Buying information: It is good for a high amperage appliance where one heavy-duty receptacle is needed.

Square Receptacle
Description: This comes in 15- and 20-amp sizes and is built just like a standard receptacle except its overall shape is square rather than round. It is also called a decor receptacle.
Buying information: Many new homes are equipped with decor

RANGE RECEPTACLE

PLUG-IN
MULTIPLE OUTLET STRIP

GROUND FAULT CIRCUIT
INTERRUPTER

receptacles, which are considered better looking than standard units but require matching cover plates.

RANGE RECEPTACLE

Description: This is the female counterpart to the range plug with slots in a "crow's foot" pattern. It has a 50-amp capacity.

DRYER RECEPTACLE

Description: This is the female receptacle for the dryer plug with the odd L-shaped prong. It has a 30-amp capacity.

MULTIPLE-OUTLET STRIP

Description: This is a long strip or box with several receptacles.
Buying information: This is an excellent device where multiple receptacles are required. It is particularly good for something like a computer/printer setup. Most multiple-outlet strips come (and should come) with a surge protector, which protects the electrical mechanism in case of a sudden surge of electricity, and a light that alerts you to the device being on or off.
How-to hints: On the back of this device are hanging slots. To mount it, drive screws in the wall, projecting enough so they can interlock with the slots.

GROUND FAULT CIRCUIT INTERRUPTER (GFCI)

Description: There are three types. One looks like a standard receptacle and is designed to be used as a receptacle. Another is a combination GFCI/circuit breaker and is installed in the circuit breaker box. The third type is portable with male and female plugs, sometimes with an integral extension cord.
Buying information: This is an important safety device. If an appliance or tool has stray current leakage of as little as $\frac{5}{1000}$ of an amp, the GFCI will sense it and shut off the current quickly to prevent a shock. They are particularly important—and in many localities are required—where water is used, such as on a line that goes to a pool, or in a bath or kitchen. There is normally a small amount of electrical leakage in house wiring and this can mistakenly trigger a combination GFCI/circuit breaker. Hence, many people opt for installing a receptacle type at the place it is needed, where the house leakage won't affect it.

GFCIs are available to protect 15- and 20-amp circuits.

How-to hints: Near a pool, inside a cellar workshop, and in garage areas on a slab, GFCIs deserve protection. When working outdoors with power tools, use a portable GFCI. Do not install a GFCI on a circuit that serves a fluorescent light. The electrical characteristics of the ballast in the light can mistakenly—and repeatedly—trigger the circuit, shutting it down. A GFCI should be installed only by the experienced do-it-yourselfer.

RACEWAY OUTLET STRIP

Description: This is a strip of plastic or metal in 10-foot lengths with outlets spaced 6 inches apart and in two or three wire types.

Buying information: Raceway outlet strips are useful where many small appliances are used, such as in the kitchen, but first determine whether the circuit can carry the electrical load.

Metal raceway strips can take more abuse than plastic ones.

PLASTIC PUSH-IN RACEWAY

Description: This is a flat strip of plastic with a lengthwise slot.

Buying information: When you push the plug into this strip, it grips the plug. The strip has a 15-amp capacity and is good for light use on such things as fish tanks.

SWITCHES

A switch is nothing more than a device to cut off or allow the flow of electrical current. When the switch is flipped or turned to the off position, the inner metal contacts separate, breaking the circuit and stopping electrical flow. Flip the switch back on and the contact is remade, allowing the current to flow again.

There is a wide variety of switches available, but most common are house switches.

Many of the things that can be said about receptacles can also be said about switches. Like receptacles, switches are designed to handle specific electrical loads. Commonly, switches come in 15- and 20-amp sizes. This means that the contacts in them can handle up to 15 or 20 amps of current without being overloaded.

Twenty-amp switches are known as "spec" or specification grade and are not only higher amperage but better made. If you plan to use the switch frequently, such as in a bath or kitchen, the spec grade is justified. Though it costs more, it will last much longer than regular grade. Switches come in white, ivory, and brown.

House switches are often referred to as "single pole" switches, which means that they interrupt the "hot" side of the circuit. "Double pole" means that they interrupt both hot and neutral sides of one circuit, or each "hot" side of two circuits, say a pair of 110-volt circuits connected together to yield 220 volts.

Most switches have screw terminals—brass, silver, or green-colored screws on which wires are wrapped to make electrical connections—as well as holes in the back or side for clamp connections. Wires can be pushed into these holes and clamped in place, rather than having to be wrapped around screws. Having clamp holes as well as screws allows you that much more capacity for accommodating the wiring connection you want to make. The holes are coded and are an integral part of the connections to screw terminals.

Switches have three kinds of on/off action, ranging from loud to silent: some switches make a distinctive click when you hit them; in others you can hear the switch, but just barely; there is also a type called a mercury switch, which is silent. The quieter the switch, the more you'll pay for it. Switches can be found on which the toggles are illuminated, handy for finding a switch in the dark.

Like receptacles, switches have metal stampings on top with tapped screw holes for ready attachment to a box, and ears so you can install the switch flush with the wall material.

In addition to house switches, there are a number of other useful switches.

House Switches

SINGLE-POLE SWITCH

Description: This is a rectangular box with a toggle switch in front and one brass screw on each side or both screws on one side.

Buying information: It is used to control one light or a group of lights from one point in a room, typically from the room entrance. As mentioned, it controls only one 110-volt circuit. As with any screw terminals, wrap the wire around them clockwise. If more than one switch is going to be in a box, wrap electrical tape around it to ensure that adjacent bare wires won't touch, which could cause a short circuit.

Single-Pole Switch

DUPLEX SWITCH

Description: This looks like a regular switch, but has two toggles.

Buying information: This type of switch is good when you need two switches in one spot for controlling two different things, such as a fan and a light in a bathroom.

DUPLEX SWITCH

THREE-WAY SWITCH

Description: This looks like a single-pole switch except that there are two brass screws and one copper screw, and perhaps a green grounding screw.

Buying information: It is used to control a light from two different locations. For example, one three-way switch could be installed at the top of the stairs to a basement, and another at the door downstairs that leads outside. You could turn on the light as you enter the basement and turn it off as you leave. In addition, you can have one switch at one end of a long hall, one at the other; one switch at one entrance to a kitchen and one at the other.

FOUR-WAY SWITCH

Description: This looks like other switches except that it has four terminal screws: two brass and two copper-colored ones, or four brass screws and possibly a green grounding screw.

Buying information: With this switch and two of the above you can control lights from three different locations.

COMBINATION SWITCH

Description: This is a regular switch, but one part is a switch and the other a receptacle.

Buying information: It is handy wherever both a receptacle and switch are needed.

How-to hint: Installs like other switches.

INCANDESCENT DIMMER SWITCH

Description: This is a rectangular switch with any of three actions: a turn knob, a toggle, or a lever that rides in a slot (the last type is best).

Buying information: Dimmer switches raise or lower the level of light. Aside from the distinctive ambience provided by a dim-

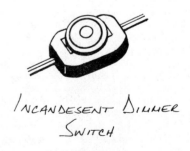

INCANDESENT DIMMER SWITCH

mer, lowering light levels lowers the wattage used. They are commonly available up to 660 watts.

How-to hints: When installing a dimmer switch, make sure the power is off. Aside from safety, if you install it while the power is on and the switch is hit by a surge of electricity—a common occurrence when connecting and reconnecting—it will destroy the switch. Instructions for installation are on the package.

FLUORESCENT DIMMER SWITCH

Description: This is about three times—6 to 8 inches—wider than a normal switch, but with the same action as the incandescent type. Special ballasts are generally required, however, for fluorescents operated on dimmer circuits. Used only for dimming fluorescent lights.

Buying information: Since these units are so large, manufacturers often sell the extra-large box and cover as a package.

How-to hint: Power should be off during installation, as detailed above.

ROCKER-ARM SWITCH

Description: This is a regular switch, but it has a flattish plate with a rocker action for turning the switch off and on. It comes in white, brown, and ivory.

Buying information: These switches do the same job as other switches, but are considered better looking.

How-to hint: Install like other switches.

ROCKER-ARM SWITCH

Specialized Switches

PILOT LIGHT SWITCH

Description: This looks like a regular switch, but it has a pilot light.

Buying information: This is a good switch when you want to see if an electrical item is on in a remote location, such as an attic or a faraway outside light that you can't see. It uses only a tiny amount of electricity.

How-to hint: Install in the same size box as a regular switch.

PILOT LIGHT SWITCH

SURFACE TOGGLE SWITCH

Description: This is a 4-inch-diameter steel plate from which a toggle switch projects.

Buying information: This is a sturdy switch that is surface-mounted. It is used in basements and other spots where appearance is not a factor.

SURFACE
TOGGLE SWITCH

WEATHERPROOF SINGLE-POLE SWITCH
Description: This is a gray rectangular metal plate with an arrow and turning knob and a built-on switch.
Buying information: This switch is intended to be screwed to a weatherproof box.

IN-LINE SWITCH
Description: This is a rectangular plate with some device to turn a switch on and off.
Buying information: It is a convenience switch; with it you can turn a lamp off and on from a remote location. There are different forms for different types of wire.
How-to hint: To use the switch, you just cut one leg of the wire, then splice it in place.

SAFETY SWITCH
Description: This looks like a regular switch, but it has a push-button fuse built in.
Buying information: It is good for use with electric motors or other items where there is a high initial surge of current that might strain wire capacity. The switch protects the wire and the device.
How-to hint: A safety switch can be installed in a handy box.

PHOTOELECTRIC SWITCH
Description: This is a small box with a clear grid.
Buying information: This switch is for turning on outdoor lights at night. It may be mounted in a post lamp or on the house itself.
How-to hint: When installing the switch, angle it so that lights of an approaching car won't trigger it.

NONTAMP SWITCH
Description: This looks like a regular switch, but instead of a toggle it has a slot for a key.

Buying information: This is an excellent choice where safety is required, such as on machines to which children may have access. No one can turn on the switch without the key.

How-to hint: Expect it to be difficult to get the key in the switch.

CANOPY SWITCH

CANOPY SWITCH

Description: This is a round switch with a knurled rotary on/off button or a toggle switch. It has wire leads.

Buying information: This is installed in a lamp or other fixture for convenience in turning the item on or off.

CORD SWITCH

CORD SWITCH

Description: This is typically rectangular; it separates into halves and has a knurled turning wheel.

Buying information: It is a good switch for controlling power to lamps, radios, and so on. It is available in a type that contains a dimmer.

MOMENTARY ON-OFF SWITCH

Description: This is a pushbutton switch; it may have two lead wires.

Buying information: This is a good switch where you want just a momentary surge of electricity, such as from a bell button, or starter button.

DESPOD SWITCH

MINIATURIZED SWITCH (DESPOD SWITCH)

Description: This is one-third the size of a standard switch, with a toggle.

Buying information: You can fit three of these switches into a spot where only one normal-size switch would go. Miniaturized receptacles and pilot lights are also available.

How-to hints: These switches require a mounting strap that accepts up to three switches (or receptacles). Place the switch in the strap and use a screwdriver to push against a pressure point and lock it in place.

FLUORESCENT STARTER SWITCH

Description: This is a small square switch with pushbutton action.

Buying information: A good switch where you don't have a lot of room, it is commonly installed under kitchen cabinets over counter.

TAPS

A variety of devices, collectively called taps, are used when you need more outlets than available at a given location.

CUBE TAP

Description: This is a cubelike piece of plastic or rubber with three outlets—two on the sides and one on the top—and prongs for plugging in.

Buying information: It accepts up to three nongrounded cords. As with any tap, it is appropriate when you have to plug in several low amperage devices whose total demand doesn't exceed the electrical capacity of the circuit being tapped.

TRIPLE TAP

Description: This is a rectangle of plastic with three side-by-side outlets and a pair of prongs for plugging it in. It comes in regular two- and three-pronged (grounded) forms.

Buying information: The grounding feature is a good idea, because it grounds all the devices plugged into the tap, provided the wall receptacle is properly grounded.

MEDIUM-BASE SOCKET ADAPTER

Description: This is an internally threaded socket with plug prongs.

Buying information: A bulb can be screwed into this device and then it can be plugged into the wall, in effect turning a receptacle into a lamp socket. These devices are made with up to 660-watt capacity.

TWIN LIGHT SOCKET

Description: Like a twin medium-base socket, this has two internally threaded sockets, but the base is like that of an incandescent light bulb.

Buying information: It converts a single bulb holder into a double holder.

CURRENT TAP

TABLE TAP

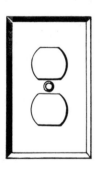

ONE-GANG
RECEPTACLE PLATE

KEYLESS CURRENT TAP

Description: This is a medium base with two side outlets and bulb socket but no switch.

Buying information: This device converts an ordinary bulb socket into two receptacles with up to 660-watt capacity, and it also contains a threaded socket for a bulb.

CURRENT TAP WITH PULL CHAIN

Description: Basically similar to the keyless current tap, this has a bead-chain pull.

Buying information: It converts a single medium base into two receptacles plus bulb holder. The bead chain controls only the bulb; the receptacles remain live.

TABLE TAP

Description: This is a three-receptacle unit with two screws projecting from the baseplate.

Buying information: Use it when you want outlets at table height.

How-to hints: Screw it into the tabletop and feed in the wires from the side. Make sure wires are secure.

WALL PLATES

Description: These are the ubiquitous flat plates that cover the mechanisms of standard switches and receptacles. They vary, from plain white plastic to painted or polished metal to decorator wood.

Buying information: Wall plates come in a tremendous array of styles for screwing to tappings on switches and receptacles; some are oversized, which is good when too large an opening was made for a switch or receptacle.

WIRE

Wires for electrical purposes are called conductors, simply because they conduct electricity. Actually, wire is a misnomer, because you don't buy bare metal. Rather the wire—the metal—comes covered with insulation, usually plastic. The conductor may consist of either solid metal or twisted strands;

solid conductors are used in most house wiring, while the stranded conductors are used in conduit wiring and other applications where flexibility is important.

Conductors are always copper (at one time aluminum was used, but this was found to be a safety hazard).

Wire is commonly spoken of in terms of a number, or gauge, that refers to the diameter of the wire. The larger the number, the smaller the wire. No. 38 wire, for example, is a little thicker than a human hair; No. 18 wire is about the diameter of the head of a pin; No. 2 wire has the diameter of a lead pencil. And it keeps getting bigger, with the number designations changing to 1/0, 2/0, 3/0, 4/0, and so forth.

The bigger the wire, the more current it can carry. You will normally be concerned with relatively few wires. Those commonly used in house wiring are numbers 14 and 12; numbers 18 and 16 are common for extension cords; number 14 is used for heavy-duty appliance cords.

Insulated wire is also classified by letter according to type of covering or insulation used, but these designations normally need not concern the do-it-yourselfer.

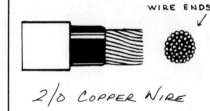

WIRE ENDS

2/0 COPPER WIRE

NM (Nonmetallic) Sheath Cable
Description: This type of cable has a flattish, cream-colored thermoplastic jacket and contains two or three wires, each covered with insulation and wrapped with spiral paper tape; it also has a paper-covered copper ground wire.
Buying information: NM cable is used for house wiring, in places that are always dry and that aren't subject to salt, oxidation, or other attacks from corrosion. This means enclosed by house walls. It comes in 25-, 50-, and 100-foot lengths but is also available in 1,000-foot lengths. However, it is illegal to use in New York City because rats can eat through the plastic, so check the building codes in your area before buying.
How-to hint: There is a stripping tool, called a cable ripper, used for working with NM cable that is inexpensive and makes the job infinitely easier.

BX Armored Cable
Description: This is a beaded steel casing with two or three insulated wires inside, each wrapped in spiral layers of tough paper. Two-wire BX has one white wire and one black wire but no ground wire. It doesn't have a third grounding wire of equal

size like NM cable, but it does have a thin aluminum bonding wire for this purpose.

Buying information: Used for house wiring, this is a tougher material than NM cable, but many electricians don't use it because it is not as easy to work with. Still, inside a wall it stands up better, and if a nail hits it, the nail may not penetrate—a good safety measure.

How-to hints: Use a hacksaw to cut it, and cut at a 45-degree angle for best results. It is used primarily in commercial establishments. Make sure the cable is braced well so the hacksaw doesn't slip.

THHN WIRE

Description: This is nylon-covered wire, and it comes in various sizes and colors, including purple, green, white, and black. It is oilproof and heatproof.

Buying information: Use this when wiring fluorescent fixtures. Different-colored wires are provided so you can make different connections. THHN is slippery and abrasion-resistant, so it can be pulled through a conduit, and it is oilproof. It is also used because the ambient temperature of a light fixture is 105 degrees, higher than NM or BX cable could readily withstand without deteriorating.

UF (UNDERGROUND FEED) CABLE

Description: This comes in various gauges and looks like NM. But unlike NM, the wires are encased in plastic rather than just being inside a sleeve of insulation.

Buying information: This is a highly abrasion-resistant material and is waterproof. As such, it is designed for burial in the ground and can tolerate temperature extremes and frost heaving. It can also withstand a blow, such as from a shovel.

How-to hint: As with NM cable, you can use a cable ripper to remove the jacket, but only if you are an experienced do-it-yourselfer.

SERVICE ENTRANCE CABLE

Description: This is neoprene-coated black wire. It comes in various gauges: 0, 00, 1, 2, 3.

Buying information: It is for use between the electric service head and the house. Any necessary attention should be left to a licensed electrician.

Low-Voltage Wire

Description: This is thin wire in 18, 20, or 22 gauge.

Buying information: It is used for bells, outdoor lights, and thermostats. Low-voltage circuits do not pose a serious shock hazard.

WIRE CONNECTORS

NM Cable Connector

Description: This is a round metal fitting with two screws.

Buying information: It is used to secure NM cable in a knockout hole in an electrical box.

NM Cable Connector

BX Connector

Description: This is similar to an NM connector, but it has teeth.

Buying information: It is used to secure BX cable to an electrical box. The teeth bite into the metal cable covering to help hold it in place.

WIRE NUT

Description: This comes in a variety of sizes and colors (usually a code for size) and is basically a fluted cap with internal threads.

Buying information: It is used to splice wires. Strip the wires, insert the bare ends in the nut, and twist the nut to fasten it on and make the connection. Make sure that these are twisted on tightly, and back them up with a wrap of electrical tape over the skirt connector for extra safety.

Wire Nut

PLUMBING
HARDWARE

FAUCETS

Faucets, known as "valves" in the plumbing trade, are available for kitchen and bath sinks, which are known as "lavatories."

The most important measurement when installing a faucet is the "center"—the distance from the center of the hot-water handle to the center of the cold-water handle. You must know this measurement. When the water and drain pipes are installed, they also have centers to which the faucet's center must correspond. If the pipes are 8 inches apart, so must the hot and cold taps be 8 inches apart.

Lavatory faucets usually have 4-inch centers, but 8 inches is not uncommon. Wall-mounted lavatory faucets usually have 4½-inch centers, but may be 6 inches. Kitchen sink faucets are usually 8 inches apart, and so are tub faucets. Utility sink faucets are normally 4 inches apart.

Faucets that use washers are called compression faucets. As you turn the handle, the washer at the end of the stem presses against and plugs up the hole, or seat, inside the faucet body where the water emerges. The washer may be made of rubber or neoprene, a plastic composition, or, the newest thing, ceramic.

In a so-called washerless faucet, which always has only one handle, there is a ball inside the faucet that is manipulated by moving the handle. The ball slides across and plugs up the hole where the water is emerging.

Faucets are made of a variety of materials: chrome-plated

brass, chrome-plated pot metal, chrome-plated plastic, and plain plastic. The latter, referred to in the trade as "builders' special," are inferior. But chrome-plated plastic is good.

Chrome-plated brass comes in two types, tubular and cast. The cast variety is much better and can be determined by hefting the faucets: the cast type is heavier.

Chrome-plated pot metal rots out readily. You can tell the difference between pot metal and cast brass also by hefting: cast brass is heavier. In addition, look on the underside in a corner where the plating didn't take for the flash of yellow indicating brass.

Compression faucets that use ceramic disks are much more expensive than ones using rubber or plastic washers, but on faucets where the water piping is new, they may be a good investment. If the plumbing is old, however, material that has scaled off from pipes may score the ceramic disk, destroying the water seal, and the faucet will leak until the disk is replaced.

Washerless, single-handle faucets are available for lavatories, sinks, and tubs. They do a better job of mixing hot and cold water and also maintaining water temperature. Single-handle faucets that keep the water temperature constant are also available.

When buying a faucet, stick with brand names, companies that have been in business for a while.

Note also that a faucet should be easy to turn even if your hands are wet and soapy. Some faucets have barrel-shaped handles or globes or other designs that are difficult to grip. No matter how well they are made, their design may make them an unsatisfactory product.

Compression Faucets

LAVATORY FAUCET
Description: Lavatory faucets come in an incredible variety of shapes, including ones that resemble fish and other creatures.
Buying information: See tips given in the introductory section above.
How-to hints: Disconnecting the old faucet and connecting the new one is made much easier by using a basin wrench, which is designed to work in limited space and reach, and turn the nuts connecting the water lines to the faucet lines. If a basin wrench is not available, you can use locking pliers. You can clamp these on a nut and exert full turning pressure on the handles without

FAUCET

having to squeeze the tool hard so the jaws stay on the nut. Before attempting any of this, however, you should turn off the water supply valves under the lavatory and shut off the water supply.

SINK FAUCET

Description: These vary greatly; the two general types are those that have separate hot- and cold-water handles of various shapes, and those that have a single-handle control.

Buying information: All the information about lavatory faucets applies to kitchen-sink faucets. Washerless faucets are the most economical; they last longer than others because there is less friction between the mating parts.

How-to hint: One thing many amateur installers forget to do is to bed the faucet deck in stainless-steel putty. It is thought that the faucet's plastic gasket is all that is required, but it isn't, and leaks can occur without the putty.

STANDARD TUB FAUCET

Description: This comes in various shapes and in several basic forms. A three-valve diverter has hot- and cold-water handles and a valve in the middle for diverting water to either the tub or the shower. A two-valve diverter has hot- and cold-water handles and a pop-up device on the spout for diverting water as needed. The two-valve shower fitting has hot- and cold-water handles for the shower only, while the two-valve tub filler has a hot- and cold-water faucet for filling the tub.

Buying information: All of the quality considerations detailed for lavatory and sink faucets apply as well to tub faucets.

How-to hints: First, of course, turn off the main water valve. To replace a tub faucet stem, loosen the nut that holds the faucet inside the wall; you can rent a socket wrench to get at it. Hardware and plumbing-supply dealers commonly lend the wrenches.

Once the faucet stem is out, take special note of where the gaskets, O-rings, and other packing items are located, and carefully reassemble them just the way they are. Ninety percent of the leaks in tub faucets are caused by defective or improperly replaced gasketing materials, and you may not even know the faucet is leaking because the water drips inside the wall, a burgeoning disaster.

Replacing an entire tub faucet is a big job if you have to open

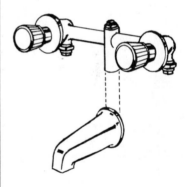

TWO-VALVE TUB FILLER

a tile wall. In many cases you can avoid this by checking for a closet or open area behind the faucet—a small section of wall may be removed and access to the faucet achieved that way. Sometimes, too, there is a panel that gives access to the tub fittings. However, most people will be more inclined to hire a plumber.

TEMPERATURE PRESSURE-CONTROL VALVE (FAUCET)

Description: This is like a standard faucet with a single handle.

Buying information: Temperature pressure-control valves take the place of standard shower faucets and, by keeping the water pressure and temperature stable, protect against a shower user getting scalded. For example, if someone flushes a toilet in one bathroom, someone in another bath could be scalded because cold-water pressure drops and hot-water pressure rises. This valve has a mechanism that senses the pressure drop and instantly adjusts hot-water pressure.

How-to hints: This type of faucet is installed in the same way as a standard faucet. One manufacturer makes a plate that allows even a ceramic-tile wall to be opened up around the faucet. After the faucet is installed, the plate or escutcheon, which is oversized, is installed and covers the damage.

UTILITY SINK FAUCET

Description: This is a 4-inch center-set faucet with a long-swing spout.

Buying information: This faucet is specifically designed for installation on a utility sink. The spout provides clearance for buckets and the like to be placed under it for easy filling.

FAUCET PARTS

STANDARD WASHER

Description: This is a small black or red doughnut-shaped item. A washer may be flat or beveled—sloped—on one side and made of rubber or neoprene.

Buying information: Neoprene washers are more durable than rubber ones, and they work better. Unlike rubber, neoprene doesn't swell, slightly reducing water flow, when the water is hot. You can get washers in boxes of 100, but for the do-it-your-

WASHERS

selfer a small boxed assortment usually contains enough sizes to handle most of the faucets in the house, as well as screws for attaching them. If you keep the washers in an airtight jar, they will stay fresh for many years.

Flat washers are often used on new faucets, but for repair work the beveled type seals better because the seat it sits on will likely be slightly pitted and the bevel is shaped for fuller contact. *How-to hints:* Sometimes the screw that holds the washer is frozen in place and can't be turned with a screwdriver. To remove it, first turn off the water. Dig out the washer around it, apply a few drops of penetrating oil, wait a few minutes, then grasp the screw head with pliers and turn the screw.

Make sure the screws you use are pure brass, not brass-colored steel, which will corrode. The package may tell you. If not, inquire, or, failing this, try to pick up the screw with a magnet: brass will not respond, but steel will.

Manufacturers make the same nominal sizes of washers in actual different sizes. For example, a so-called quarter washer from one manufacturer will be different from that of another. The only way to ensure a correct fit is to try it.

NO-ROTATE WASHER

Description: This is a standard washer set in a brass cup, with two prongs for attachment to the faucet stem.

Buying information: In some cases the cup or rim on the stem where the washer has been mounted is so worn that an ordinary washer will not seal. Or you may have difficulty getting the right size stem. Here, a no-rotate washer is suggested. It is a washer and seat in one. Various sizes are available. They don't rotate like regular washers, so they don't get the same kind of harsh wear.

How-to hints: To use a no-rotate washer, first file or pull off the end rim of the stem with pliers. Snap the washer into the screw hole in the stem.

No-Rotate Washer

O-RING

Description: This is a slim circle of neoprene rubber in various sizes.

Buying information: O-rings fit around the stems of some faucets; their purpose is to keep any water that slips by the washer from leaking out. You can buy a single O-ring or a small assortment; the latter is a good idea.

How-to hint: As mentioned earlier, in replacing an O-ring, make sure that it is in exactly the same spot as the old one.

SEAT

Description: This is a small, circular metal disk partly threaded on one end with a square or hexagonal hole in it.

Buying information: Some faucets have removable seats, against which the washer presses. These sometimes become worn and require replacement. Hundreds of sizes are available, so the best bet is to take the existing seat in to the dealer and get a match.

How-to hints: A good tool for removing a seat is an L-shaped faucet seat wrench. Its ends are machined to fit into the hole in the seat so it can be turned up and out. Allen wrenches can also be used. If corrosion has enlarged the hole and a wrench slips, use a screw extractor, which can be inserted in the hole in the seat with a minimal risk of deforming the threads in the faucet body.

A few faucets don't come with replaceable seats. In that case you must replace the entire faucet. It is sometimes possible to tell what type you have by peering down into the seat, using a magnifying glass if necessary. A round hole, rather than a square or hexagonal opening, indicates that the seat is not replaceable.

FAUCET STEM

Description: This is a metal shaft with one end threaded and one end (the top, when installed) fluted or grooved.

Buying information: Stems come in a tremendous array of sizes, even within brands. The best way to get the right size is to take the old one to the store with you.

Sometimes it is difficult to find the right stem, and a dealer has to order it, a time-consuming process. If so, you can obtain a spring-actuated stem, which you can secure into the faucet hole and tighten down, to cut off water flow until the proper replacement can be installed. This temporary stem has a knurled end that you can grip to turn the water on and off.

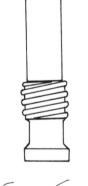

FAUCET STEM

STANDARD HANDLE

Description: This comes in a great variety of sizes, and styles ranging from clear to chrome.

Buying information: As with stems, manufacturers make

many different kinds, so handles can be hard to replace unless they are a popular style. Your best bet is to take the old handle to the store.

How-to hints: If you have trouble removing a handle because it's frozen in place by corrosion, try to loosen the screw on the handle two or three threads. Use a small hammer to rap the screw. The resulting vibration often is enough to jar loose the parts held fast by corrosion. A little penetrating oil doesn't hurt, either.

Failing this, you can use a device called, appropriately enough, a "handle puller," which can be bought at hardware stores and home centers. This works like a steering-wheel puller on a car. Hooklike projections on the side grip the handle while a rod presses against the handle screw. As the puller is turned, the screw presses down against the handle screw and the hooks pull the handle gradually up and off.

UNIVERSAL HANDLE

Description: This looks like the standard handle and, like a standard handle, comes in a variety of styles and sizes.

Buying information: Different manufacturers make universal handles. Designed to fit over any stem, they slip onto the stem and are clamped in place with an Allen set screw. The necessary wrench is provided.

How-to hints: Usually, when the handle slips off, it means the stem is also ruined—the fluted top is worn—and it must also be replaced. But you can always try affixing a universal handle first.

UNIVERSAL HANDLE

AERATOR

Description: This is a small, barrellike metal item with a screen.

Buying information: Aerators are designed to add air to water. Some are adjustable to vary the consistency of the stream obtained. Most aerators come with three or four plastic threaded adapters so they will fit any faucet.

How-to hint: To clean an aerator, invert it and place it under running water.

SWIVEL AERATOR

Description: This looks like a standard aerator but is slightly larger.

Buying information: This aerator swivels 360 degrees and allows you to direct the water stream anywhere in a sink, which can be handy for cleaning and other purposes. The spray pattern can also be varied.

UTILITY SINK AERATOR

Description: This is a standard aerator.

Buying information: Utility sinks usually come with faucets designed with aerator threads. But there are adapters available for converting these threads to threads that will accept a hose coupling. So if the sink has hose threads, adapters are available to convert it to aerator threads.

Washerless Faucets

Washerless faucets are, as mentioned earlier, always of the single-handle type, and though termed washerless they are not—they have replaceable parts, including a part that resembles a washer.

The washerless faucet comes in two basic styles—ball and cartridge—and both work essentially the same way. On the ball type, the water emerges from either of two holes in the faucet body; the holes contain springs and washerlike pieces. When in the off position, the ball is located—manipulated by the single handle—so that its solid parts block the water ports. To turn it on, the ball is manipulated so that holes in the ball align with the water ports and the water flows through them and out the spout.

The same thing happens with the cartridge type, which is a one-piece cylinder with holes on one end. When these holes are aligned with the water ports, the water flows.

Though individual parts are available for cartridge and ball faucets, the best bet when repair is needed is to get a new cartridge, or the complete kit for replacing all parts of the faucet.

CARTRIDGE FOR SINGLE-HANDLE FAUCET

Description: This is a metal cylinder with a series of O-rings and water ports at one end.

Buying information: Individual parts and kits are available for cartridge-style single-handle faucets, but a cheaper, easier, and better repair is to replace the entire cartridge.

How-to hint: Instructions for installing the new cartridge will be on the package. Cartridge models can vary. To find out which one is needed, check at the base of the spout. The model number is often embossed there.

BALL-TYPE SINGLE-HANDLE FAUCET KIT

Description: The heart of this kit is a stainless-steel ball with water ports in it, but there are other parts as well.
Buying information: Same as for a cartridge-type faucet.
How-to hint: Same as for a cartridge type (including getting the model number off the spout).

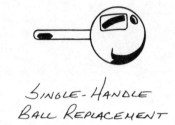

SINGLE-HANDLE
BALL REPLACEMENT

FITTINGS

In plumbing, fittings perform three jobs: (1) they continue straight runs of pipe; (2) they enable pipe to make turns; and (3) they allow changing from one type of pipe to another, for instance, galvanized to plastic.

There are fittings for water and for waste, as well as for the different pipe materials used. Fittings for waste and water come in essentially the same shapes, though drain or DWV (drain-waste-vent) fittings are bigger.

You can assume that any fitting you need to join pipe will be available. Following are examples of the kinds of fittings available:

Elbow:	Curved, shaped roughly like an elbow. Its purpose is to change a pipe's direction. It comes in 90 or 45 degrees.
Tee:	A T-shaped fitting with one vertical section and two straight sections coming off it and forming the top of the T. It enables water or waste to travel in three different directions.
Wye:	A Y-shaped fitting
Tee wye:	As the name suggests, a blend of a T and a Y
Nipple:	A short pipe section used to extend the length of pipe in conjunction with another fitting
Coupling:	Used to join two pieces of pipe together

GALVANIZED PIPE
(NIPPLE)

Fittings for Copper

SWEAT FITTING

Description: This is a smooth copper fitting in various shapes. It also comes in cast brass, which is lighter-colored than copper or wrought (extruded copper).

Buying information: This is used for both water and waste. A more accurate name for this fitting would be "solder fitting," because hot solder is used to join the fitting to the pipe. This method of joinery is used for both water and DWV pipe. Brass is used wherever water is corrosive.

How-to hints: See the section on pipe for how-to hints on joining copper pipe to fittings by sweating. Note also that cast brass is somewhat more difficult to solder than copper, because copper heats evenly, brass less so. In addition, the thickness of the fitting inhibits joinery.

SWEAT-SOLDERED FITTING

COPPER SWEAT FITTING

COMPRESSION FITTING

Description: This is a short, threaded sleeve with a compression ring and a nut.

Buying information: Compression fittings are used only for joining water pipe. They are good to use where it may be difficult to solder the pipe in place or where soldering—using an open flame—might be difficult or where the heat might damage a component, such as a valve.

How-to hints: Clean the pipe and then slip the nut onto the pipe. Slip the compression ring onto the pipe, insert the end of the pipe into the fitting, then screw the nut on the fitting and tighten. Use a small amount of Vaseline on the fitting so that the fitting and compression ring make up evenly.

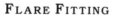

FLARE FITTING

Description: Externally, this looks like a compression fitting, consisting of a short fitting threaded on each end as well as a nut on each end.

Buying information: Flares are more secure than compression fittings. For this reason they are most often used for oil, gas, and other lines carrying flammable liquids.

How-to hints: Use a flaring tool to expand the end of the pipe, into which the fitting then fits snugly and is held tight by a nut. Apply nut onto pipe before making flare to end of pipe.

Fittings for Galvanized Pipe

STANDARD GALVANIZED FITTINGS

Description: These are short, variously shaped sections of silvery pipe with internally threaded ends.

Buying information: Standard galvanized fittings are about ⅛ inch thick. They are always female; male ends of pipe are screwed into them. Used for both water and waste pipe.

GALVANIZED FITTING
(UNION)

DRAINAGE FITTINGS

Description: These look like standard galvanized fittings, but the walls are much thicker.

Buying information: They are used in the same way as standard galvanized fittings; when in place, the insides form a smoother surface for water (or waste) to flow over, greatly minimizing the chance of blockages.

Fittings for Plastic Pipe

INSERT FITTINGS

Description: Tubular plastic pieces, these are cone-shaped at the ends and held on pipe with stainless steel clamps.

Buying information: Used to join lengths of tubing in sprinkler systems.

PVC, CPVC, OR ABS FITTINGS

Description: These look like standard fittings, but are made of plastic.

Buying information: PVC fittings are used on cold-water pipe or drainpipe, CPVC is used on hot-water pipe, and ABS is used on drainpipe. These kinds of pipe are assembled with a solvent that actually melts the plastic and welds the fitting and pipe end together. It acts very quickly, so it's important first to assemble the fittings and pipe dry, and mark where they are to align and the depth that the pipe is to penetrate the fitting. Then, when you assemble them with the wet solvent applied, you can do it with little fear that you'll get it wrong and have to tear things apart and start over.

Fittings for Cast-Iron Pipe

STANDARD FITTINGS
Description: These come in a variety of shapes and have hubs, or rims, at the ends.
Buying information: Cast-iron fittings are heavy and unwieldy to work with, but are required in many localities. Joinery is with hot lead and oakum. Use for waste pipe only.
How-to hint: Only an experienced plumber should use this method of joinery. It's too dangerous for amateurs.

No-Hub Fitting (Cutaway View)

HUBLESS FITTINGS
Description: Made of neoprene, these look like short sections of pipe. In place, they are secured with pairs of stainless steel worm-gear clamps.
Buying information: This type of fitting is designed to be used with hubless cast-iron pipe—that is, pipe with no rims, just plain ends. Use for waste pipe only.
How-to hints: You can install cast iron using this method. Indeed, hubless joinery is easy and reliable. Note: Formed neoprene gasket fittings are also available, but the consensus among plumbers is that they don't work well.

Fittings for Fiber Pipe

FIBER PIPE FITTINGS
Description: These are dark gray fittings made of a compressed-fiber material.
Buying information: Used outside underground for connecting house lines with sewer, septic tank, or cesspool, a limited number of fittings are available, and they are joined to the waste pipe with rubber coupling pieces.

Other Fittings

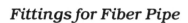

Dresser Coupling

DRESSER COUPLING
Description: This is a short length of pipe with washers and nuts, in plastic, brass, or galvanized.
Buying information: When a water pipe leaks, a dresser coupling can save expensive disassembly of the pipe to make a repair.

How-to hint: Use a hacksaw to cut the pipe where the leak is. Spread apart the pipe ends and slip on the coupling. Tighten the nuts on the coupling (using a pair of wrenches) to create a water-tight seal.

Pipe Coupling

Transition Fittings
Description: These come in various shapes for different types of water and DWV pipe.
Buying information: Transition fittings let you go from one type of pipe to another—plastic to galvanized, copper to plastic, and so on. Your best bet is to tell the dealer what you want.

Adapter
Description: This is usually a short coupling-like fitting with threaded and unthreaded ends.
Buying information: Adapters let you change size from a smaller to a larger diameter pipe, or vice versa.

Flexible Coupling
Description: This is a black, flexible device used with clamps.
Buying information: It comes straight and in shapes, and is good for connecting pipe of all kinds. Since it's not rigid, it forgives error.

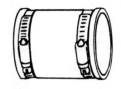

Flexible Coupling

LAVATORY PARTS

All lavatories have traps—the assembly of pipes whose job is to drain off waste after the basin is emptied, but at the same time "trap" a little water as a seal against gases or vermin entering the house.

For basins there are P-traps and S-traps, so called because when installed that's what they look like. A P-trap is characterized by a pipe that goes into the wall, while an S-trap goes into the floor.

The traps may be plastic or, more commonly, "tubular goods," which means chrome-covered brass.

The parts are assembled with large nuts and sealing washers so that the pipes can be taken apart in case the trap has to be cleared.

J-BEND

J-bend

Description: This is a J-shaped piece of pipe, usually 1½ by 1½ inches, but occasionally 1¼ by 1¼ inches.

Buying information: The J-bend is the heart of the trap. It comes with or without a cleanout, which is a threaded metal plug that screws into the bottom of the bend and can be unscrewed for clearing the trap when it gets clogged. The value of a cleanout plug is debatable, although it is certainly useful if you drop something valuable down the drain.

How-to hints: Trap pipes are held together with large nuts and washers, and can be taken apart easily using water-pump pliers. But take care in reassembling them so that you don't strip the threads.

Wall Bend

Description: This is a straight piece of pipe with a slight bend at one end. It has the same diameter as the J-bend.

Buying information: It extends the J-bend to the wall. You can buy the wall bend and J-bend individually or packaged together.

How-to hint: See above.

Waste Bend

WASTE BEND

Description: This is a straight piece of pipe with one bent end.

Buying information: It does the same job as a wall bend, except it does so for an S-trap.

How-to hint: See above.

Pop-up Drain Assembly

Description: This is basically a hollow tube on the top of which is a chrome stopper and below, jutting from a hole in the tube, a lever for controlling the stopper. Much of the device is inside the lavatory.

Buying information: The purpose of the pop-up drain is to stop and open up the lavatory for draining. If you buy the drain with a faucet, it will be much cheaper. You can replace just the plug, but only the specific manufacturer's size will work. Finding the plug needed might be difficult; the best course is probably to replace the entire assembly. These are commonly interchangeable.

How-to hint: To make removal of the assembly easier, use a special plug wrench designed for that purpose.

PIPE

The basic stuff of plumbing is, of course, pipe. Pipe is divided into two basic types: pipe for water and pipe for waste. In both cases, when size is given it always refers to internal diameter. A 1-inch pipe, then, has a 1-inch inside diameter; its outside diameter will be greater, depending on the thickness of the material.

All pipe is male. That is, it is designed to fit into fittings that are always female. Understanding this concept can lead to a quicker understanding of other plumbing parts, which are described in terms of male/female designations.

Water pipe is just that. But waste pipe is also called DWV pipe, which signifies its functions: drain-waste-vent. It drains away water and waste, and vents the system to the outside.

As detailed earlier, with the proper fittings any kind of pipe can be joined to virtually any other. For the do-it-yourselfer, this is a boon, because it makes things doable without great experience. In all cases, though, follow local plumbing codes.

Waste Pipe

GALVANIZED PIPE
Description: This is iron pipe that has been galvanized and has threaded ends. The standard length is 21 feet, and it commonly comes ½- or ¾-inch diameter, and larger.

Buying information: Used for straight runs of water pipe all over the house, galvanized pipe is not used much anymore because it must be threaded, sometimes on site, a difficult job. Also, it tends to scale, which can lead to blockages.

How-to hint: While the standard length is 21 feet, plumbing-supply outlets, for a small charge, will cut it to the size needed.

CAST-IRON PIPE
Description: Standard cast-iron pipe is heavy, thick-walled pipe with a variety of forms at the end. It may be straight on both ends or bell-shaped at one end (known as the hub or spigot end). It is shaped with hubs so that it can be joined with hot lead and oakum, a fibrous material.

Newer cast-iron pipe is "hubless"—both ends are plain—and this permits much easier joining.

Cast iron commonly comes in 5- and 10-foot lengths and in 2-, 3-, and 4-inch diameters for home use.

Buying information: Because it is lighter and easier to work with, plastic waste pipe has displaced cast iron in many situations.

How-to hints: The old method of joining cast-iron pipe was to insert the plain end into the spigot end and seal it with oakum and hot lead, a time-consuming, difficult, and dangerous job best left to a plumber.

Hubless cast iron is joined by slipping the ends into a neoprene gasket with stainless-steel clamps; the clamps are tightened with a torque wrench to a specified torque. This is a far better material for the do-it-yourselfer. Indeed, plumbing codes may not allow anyone but licensed plumbers to work on old-style pipe.

FIBER PIPE

Description: This is gray composition pipe in various lengths and diameters, tapered at the ends.

Buying information: Fiber pipe is commonly used underground for cesspool and septic tank connections.

How-to hint: Connect with rubber gaskets.

COPPER PIPE

Description: Copper waste pipe is standard copper color and comes in various large diameters and in 10-foot and 20-foot lengths. For home use, 3-inch diameter is common.

Buying information: Copper pipe, also known as DWV tube, is expensive, but it is better looking than most other pipe. It is a thinner gauge than copper water pipe.

How-to hints: Copper pipe is commonly joined to fittings by sweating, a process using hot solder. Soldering seems difficult, but is easy once you get the hang of it. One key is cleanliness. When the pipe is cleaned and properly heated and fluxed (flux is a salvelike preparation used for cleaning), the solder is readily sucked into the joint. Another key is to heat the copper directly, not the solder, and to heat evenly: Keep the torch moving over the surface being heated.

PLASTIC PIPE

Description: This is black or cream-colored, depending on the plastic. It commonly comes in lengths of 10 and 20 feet and in diameters of 1½, 2, 3, and 4 inches.

Buying information: The most popular materials for plastic DWV is PVC (polyvinyl chloride) and ABS (acrylonitrile butadiene styrene).

How-to hints: The main appeal of plastic pipe is that it's easy to work with. It is light and can be cut with a hacksaw and joined with a special primer and cement. If it is laid underground, however, it must be carefully supported by solid earth.

Water Pipe

As mentioned previously, many of the same materials used for the DWV system are used for the water lines, but are available in smaller diameters. For the average home, pipe inside the house is ½ inch; the main pipe coming into the house is ¾ inch.

GALVANIZED PIPE

Description: This is silvery in color, threaded at the ends. Common sizes are ⅜, ½, ¾, and 1 inch. It is normally available in 21-foot lengths.

Buying information: Galvanized pipe starts out as black iron pipe, and then is dipped in zinc—galvanized. Galvanized water pipe has the same drawbacks as galvanized DWV—it scales. When replacing a section of galvanized pipe, many plumbers use copper.

How-to hints: Dielectric fittings are available for joining copper to galvanized iron; this prevents an electrolytic corrosion that occurs when copper makes direct contact with galvanized iron.

You can cut galvanized pipe easily with a snap cutter, which you can rent. The dealer will show you how to use it.

COPPER TUBING

Description: This is copper-colored pipe, straight or coiled, depending on the type. Straight copper comes in 10- and 20-foot lengths and in diameters ranging from ¼ inch to 2 inches. Coiled copper tubing comes in various lengths from 45 feet to 200 feet.

Buying information: Copper pipe comes in three types, K, L, and M, depending on pipe-wall thickness.

Type K, whch comes in rigid lengths and coils, is designed to be buried in the ground.

Type L is used inside the house. It is available in rigid lengths and coils, but the rigid material also comes in type LBT, or bending temper. The pipe can be bent with a special bending tool. This is expensive, however, so most do-it-yourselfers opt for straight runs and fittings, one function of which, as mentioned earlier, is to allow straight pipe to make turns.

Type M is used for heating applications.

Overall, copper is the most expensive pipe you can buy.

How-to hint: A key consideration in sweating pipe is that the ends be dry. A good trick to get any water out of a pipe near the joint you are sweating is to push a piece of bread in the tube. This will soak up the water.

PLASTIC PIPE

Description: This is usually cream-colored and is available in 10- and 20-foot lengths and in various diameters.

Buying information: Plastic pipe for water may be polyethylene (PE), a flexible material available in several densities and often used for lawn-sprinkler pipe; PVC (polyvinyl chloride); and CPVC (chlorinated polyvinyl chloride). CPVC can be used for both hot and cold water. Some plumbers dislike CPVC, saying it distorts or "spaghettis" when the water gets too hot.

How-to hints: Like plastic DWV, plastic water pipe can be cut and joined with adhesive. It can also be joined to other types of pipes, as mentioned previously, with appropriate fittings called transition fittings.

BRASS PIPE

Description: This comes in various diameters; ¾ inch is common. It is available in lengths up to 20 feet.

Buying information: Brass pipe is good where water is very corrosive. It lasts longer than other types of pipe (it doesn't scale or clog), so it is a favorite of plumbers in certain situations, such as the run between the water company pipe and the house water meter.

How-to hint: If brass pipe is connected to galvanized, dielectric fittings must be used to prevent corrosion.

WATER SUPPLY TUBE

Description: Standard water supply tube comes in four different forms: chrome-covered copper, plastic, rough copper (no chrome), and corrugated copper, and in small diameters (usually ⅜ or ½ inch).

Buying information: Sinks, toilets, and lavatories have water supply tubes leading to them, and are connected to fixtures by some sort of compression fitting—basically a nut that screws parts tight. Cut-off valves control the water supply.

How-to hints: The most important task when installing a water supply tube is to cut it exactly right—not too long and not too short. With copper this is not so easy; consequently, plastic tube is usually best for people without great skills. It bends and is forgiving of error.

POLY FLEX CONNECTOR

Description: This is a flexible connector with fittings in place at both ends.

Buying information: These connectors are made of tough, hoselike material with the fittings to be hooked up. They are expensive, but available in various sizes for use on sinks, lavatories, and toilets, and make installation of supply tubes simple.

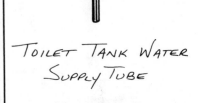

TOILET TANK WATER SUPPLY TUBE

SINK PARTS

Sink pipes are slightly larger in diameter than lavatory pipes.

TAILPIECE

Description: This is a straight length of tubing, 1½ inches in diameter and usually 8 inches long, with a rolled or collared edge. It is also available in 6-, 10-, and 12-inch lengths.

Buying information: This is the part that projects straight down from the sink and is secured to the sink with a large locknut that screws to the drain strainer.

How-to hints: To avoid having to cut it, buy a tailpiece as close in length as possible to the distance to be covered between the sink and the J-bend.

If necessary, you can cut the brass with a hacksaw or a very large tubing cutter. The latter does a better job—the cut edges are not ragged. Though most people don't have a tubing cutter that's large enough, many hardware and plumbing-supply stores will do it free. Plastic cuts easily with a hacksaw.

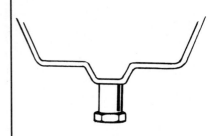

SINK AND TAILPIECE

DRAIN PIPE

Description: This comes in various shapes including J-bends, waste bends, and more.

Buying information: Like a lavatory, sinks have P- and S-traps, and parts are readily available. In instances of a double sink, or some other pipe arrangement, the parts are also available and in the same materials as for a lavatory. You just have to determine what you need.

How-to hint: Follow the tips given above.

DUO STRAINER

DUO STRAINER

Description: This is a threaded, chrome-plated cylinder of metal with an insert that can be raised or lowered.

Buying information: This is called a duo strainer because it allows the water either to flow or not to flow, and catches debris that might otherwise build up in the trap.

How-to hints: When installing, don't forget to put plumber's putty under the lip of the strainer to prevent leaks.

For ease in removing or installing a strainer, there is, in the first instance, an internal spud wrench and, in the second, a regular spud wrench.

TOILET TANK PARTS

The toilet is an ingenious device whose operation has not fundamentally changed since it was invented over 100 years ago. Before discussing its parts, it's essential to understand how it works.

The toilet handle is connected to a rod called a trip lever. Connected to the end of the lever are a couple of linked vertical rods or a chain. At the end of the rods or chain is the tank ball, or flush valve, which sits in a hole called the flush valve seat. When you push the handle, the trip lever rises, lifting the rod or chain and the ball or valve off the flush valve seat, and the water in the toilet tank rushes out, flushing the bowl.

The tank is refilled by the action of the ball cock. As the water level in the tank lowers, a float ball goes down with it. The float ball is screwed to a rod that is linked to the end of the ball-cock mechanism, that serves as a water inlet valve. The valve opens as the float ball drops down and new water starts to rush in. At the same time, the tank ball drops into the hole, sealing off the tank, and it starts to fill again. As the water level rises, lifting the float ball, the inlet valve closes and stops the tank from filling. There is an overflow tube so that the tank can't overflow, in the event the valve doesn't shut off completely. There is also a small tube that routes some water into the bowl to fill it as the tank is being filled.

BALL COCK

Description: This is basically a tubular metal device with one threaded end that goes into a hole in the toilet tank and a plungerlike valve on the other end.

Buying information: You can replace a part on a faulty ball cock, but since there are hundreds of models available—each with different parts—and finding the part you need can be very difficult, you should buy a new ball cock—almost all the makes will fit the same toilet. If you buy a ball cock loose, it will come with a refill tube and a float rod. You can also buy packaged kits (at much greater expense) that come with all components required to replace everything in the tank.

How-to hints: Replacing a ball cock is a relatively simple job on a two-piece toilet, and it can be eased by using plastic water supply pipe instead of metal. Plastic pipe is flexible, which allows it to be bent into position, and requires less-precise cutting than metal tubing.

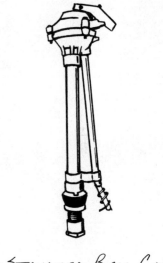

STANDARD BALL COCK

DIAPHRAGM-TYPE BALL COCK

Description: This is basically a plastic tube on top of which is a plastic canister that houses a diaphragm mechanism.

Buying information: This costs less than a standard ball cock and can be installed in most toilets. It is also quieter (it operates by water pressure) than a standard ball cock. It comes in two models, one of which has an anti-siphon feature, which ensures that waste water will not be siphoned into the water supply system.

How-to hints: Sometimes connecting the bottom of this type of ball cock to the top of the water supply tube can be difficult without danger of leaking when the top of the supply tube has a plastic insert. This means that hard plastic—the top of the supply tube—is contacting hard plastic, the bottom of the ball cock. To avoid the problem, place the rubber washer supplied by the manufacturer on top of the supply tube. This will ensure a tight seal.

A way to save having to put in a new water supply tube when

installing the diaphragm-type ballcock is to use the brass nut securing the existing ball cock. In other words, when removing the existing ball cock, loosen the brass nut on the bottom and drop it down along the water supply. Install the diaphragm ball cock and use this nut to secure it in the tank, rather than using the plastic nut supplied by the manufacturer, which, as mentioned, makes it necessary to install a new supply tube.

DIAPHRAGM BALL-COCK WASHER

Description: This is like a solid washer, about the size of a quarter.

Buying information: Diaphragm ball cocks are very reliable. When they go bad, it's almost always because of a bad diaphragm washer. Replacing this will renew the device for years.

How-to hint: The manufacturer supplies installation instructions.

TANK BALL

Description: This is an elliptical ball made of black plastic or formed copper.

Buying information: Tank balls are available in plastic and copper, but plastic is the better buy. It costs half as much as copper and works just as well.

FLUSH VALVE SEAT

Description: This is a threaded section with a smooth circular rim on the top side when installed.

Buying information: Flush valve seats are of two kinds. One type is installed in a hole in the tank, and the tank rests on a short piece of pipe that is connected to the bowl. In the other situation the tank sits directly on the back of the bowl; this is called a close-coupled toilet.

How-to hint: Installing a new seat in a tank connected to a flush elbow is difficult to do and should only be attempted by the experienced person; replacing a valve on a close-coupled toilet is much easier.

FLUSH VALVE RENEWAL SEAT

Description: This consists of a plastic ring and strips of epoxy adhesive to secure it.

Buying information: The main problem with a flush valve seat is that it gets pitted so that the seal between it and the tank ball is not perfect, and water leaks from the tank into the bowl.

Sometimes just scouring the seat with steel wool can smooth it enough to make the seal work, but occasionally it is so badly pitted that the seat has to be replaced or a flush valve renewal seat used.

A renewal seat is basically a plastic ring that is glued over the old seat.

How-to hint: Instructions for securing the renewal seat to the existing seat are on the package. The key is to make sure the old seat is clean and dry so that the epoxy adhesive, which has a puttylike consistency, makes a good bond.

FLUSH VALVE (BALL)

FLOAT BALL
Description: This comes either as an elliptical ball or a so-called flapper ball. There is a ring of rubber on the ball, which is designed to be slipped down over the overflow tube. Some other balls attach to the overflow tube by a built-in clamp.

Buying information: As mentioned above, the purpose of the flush valve is to regulate the control of the flow of water out of the tank to flush the bowl.

FLAPPER FLUSH VALVE

LIFT ROD
Description: This is a rod that is threaded at one end and has an eye on the other.

Buying information: It is sold in pairs (upper rod and lower rod).

OVERFLOW TUBE
Description: This is 10 inches long, made of brass or plastic. Usually 1 inch in diameter, it can also be found in 1⅛-inch and 1¼-inch sizes, and threaded at one end.

Buying information: Brass overflow tubes come in various gauges; the heavier gauges last much longer than the thinner gauges.

How-to hints: Plastic overflow tubes work well, but only on new work. They are difficult to screw in where a brass tube has been. Brass is a better choice, but, before screwing it in place, make sure all remnants of the old overflow tube are gone from the threads. To ensure a watertight seal, apply pipe joint compound before screwing the tube in place.

HANDLE

Description: Handles come in a wide variety of styles, with a trip lever attached.

Buying information: Unlike most hardware items, toilet bowl handles have a reverse-thread nut inside the tank. Otherwise, every time the handle is pushed down it would loosen.

TOILET BOWL/SEAT PARTS

In addition to the parts used in the toilet tank, other parts are required when you install a toilet to ensure that it is set securely in place and is tightly sealed. There is also hardware available for securing the tank to the bowl, and for securing the seat to the bowl. Collectively, the parts are called toilet trimmings.

When you take the toilet out, place a board over the open drainpipe so that if you drop a part it won't fall down the drain. Or stuff something in it that won't fall through.

WAX RING

Description: This is a large, doughnut-shaped ring made of wax.

Buying information: Wax rings are pushed against the top of toilet soil pipe, and the horn or bottom of the toilet bowl is pressed into this, making a watertight seal. Wax rings come single size and double as well as with a plastic sleeve. The latter is the best ring to buy. It ensures a leak-free seal and also can help if the bowl is a little lopsided; the ring with sleeve will still do the job.

PLASTIC CLOSET FLANGE

Description: This is a circular plastic disk with cutouts.

Buying information: The flange is the part that is screwed to the floor; the toilet, in turn, is bolted to the flange. A plastic flange is also glued to the top of the drain pipe. It has a movable interior portion that helps align the bolts inserted in it.

How-to hints: You can install a plastic flange because it just involves gluing and screwing it in place; a brass flange requires soldering it to the soil pipe with hot lead, a professional job.

TOILET BOWL BOLTS

Description: These come as a kit—two large-headed brass bolts and nuts, with rubber and metal washers.

Buying information: These are used to secure the toilet to the closet flange.

How-to hints: To use the bolts, turn them upside down and slip their heads under the cutouts in the closet flange so they stand upright. Thread the bowl base over the bolts and then slip the washers and nuts over the bolts. As you tighten the nuts, the bowl becomes secure.

CLOSE-COUPLED TANK-TO-BOWL KIT

Description: This consists of various brass bolts and washers, in kit form.

Buying information: It is used to secure the tank when it sits directly on the back of the bowl (a close-coupled toilet).

TOILET SEAT HINGE

Description: This is chrome-plated brass, and consists of a horizontal rod on top of which are short arms that connect to the seat, and bolts that connect to the toilet.

Buying information: Chrome-plated brass hinges are expensive. Today most seats come with plastic hinges. However, standard chrome hinges cost just as much as plastic ones.

HINGE BOLT

Description: This is a brass bolt with nuts and washers.

Buying information: It is used on toilet seats.

TUB PARTS

SHOWER HEAD

Description: The old type has a ball on the end of the shower arm, to which the head is attached; the arm and head are one piece. The newer type is threaded and can be detached from the shower arm.

Buying information: You can, of course, connect flexible hoses to heads, or replace the heads.

How-to hint: Take care in removing the old type not to break off the pipe.

SHOWER ARM

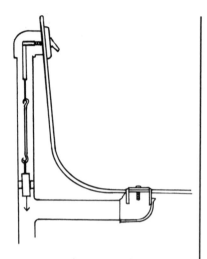

WEIGHT DRAIN MECHANISM

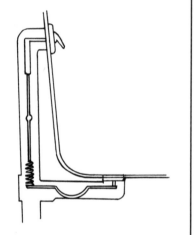

SPRING MECHANISM

BALL VALVE

DRAIN MECHANISM

Description: There are two basic types. The weight type has a weight/stopper connected to a linkage of rods that are raised and lowered by a lever that juts through the middle of an escutcheon on the tub. The spring type has the same kind of lever, but it is connected to a vertical linkage that pushes a rocker arm up or down on a chrome stopper.

Buying information: Either type can be removed and replaced (and so can the escutcheon), but it is also possible to get around replacing the weight-type mechanism, as indicated below.

How-to hints: To remove either linkage, first unscrew the escutcheon plate, then grasp the lever and pull the mechanism up and out. To avoid having to replace either mechanism, you can remove the drain and replace it with a plug. In some cases removal means inserting a screwdriver into the cross-hatching of the drain and turning it counterclockwise until it comes out. On others a spud wrench—a forklike tool—is required to mate with projections on the inside of the drain. Blank escutcheons are available for covering the hole where the drain mechanism lever was located.

PLUG

Description: This comes in various styles and materials and is sized to fit standard drains. Also available is a type that has a plug and a rubber lip.

Buying information: The rubber-lip type is used when you don't know the size of the drain. It will work on any drain.

VALVES

BALL VALVE

Description: This is a pipelike mechanism with an angled handle.

Buying information: The ball valve works like a washerless faucet in that a Teflon seated, stainless steel ball inside the valve covers or uncovers the water opening. It's easy to see, from the position of the handle, whether the valve is off or on.

GATE VALVE

Description: This is a ridged circular handle connected to a vertical pipe assembly inside of which is a metal plate that rides up and down into a seat.

Buying information: The great asset of a gate valve is that it allows almost unrestricted water flow—more than other types of valves. It is commonly used as the main valve in the house, and therefore must be of high quality.

How-to hints: Every now and then, turn the handle on and off. Valves that are never turned deteriorate more quickly than ones that are occasionally turned.

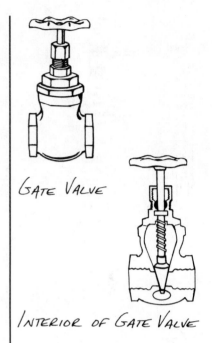

GATE VALVE

INTERIOR OF GATE VALVE

GLOBE VALVE

Description: This is a ridged, circular metal handle on a vertical stem set into a globelike assembly.

Buying information: The globe valve operates like a faucet. It has a stem inside, on the end of which is a washer that presses against a seat to close and open water flow.

How-to hint: The letter *L* or *R* or arrows will be stamped on a globe valve, which tells you which way to install it according to water flow, so that when it is in the off position, the water may be drained out of the other side of the valve, facing vent, cap down.

GLOBE VALVE

CUTOFF VALVE

Description: This looks something like a coupling with a small round or elliptical handle on it.

Buying information: Cutoff valves come in a number of sizes, but all do the same job: control water flow. On sinks and lavatories there are two stop valves, one for hot and one for cold water, while on a toilet there is only one—it controls water supply to the tank.

Stop valves have the internal mechanism of globe valves; washer and seat are replaceable.

CUTOFF VALVE

CHECK VALVE

Description: This resembles a coupling.

Buying information: Used on an oil burner, this keeps water from flowing in or out of a boiler too quickly.

VALVE AND SADDLE CLAMP

SADDLE VALVE

Description: This is a pair of clamps or a U-bolt to screw on pipe, with a turn handle. It has a cast brass body.

Buying information: It is used to tap into a pipe when you want to supply water to a refrigerator ice-cube maker.

How-to hint: It comes with instructions and is easy to install.

MISCELLANEOUS

ADHESIVES

Adhesives and glues do the same job, but technically the former is a man-made product, while the latter are products of nature. Here, the terms are used interchangeably.

CARPENTER'S GLUE
Description: This is a fairly heavy but pourable yellow glue that dries fairly clear.

Buying information: Yellow glue is strong and heat-resistant, with good gap-filling properties, and is ordinarily *the* glue for woodworkers. It sets in 30 minutes, and no clamping is required.

How-to hints: If you buy a large container you can make a good applicator for yellow glue with a small, empty jar and an acid-paste brush. Make a hole in the lid for the brush, stick it in the lid, then fill the jar with glue. Every time you want to apply glue, just swab it on with the brush. The glue will stay fresh and you'll have some precision in application. Take care when applying glue not to get it on areas of the wood that are to be stained. The stain won't take where glue has spilled because the wood pores will be clogged with glue residue.

CASEIN GLUE
Description: This comes as a brown powder that is mixed with

water. Depending on type, it dries either brown or clear.

Buying information: Because it is of a heavy consistency, it is often used for loose furniture joints where some gap-filling is required.

How-to hint: To make glue even thicker, mix with sawdust.

WHITE GLUE

Description: This is a white, viscous liquid that dries clear.

Buying information: It is used for bonding paper and in light woodworking. It isn't quite as strong as yellow glue, nor is it as water-resistant. Excellent for book repair because it's flexible when dry. It is also good as an edge sealer for plywood.

How-to hints: Don't get it on areas to be stained—wipe off spills immediately with a damp towel. To maximize strength, apply a zigzag bead rather than a straight one.

HIDE GLUE

Description: This is a dark brown liquid that dries dark brown.

Buying information: It is used for repair or construction of furniture.

How-to hints: Hide glues take longer to set (overnight) than wood glues, but this can be an advantage in that for several hours after a joint has been glued, it can still be adjusted. Hide glues also require clamping.

HOT-MELT GLUE

Description: This type of glue usually comes in solid, clear, pencillike sticks 2 to 4 inches long. Sticks are hot-melted in an electric glue gun and extruded either by trigger action or with thumb action. Cool-melt glues—which liquify under 200 degrees Fahrenheit—are also available, as are white caulking sticks and a variety of other glues designed for different materials.

Buying information: It is good for quick repair or clamping something together before permanently fastening it. The white caulking glue is simply regular glue colored white, but it works well on some caulking jobs.

How-to hints: Hot-melt glue sets in seconds, so you have to know exactly what is to be glued and how. Take care not to get the glue on your skin; it gets to be around 300 degrees Fahrenheit.

RESORCINOL
Description: This is a powder and a liquid that are mixed together.
Buying information: It is waterproof, good for repair or construction of outdoor furniture.
How-to hints: Apply glue to both surfaces and clamp well. To make a thicker, stronger material, use less liquid than specified.

ACRYLIC CEMENT
Description: This is white glue that comes in two parts that are mixed. It dries clear.
Buying information: Acrylic is waterproof, particularly good for fixing plastic eyeglass frames.
How-to hint: Wipe off excess quickly.

ANAEROBIC CEMENT
Description: This is thin, clear glue.
Buying information: It is good for securing nuts where vibration is a problem, and for securing screws in eyeglass repairs.
How-to hints: Use sparingly—a drop or two should do it, and the bond is very strong.

CONTACT CEMENT
Description: This is amber-colored liquid.
Buying information: Contact cement bonds instantly—on contact. It is *the* glue for adhering plastic laminate to countertops and other surfaces. It comes in two versions, water-based and solvent-based. The latter is available in low-flashpoint and high-flashpoint types. The high-flashpoint type is used where there is a danger of explosion (contact cement vapors are flammable). Most installers do not have high regard for water-based contact cement. There is also a nonflammable solvent-based type.
How-to hints: Apply cement to both surfaces, wait until the adhesive gets tacky, and then press them together. The main idea is not to rush to press the pieces together. Make sure they are dry to the touch. If you can place a piece of paper on the surface and lift it without its sticking, the surface is ready. For faster, easier spreading of contact cement, use a paint roller.

CYANOACRYLATE ADHESIVE

Description: This is clear liquid that comes in a tiny tube.

Buying information: There are two types of this adhesive, one for nonporous (glass, ceramic) items and the other for porous (paper, cardboard) items. Both are supposed to work instantly.

How-to hints: The instructions say to apply just a drop or two, but in many cases people have found that the adhesive does not work. The glue is also dangerous to use—read the instructions carefully. A tip that might help is to breathe on the joint if the glue doesn't hold. The water vapor can help it set.

EPOXY

Description: This is a two-part material consisting of a catalyst and a hardener.

Buying information: Epoxy components are mixed together before use. It is a very strong adhesive and can be used to bond things like metal, glass, and ceramics that other adhesives can't glue. It sets in any time from 1 minute to overnight.

How-to hints: Some epoxies dry amber; this may be objectionable on ceramics and the like. After bonding parts, you can add extra strength by applying additional epoxy over the bond line.

EPOXY PUTTY

Description: This is a two-part liquid mixed into a white, dough-like consistency.

Buying information: It is excellent for plugging holes in drainage pipes and readhering cement sections to walls.

How-to hint: All epoxies are irritating and should be washed off immediately.

CONSTRUCTION ADHESIVE

Description: This is a thick, doughlike adhesive that is gray or tan.

Buying information: It is dispensed from a caulking gun or from squeeze tubes, and is a strong adhesive for a variety of jobs but used mainly for installing wood paneling.

How-to hint: Construction adhesive stays workable for a long time, giving you time, perhaps, to align something, but once dry it is virtually permanent.

CAULK

Before applying any caulk, scrape the joint clean.

LATEX WITH ACRYLIC CAULK

Description: This comes in cartridge form. The cartridges are loaded in a caulking gun, which dispenses it. It is available in a variety of colors.

Buying information: This is a medium-priced caulk that is very popular for general use, such as sealing around windows and doors. It is also good for sealing the joint between tub and wall. Note that many caulks are labeled latex but contain no acrylic, which is an important ingredient.

How-to hints: A common mistake is to make too large a hole in the cartridge spout, resulting in dispensing too large a bead of caulking.

A good trick for making an even, neat line in the tub/wall joint is to lay down two parallel strips of masking tape, one on the tub and one on the wall, about a half inch apart. Extrude the bead of caulk between the tape strips, then use a finger wrapped in thin plastic that has been dampened to form the bead. Once the bead is formed, immediately strip off the tape.

BUTYL RUBBER CAULK

Description: This, too, comes in cartridges, but only in white or gray.

Buying information: Butyl is excellent for use with masonry where there is a lot of movement, such as along the joint between the house wall and the patio slab or cement walls. It is also good for filling cracks in sidewalk.

How-to hint: Butyl caulk will stick to just about anything; once a bead is laid down, it should be left as is. If you try to smooth it, it will stick to the applicator. In sum, it's a difficult material.

CAULKING CORD

Description: This comes in a flat, beltlike band segmented into six beads of various sizes.

Buying information: Beads can be stripped off for use as needed. It is good for setting a sink drain (less messy than plumber's compound) and for permanent as well as temporary caulking. For example, the cord can be pressed into the cracks around a window in the winter, and it will be soft enough to strip off in the spring (you can't do that with regular caulk).

How-to hints: During warm weather, store the cord in the refrigerator and it will be in good condition for the following winter. Or, at the very least, keep it in a plastic bag. Take care that it is not accessible to a child.

OIL-BASE CAULK

Description: This comes in cartridges like other caulk, and may be gray, black, or white. It is a smooth, dense material.

Buying information: It may be used for standard house sealing, but is particularly good for back sealing—applying a bead of caulking to the edges of cedar shingles that abut window frames. The caulk keeps water and drafts from getting under the shingles. Oil-base caulk is the cheapest you can buy and resists deterioration. Available in gallon containers for professional use.

How-to hints: Oil-based caulk is difficult to clean from tools; you must use thinners. If so, use thinners in a well-ventilated area.

SILICONE CAULK

Description: This comes in many colors and is the only household caulk that is available in clear form (except for hot-melt glue, which also may be used as caulk). It applies clear and dries clear.

Buying information: Silicone caulk is the best caulk available—and is also much more expensive than the others. It will stick to almost anything. Unlike most other caulks, standard silicone cannot be painted, though silicone you *can* paint exists as well.

How-to hint: Silicone is easy to work with. After applying, you can smooth it with a finger covered with plastic film (such as plastic wrap) and dipped in water—but only within two minutes of application. After this it starts to set and can't be worked easily.

AEROSOL CAULK

Description: This comes in a can with a nozzle applicator. When dispensed, it looks like white foam, but it dries very hard.

Buying information: This product is excellent for filling very large cracks, such as where shingles meet foundation and where pipes protrude from masonry.

How-to hint: When applying foam, keep the nozzle moving rapidly. Otherwise, foam can build up in one spot or produce an uneven bead.

BATHTUB CAULK

Description: This comes in a tube or a cartridge and in several bathtub colors.

Buying information: This caulk is specifically designed for sealing the tub/wall joint. It is particularly good where children are present because it is nontoxic. Before applying the caulk, scrape the joint clean and swab it with denatured alcohol, which does an excellent job of removing gummy film. Do not use denatured alcohol near an open flame.

FLASHING

Flashing is the material used to seal the seams between roof shingles and around windows and doors.

METAL FLASHING

Description: This is bright aluminum sheet. It comes in various gauges (most common is 26 gauge) and 6-, 8-, 12-, 14-, and 18-inch widths, and in 50- and 100-foot rolls.

Buying information: It can be bought a few feet at a time as well as by the roll.

How-to hints: Purchase flashing that is as close to the gap in width as possible. This makes it easier to work with. For example, if the gap is 8 inches, get 10-inch-wide material. It cuts easily with tin snips.

COPPER FLASHING

Description: This comes in rolls of different gauges, but is usually only 12 inches wide.

Buying information: Copper is much more expensive than aluminum.

How-to hints: It can be cut with tin snips. Copper is not as springy as aluminum, and therefore is easier to work with. In a special situation it may pay to use copper rather than aluminum, which will eventually deteriorate and have to be replaced. Copper will last virtually forever.

PREFORMED VALLEY FLASHING

Description: This is V-shaped like the roof valleys it is meant to seal, and is bright aluminum. It comes in 10-foot lengths and is 9 or 10 inches wide.

Buying information: This is easy material to handle and install, easier than flashing off a roll.

How-to hint: Overlap sections and fasten the flashing with roofing nails.

W FLASHING

Description: This is copper material that comes 4½ by 4½ inches wide and in profile looks like the letter W.

Buying information: It is designed to seal the roof valleys, and lasts longer than regular or preformed flashing because it has two troughs for water to run out of rather than one.

METALLIZED FLASHING

Description: This looks like brown tarpaper, and consists of two dark pieces of paper sandwiching a thin-gauge copper sheet.

Buying information: Use it on top of foundation walls as a termite shield. It is easier to handle and install and is more durable than aluminum.

How-to hint: Thread it over bolts protruding from the foundation and press it in place.

PLASTIC FLASHING

Description: This is black plastic in 6-mil, 12-inch wide rolls of 50 feet.

Buying information: It is used around windows, before installing some shingle courses, underneath doorsills, and more.

How-to hint: Cut with a drywall knife or scissors.

GLASS

WIRE-REINFORCED GLASS

Description: This is ¼-inch-thick clear glass in which are embedded thin wires, which are visible.

Buying information: It is good wherever you want security against break-ins, such as in a garage-door window. A burglar could crack the glass but would have difficulty getting through the wire.

How-to hint: Cut with a standard glass cutter, but hinge it—bend it back and forth—to separate pieces. Bending works much better than using snips to cut the wires.

SINGLE-STRENGTH GLASS

Description: This comes in variously sized sheets 3⁄32 inch thick.

Buying information: It is good for ordinary windows around the house.

How-to hints: Cutting glass is not simple, and it can be cut professionally and cheaply. If not done professionally, a number of techniques must be observed when cutting:

- Use a sharp glass cutter.
- Dip the cutting edge in kerosene before cutting to help lubricate the cutting action.
- Draw the cutter all the way across the glass in one uninterrupted stroke; do not stop.
- Break the glass by applying pressure at the end of the score line.

It also helps if the glass is warmed. The glass should also be new (old glass gets brittle). Warm the glass in the sun; direct heat is not likely to be uniform enough.

If the first score is not completed properly, turn the glass over and try from that side.

DOUBLE-STRENGTH GLASS

Description: This is standard glass, but 3⁄16 inch thick—twice as thick as single-strength glass.

Buying information: It is good for cellar windows or wherever there is a possibility of a window being hit by an object (such as near where children play).

How-to hint: Follow the cutting tips for single-strength glass, above.

PLATE GLASS

Description: This comes ¼ inch thick and in various sizes, with beveled edges.

Buying information: It is used on coffee tables, countertops, and other surfaces.

How-to hints: It takes more skill, but it can be cut the same way as single- and double-strength glass; warming it in the sun makes the job easier. The edges can be sanded smooth after cutting to make them less likely to chip and crack, but do this only with silicon carbide sandpaper.

TEMPERED GLASS

Description: This looks like regular glass.

Buying information: It is excellent for use in storm doors. It breaks into small, relatively dull pieces rather than sharp shards.

How-to hint: Tempered glass has to be measured and custom-ordered. It is "drawn" to the size needed and, once manufactured, cannot be cut.

JALOUSIE GLASS

Description: These are narrow strips (3½, 4½, or 6 inches wide) beveled on the side edges, up to 48 inches long, and of plate-glass (¼ inch) thickness. Length is cut to size.

Buying information: It is used on jalousie doors and windows. The 3½-inch size is still popular as shelving.

How-to hint: After cutting, smooth edges with silicon carbide sandpaper.

LUBRICANTS

LIGHT (HOUSEHOLD) OIL

Description: This is a light amber-colored oil in a metal can with a spout.

Buying information: It is used around the house for light machines (sewing machines), garage door tracks, door hardware, and other things.

How-to hints: Sometimes it is difficult to get the oil where you want it. A good trick is to place a straw in the spot, then dispense the oil into the straw. Another trick is to slip the plastic casing off type THHN No. 10 or No. 12 wire, cut a 6-inch piece, and slip it onto the spout. It makes an excellent dispensing extension. Or, invest in a good pump-type oil can with a long, flexible spout.

20-WEIGHT OIL

Description: This is oil that is slightly thicker than light oil.

Buying information: This oil is better to use on larger motors, such as those on electric fans and oil pumps, because its viscosity is better suited to heavier loads, and it doesn't ooze out of the machinery as readily. Get the nondetergent oil for use in pump motors because it will not attack the rubber seals in the motor, as detergent oil can.

GRAPHITE

Description: This is black dust dispensed from a squeeze container.

Buying information: It makes locks work more smoothly, and does not collect dirt as liquid oil does.

How-to hints: You can get a bellows dispenser that holds and dispenses a large amount of graphite. Wipe up any excess that falls to the floor, because it can make the floor slippery.

LOCK FLUID

Description: This is a thin lubricant with graphite.

Buying information: It is used to make any kind of lock work more easily. The liquid seeps into nooks and crannies better and keeps the graphite in place longer.

PENETRATING OIL

Description: This is a very thin oil that looks like household oil.

Buying information: It is used to break down rust and corrosion that makes nuts, bolts, and the like difficult to loosen.

How-to hints: Most items yield to an application or two of penetrating oil. If not, use a propane torch to heat the object until cherry red, allow to cool until the redness disappears, then apply the penetrating oil. The heat and absorption by the surface of oil will make it highly likely that you can loosen the item. When using the propane torch make sure to keep the flame away from any flammable materials. If it still doesn't budge or you don't want to use heat on the item, give a couple of raps with a hammer; the vibration may break the rust bond.

SILICONE

Description: This is a clear substance that comes in rub-on stick form and in spray cans. The spray liquid dries to a clear, slick film.

Buying information: A dry lubricant for use on door and window tracks, it is also good for sticky drawers and lubricating locks and latches. Stick-applied silicone lasts longer than the spray, but sometimes the surfaces are not readily accessible for application of the stick. The best application is on a door track.

WHITE GREASE WITH LITHIUM

Description: This comes in a tube and has the consistency of soft butter.

Buying information: Good for garage door tracks, bicycle chains and bearings, lawn equipment, and so on. It lasts longer than other lubricants.

How-to hint: Use it for lubricating surfaces where the penetration of oil is not required. Just spread on a thin coat with a cotton cloth.

PATCHERS

There is a wonderful array of patchers available for use inside and outside the home. Indeed, products have been fine-tuned to a degree that it is highly likely you'll be able to get just what is right for the job.

Masonry Patchers

For masonry patching jobs, you can get the components for concrete and mortar, mix then up, and add water.

But for a smaller job, premixed cement material (though in fact cement is only one component in the mix) works well; just add water and it's ready to use. Premixes come in 20- to 60-pound bags.

There are three basic premixed cements: mortar, concrete, and sand mix. They can be used for building things from scratch as well as for patching. It is amazing how big a bag of masonry mix looks when dry, but when mixed with water it can reduce to a surprisingly small amount of usable material. On a big job this can get costly.

Mortar Mix

Description: A smooth tan/gray powder.

Buying information: Mortar mix has plasticity, and is the material to use for the joints between brick or block, either new or repair work. It has more ability to stick to a vertical surface than other cements, and as such is good for filling in around windows and the like.

Concrete Mix

Description: This is a gray powder mixed with tiny stones or gravel, called aggregate.

Buying information: Concrete is by far the strongest of the pre-mix cements. It can be used for making large patches in concrete as well as for building things. As mentioned above, however, premixed concrete can get expensive for a large project, so you may prefer to mix it from scratch.

How-to hints: If you have a large area to fill, you can first dump in anything solid—big stones, pieces of block, and so on—before pouring the concrete mix. This will save money spent on mix without sacrificing strength.

Sand Mix

Description: This is a tan, sandlike product that is coarser than mortar mix.

Buying information: It is used for small holes in concrete as well as for filling cracks and resurfacing. Apply a skim coat of sand mix to a badly pockmarked or damaged area.

How-to hint: As with concrete mix, you can use large stones or other solid filler pieces.

Hydraulic Cement

Description: This is a gray powder.

Buying information: Hydraulic cement is used to patch masonry through which water is leaking. It comes in 1½- and 3-pound cans and 6-pound tubs. Mix with water before use.

How-to hint: The cement mix is applied to the crack and pressed with a trowel until it hardens, a matter of three to four minutes.

Epoxy

Description: This is a two-part material consisting of a powder and a liquid.

Buying information: Epoxy comes in quarts and gallons. It is used wherever great strength is required, such as to patch glass and steel and to set patio and paving stones. Because it is compliant like concrete, it makes an excellent material for sidewalk joints.

How-to hint: To create a neat bead of epoxy, apply masking tape on both sides of the joint to be filled, and peel off the tape immediately after application.

LATEX PATCHER/WATERPROOFING SURFACE COMPOUND

Description: This comes as a powder and a liquid that are mixed together before use.

Buying information: It is excellent for patching pockmarked concrete walks as well as resetting loose slates and tiles.

How-to hints: This material can be thinned to brushing-on consistency, making it good as a resurfacer. It dries white, much lighter than regular concrete, so it is usually a good idea to use it over a broad area rather than as a patch, where its color would make it stand out.

ANCHORING CEMENT

Description: This is gray powder that looks like hydraulic cement.

Buying information: It is used to anchor wrought-iron gates and fencing, bolts, and the like.

How-to hint: When anchoring something, make sure the hole drilled for the item is large enough to accommodate an ample amount of anchoring cement. Make a hole twice the diameter of the item.

BLACKTOP PATCHER

Description: This is a black cementitous material with rocks in it.

Buying information: This is *the* material for repairing holes in asphalt driveways.

How-to hints: To save on patcher, first dump rocks or other masonry material in a hole if it is large, then follow with the patcher.

BLACKTOP SEALER

Description: This black liquid is available in various thicknesses and comes in 5-gallon containers.

Buying information: Blacktop sealer is used to protect an asphalt driveway against weather and wear. Many types are available, including asphalt-based, latex-based, and coal-tar-based. Asphalt is difficult to apply, and latex comes off. The best material to use is coal-tar based.

How-to hints: Most people apply this material too thickly. Apply it thinly, using a special brush/squeegee tool designed for this purpose.

Roofing Cements

ASPHALT CEMENT

Description: This is thick, viscous black material, about the consistency of tar.

Buying information: It is used for a variety of jobs, including sealing patches for flat roofs, sealing flashing, and patching gutters. It comes in 1- and 5-gallon cans, and in regular and flashing grade; the latter is thicker and better.

How-to hints: Asphalt cement must be applied to a dry surface. Use a trowel.

QUICK-SETTING ASPHALT CEMENT

Description: Resembles regular asphalt cement, but thinner.

Buying information: This is used for adhering shingles in windy areas.

PLASTICS

POLYETHYLENE SHEETING

Description: This comes in various thicknesses (1 mil, 2 mil, and 6 mil), various widths (3, 6, and 12 feet), and in rolls 25, 50, and 100 feet long. As the film gets thicker it gets cloudier, with 1 mil quite clear and 6 mil milky. It also comes in black.

Buying information: Different forms of "poly" have different uses. The 3-foot-wide, 2-mil material is commonly preferred for drop cloths. The 1-mil material is very thin but drapes well and can even be used as a drop cloth on furniture.

How-to hints: Masking tape can be used to secure plastic sheeting, but not for more than a few weeks. After this it tends to fall off. Duct tape or package tape is much better.

VINYL SHEETING

Description: This is absolutely clear, 36-inch-wide, heavy vinyl film.

Buying information: This material is sold by the foot (it's expensive) and makes an ideal material as a storm-door window. Unlike rigid plastics, it does not scratch or cloud up. It can be removed after the cold-weather season and put away for reuse the next year. A good storm window can be made using a metal screen frame. Follow the same procedure you would in replacing screening (see pages 51–52), but use a spline that is one size larger than you would normally use.

RIGID PLASTIC SHEETING

Description: This comes in two sizes: 2 by 3 feet, and 38 by 42 inches. It is clear and $\frac{3}{32}$ inch thick.

Buying information: It is used for storm doors. It can be scratched and may turn cloudy as it ages, but it is a lot less costly than tempered glass.

How-to hints: Rigid plastic must be cut with a toothed carbide tool. Scribe the material at least six times, then place the core mark over a broom handle or dowel and press down on a few inches of the line near one end. When this cracks, press down a few inches farther along, gradually "walking" the crack up until the plastic is severed.

The plastic can be secured in the frame with a bead of acrylic adhesive.

TAPES

ANTISLIP TAPE

Description: This is closed-cell mottled vinyl tape that looks a bit like Styrofoam. It comes in 1-, 2-, 3-, and 4-inch widths.

Buying information: This tape is excellent for making surfaces slip-proof. It is used on steps, running boards of vehicles, and the like, as a safety measure. It sticks well to nonporous surfaces, but not so well to porous ones.

How-to hints: Peel off the pressure-sensitive backing, then lay tape in place. It is important for adhesion that the surface be clean and dry. Cleaning the surface beforehand with isopropyl alcohol is a good idea. Do not use alcohol near an open flame.

PURE VINYL TAPE
Description: This comes in a wide variety of colors and in rolls of various sizes, usually ¾ inch or 1½ inches wide.
Buying information: It is good for repair of torn vinyl items.
How-to hints: Vinyl can be cut with scissors. Do not store in direct sunlight.

ELECTRICAL TAPE
Description: This is black, shiny material that comes in rolls ½ inch, ¾ inch, and 1 inch wide.
Buying information: The chief quality of electrical tape that makes it useful in electrical situations, is that it is flame resistant: when direct heat is applied, it simply shrivels up rather than catching fire. Electrical tape has considerable stretchability, and you can wrap it very tightly around devices.

DOUBLE-FACE TAPE
Description: There are two types of double-face tape. One is a thick foam; the other is thinner, like cellophane tape that is sticky on both sides.
Buying information: Foam double-face tape is very strong and is considered permanent. Indeed, it can be used to secure something as heavy as mirror tile, but it is also commonly used to secure carpet, hang soap caddies, and much more. The cellophanelike tape is considered semipermanent, and can be used to secure signs, name tags, and the like.
How-to hints: It can be used on any nonporous material. The protective covering is peeled away and the tape applied, but the surface must be very clean. Clean it first with isopropyl alcohol. Take care to keep alcohol away from flame.

DUCT TAPE
Description: This is gray metallic tape that comes in rolls, usually 2 inches wide and 60 yards long, but also in 30-yard rolls.
Buying information: This is an all-purpose tape for sealing

ducts, smoke pipes (though not stove pipes) and temporary drain repairs, taping off glass to protect it against shattering, taping down wires . . . the list goes on. Duct tape comes in various grades, but hardware stores normally carry only good-quality material.

How-to hints: Strong as it is, pieces of duct tape can be torn off the roll by hand. Keep it out of the sun, and, if carried in the car, out of the glove compartment. A good spot is in a paper bag under a seat.

FOIL TAPE

Description: This is pure aluminum in rolls 2 inches wide and 60 yards long.

Buying information: Foil tape will stick to surfaces extremely well and not break down. It is good to fill gaps in duct work.

How-to hints: Keep the roll out of the sun. Cut with scissors.

MASKING TAPE

Description: This is tan tape that comes in widths of ½ inch to 3 inches.

Buying information: This tape is used for masking or protecting areas prior to painting. The 2-inch size is generally most useful.

How-to hints: It is extremely important to remove masking tape immediately after use. The longer it stays on a surface, the more difficult it is to get off, and after a day or so it is virtually welded on, so that when you try to remove it, any paint underneath comes with it.

PACKAGE SEALING TAPE

Description: This is light brown, thin, shiny plastic tape.

Buying information: It is extremely strong tape that is excellent for sealing packages.

How-to hints: This is very sticky tape that tends to cling to itself. There is an inexpensive small machine sold for dispensing the tape, and it is heartily recommended.

MYLAR-COATED TAPE

Description: This tape has adhesive on one side and mylar film on the other. It comes in rolls 10 yards long by 1 inch wide.

Buying information: Mylar tape is slick and slippery and is often used inside chests to increase slidability of drawers, or on the base of a circular saw to make the saw slide more easily.

WEDGES

WEDGE/SHIM

Description: This is a tapered length of wood usually cedar shingle. It is also available in plastic.

Buying information: Wedges or shims are very useful for a variety of jobs including leveling kitchen base cabinets, leveling door frames, leveling under carpeting, and more.

Appendix A

METALS AND FINISHES

Hardware comes in a variety of metals and has a number of different finishes, factors that affect quality and use of the items. For example, if you want to use an item outside, you need to know if it is weatherproof.

Appearance, of course, is another factor. Brass certainly has a different look from hot-dipped galvanized items.

Black iron: This is iron that has no finish on it, but resembles iron when it's manufactured—grey black. If it is real black—the wrought-iron look—it is actually painted.

Brass: A soft, yellowish metal that has excellent weather resistance but can turn green (oxidize) to a degree if under constant exposure to weather, particularly near salt water.

Bronze: Brownish metal that has even more weather resistance than brass—it doesn't turn green—and is harder. Bronze is considered the ultimate metal for use outdoors. For marine applications there is silicon bronze, which is even better than the ordinary kind.

Cast iron: Very hard, heavy metal that will last forever but tends to be brittle. If smacked with a heavy hammer, it can shatter.

Steel: Most hardware items are made of steel, which requires painting or plating for protection against rusting. This versatile material comes in various alloys and finishes, as follows:

- *Blued.* A finish, of limited protection, often given to nails to keep them from rusting while waiting to be sold.
- *Brass-plated.* Steel that has been coated with a plating of brass. It is attractive and strong, and is somewhat, though not completely, weatherproof. A clear, lacquer spray will do much to extend its life.
- *Bright.* A term used for steel items that are not coated after manufacture. Nails commonly have this "finish."
- *Bright zinc.* A plating that protects items against tarnishing and gives them some degree of weather resistance. Bright zinc-finished items can be painted.
- *Bronze-plated.* Provides some weather resistance, but the usual reason for the plating is that bronze is attractive.
- *Cadmium-plated.* Refers to an item that has been coated with cadmium to make it rust-resistant. Many different hardware items are cadmium-plated, which is more wear-resistant than zinc.
- *Chrome-plated.* Bath items—plastic as well as steel—commonly come chrome-plated. Chrome resists corrosion and water very well.

- *Electroplated.* A broad term that includes items that are coated by various metals in an electrochemical process. The plating is usually thin, and items with this finish are weather-resistant rather than weatherproof.
- *Galvanized.* Steel that is coated with zinc to make it weather-resistant or weatherproof. Only items that are called "hot-dipped galvanized" are relatively weatherproof. The finish is silvery and rough.
- *Nickel-plated.* Refer to items that have been coated with nickel, not quite as garish as chrome. Such items are more attractive than cadmium-plated pieces and are durable, though not weatherproof.
- *Oiled.* Not a true finish, this simply means that a light coat of oil has been applied to retard rusting while an item is waiting to be sold.
- *Stainless:* Made with nickel and chrome, this shiny metal is generally weatherproof and strong, but stainless comes in degrees of quality.
- *Zinc-plated.* Similar to bright zinc but the plating may be thicker and less shiny.

Appendix B

SAFETY EQUIPMENT

Ear Protectors
Description: These range from earplugs to earmuff-like devices.
Buying information: What you use will depend on what you are protecting yourself against. With power tools, ear protectors are a good idea.
How-to hint: Be careful moving around when using ear protectors. With your hearing muffled, you are less aware of what is going on around you, and more vulnerable to harm.

Hard Hat
Description: A protective helmet, flat-domed, available in various colors, as well as metal and impact-resistant plastic.
Buying information: Though mainly thought of as safety equipment for the construction industry, it can be useful to do-it-yourselfers who are involved in demolition and renovation.

Gloves
Buying information: A wide variety of gloves are available, including cotton gloves that keep paint off hands, neoprene gloves that can withstand harsh chemicals, heavy canvas gloves for handling rough or splintery materials, and rubber gloves that keep harmful chemicals from being absorbed through the skin.

Glasses

PROTECTIVE GLASSES
Description: Protective glasses have shatterproof lenses that protect eyes against flying debris. They can be bought in plain and prescription types, and in plastic or hardened glass. Many tools carry a printed notice advising the user to wear protective glasses when using the tool.

GOGGLES
Description: These are large glasses with protective side pieces.
Buying information: Goggles are mainly used for protection against errant splashes of harmful chemicals, but some types are also made to withstand impacts.

Breathing Masks

A number of products are on the market that protect you to varying degrees against harmful vapors and dust. Before purchasing any breathing apparatus, make sure it is adequate for the task at hand. Any mask must fit tightly. An ill-fitting mask may leak and is extremely dangerous, offering only the illusion of protection. Make sure a mask is government-approved.

PAPER MASK
Description: This is a cone-shaped white paper mask with a rubber band to affix it to the wearer's face.
Buying information: These vary in the protection they afford. Some can protect only against house dust; others protect against vapors.

FILTER-TYPE MASK
Description: This type of mask is of plastic, with a replaceable filter.
Buying information: It will do an adequate job of protecting the wearer against sanding dust.

CARTRIDGE RESPIRATOR
Description: This resembles a military gas mask with two protruding filter cartridges and a heavy rubber strap to hold the mask to the head.

Buying information: It comes in two models, one of which covers half the face; the other is a full-face version. These are the ultimate in breathing mask protection, but check to make sure that the respirator is designed to protect against the specific substances you will be working with or around. Look for the label that says the mask is government-approved against the particular vapor. One mask, for example, may be approved for paint fumes (typically, ''organic'' vapors), but not for radon.

Appendix C

OTHER PRODUCTS FOUND
IN A HARDWARE STORE: THE RATINGS

Anyone preparing to tackle a do-it-yourself project, no matter how large or small, needs accurate, unbiased information about products and materials that will be used. The Ratings from *Consumer Reports* will help you choose the right products for your needs.

The Ratings

Individual brands and models are rated based on the estimated quality of the tested product samples. The Ratings order is derived from laboratory tests, controlled use tests, and/or expert judgments. Products judged high in quality and appreciably superior to other products tested receive a check (✔) rating. If a product is both high in quality and relatively low in price, it is designated A Best Buy. The Ratings offer comparative buying information that greatly increases the likelihood you will receive good value for your money.

When using the Ratings, first read the introduction preceding each chart, then the notes and footnotes in order to find out about the features, qualities, and deficiencies associated with each product in the test group. You will often find out, in a sentence that starts with "Except as noted," what qualities the rated products have in common.

The first sentence in the introduction to each Ratings chart tells you the basis of the Ratings order. Sometimes groups of products may be listed alphabetically or by price when the quality differences are small. Usually, however, Ratings are "Listed in order of estimated quality." That means Consumers Union's engineers judged the brand (or product type) listed first to be the best, the one listed next to be second best, and so on. When two or more products are about equal in estimated quality, they are listed in a special fashion, perhaps alphabetically, within brackets.

Prices. Where there is a listing of brands and models, there is a notation of the month and year in which the Ratings appeared in *Consumer Reports*. Usually the prices are listed as published at the time of the original report. Whenever possible, it pays to shop around and buy from the dealer or source that offers the best price and also provides satisfactory return and servicing arrangements.

Model changes. Even though the particular brand and model you select from the Ratings may be out of stock or superseded by a later version, the information given can be of great help in understanding and sorting out product features and their characteristics.

Listed by types. Within types, listed in order of increasing number of zones.

❶ Brand and model. We included systems ranging from one-piece area detectors to sophisticated perimeter systems. Wireless units are relatively easy to install; you may need a professional to install a wired system. Most wired systems come with a control box only; other parts of the system must be purchased separately.

❷ Price. Manufacturer's list, if available, and what CU paid in the New York City metropolitan area.

❸ Transmitters/price. How many transmitters are included in the base system and the price, if available, of additional units. Wireless perimeter systems use a transmitter with sensors you mount on doors and windows you want to monitor. The more transmitters that come with the unit, the less you have to spend to complete your system.

❹ Zones. An indication of a system's sophistication and complexity. A zoned system divides your house into identifiable security areas—such as one zone for each room—and makes troubleshooting easier. Only the

most sprawling mansion would need the full 64-zone capability of the *Ademco Alert III*.

❺ Controls. System controls and displays can be on the system's main box, mounted separately by the door, or on a remote device like a keypad. A keypad turns the alarm on and off (older systems use instead a key switch by the door). You mount the keypad just inside the door or doors you most use; the system, when armed, gives you enough time to deactivate the alarm by entering a code. Most systems come with one keypad; with a few, it's an option (O). An alphanumeric display on

As published in the February 1990 issue of Consumer Reports.

Specifications and Features
Except as noted, all: • Accept both perimeter and area sensors. • Can be tested without sounding alarm. • Include remote control. • Have alarm that automatically stops after a preset time. • Can be powered by household current or battery. • Have control unit that you can mount on the wall.

Key to Advantages
A—Telephone dialer transmits your messages, not prerecorded message.
B—Has a low-battery indicator.
C—Has an adjustable entrance delay.
D—Has an adjustable exit delay.
E—Automatically bypasses open or tripped zones.
F—Supervised system.
G—Provides voice prompts for programming the system.
H—Allows for more than one user code.
I—System can be customized by programming the keypad.
J—Allows some zones to remain monitored while the rest of the system is off.
K—Has adjustable loop response; helps system detect breaking glass.
L—Has an alarm memory indicator, useful for troubleshooting.

Key to Disadvantages
a—System cannot be turned on or off remotely.
b—Requires use of an external device to program the system.
c—Battery-powered only.
d—Dialer preprogrammed to dial only company's selected central alarm.
e—Has no test mode.
f—Transmitter takes special 12-volt battery; may be hard to find.

Key to Comments
A—Control unit cannot be wall mounted.
B—Has relay for extending transmitter range.
C—Sensor transmits an audio signal.
D—Can be programmed via the phone line.
E—Unlike most wired systems, sold as package.
F—Highly technical installation manual and difficult programming; may require professional installation.
G—Price for control box only.
H—Can be modified to monitor more zones.
I—Discontinued but may still be available.
J—Alarm imitates barking dog.

❶ *Brand and model*

Wireless systems
Radio Shack Safe House 49-308 ①
Hyundai HS-100
Universal PT-2200
Black & Decker 9105B
Schlage Keepsafer 71-102
Dicon 9000
Audiovox RSS-2000
Hyundai HS-672
Linear Advantage Console System 7
Schlage Keepsafer 71-152
Transcience The Supervisor
Wired systems
Heath Zenith SD-6000 ①
Fortress DA-9700
Moose System 911
Napco Magnum Alert 825HS
Radio Shack Safe House 49-470A
Heath Zenith SS-5910 ②
Ademco Vista XT-KT 5130
Moose Z1100 System II
Napco Magnum Alert 2600
Ademco Alert III 5720 ②

① *Area system only.*

the control panel shows the system's status in words and numbers, which helps you pinpoint trouble. A panic button, part of the remote control on some units, part of the keypad on others, lets you sound the alarm if you want to frighten an intruder or summon help.

❻ Battery pack. Backup battery power keeps your system working during a blackout or when an intruder cuts your wires. The packs, an option (O) on most of our systems, cost $10 to $25.

❼ Other attachments. All but the simplest units will let you add door and window sensors. Most also provide for other devices, either as part of the package or as an option (O): glass-break detectors trigger the system if someone has broken a window; area sensors detect intruders' motion in a room; smoke detectors; automatic telephone dialers; and external sounding devices (sirens, bells, horns) and strobe lights you can mount where they'll be seen or heard outside the house. Auxiliary alarm contacts and appliance controllers let the system turn outlets or light switches on and off.

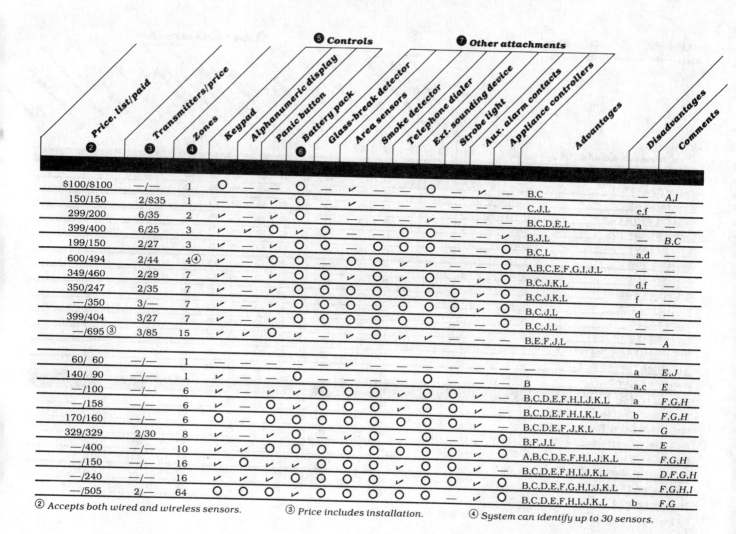

Price, list/paid ❷	Transmitters/price ❸	Zones ❹	Keypad	Alphanumeric display	Panic button	Battery pack ❻	Glass-break detector	Area sensors	Smoke detector	Telephone dialer	Ext. sounding device	Strobe light	Aux. alarm contacts	Appliance controllers	Advantages	Disadvantages	Comments
$100/$100	—/—	1	O	—	—	O	—	✓	—	—	—	O	—	✓	B,C	—	A,I
150/150	2/$35	1	—	—	✓	O	—	✓	—	—	—	—	—	—	C,J,L	e,f	—
299/200	6/35	2	✓	—	✓	O	—	—	—	✓	—	—	—	—	B,C,D,E,L	a	—
399/400	6/25	3	✓	✓	O	✓	O	—	O	O	✓	—	—	—	B,J,L	—	B,C
199/150	2/27	3	✓	—	✓	O	O	—	O	O	O	—	—	O	B,C,L	a,d	—
600/494	2/44	4④	✓	—	O	O	—	O	O	O	O	—	—	O	A,B,C,E,F,G,I,J,L		—
349/460	2/29	7	✓	—	✓	O	O	—	O	✓	✓	—	—	O	B,C,J,K,L	d,f	—
350/247	2/35	7	✓	—	✓	O	O	O	O	✓	O	—	✓	O	B,C,J,K,L	f	—
—/350	3/—	7	✓	—	✓	O	O	O	O	O	O	O	✓	O	B,C,J,L	d	—
399/404	3/27	7	✓	—	✓	O	O	O	O	O	O	—	—	O	B,C,J,L	—	—
—/695③	3/85	15	✓	✓	O	✓	—	✓	O	✓	✓	—	—	—	B,E,F,J,L	—	A
60/60	—/—	1	—	—	—	—	—	✓	—	—	—	—	—	—		a	E,J
140/90	—/—	1	—	—	O	—	—	—	—	O	—	—	—	—	B	a,c	E
—/100	—/—	6	✓	—	✓	O	O	O	✓	O	O	✓	—	—	B,C,D,E,F,H,I,J,K,L	a	F,G,H
—/158	—/—	6	✓	—	O	O	O	O	✓	O	O	✓	—	—	B,C,D,E,F,H,I,K,L	b	F,G,H
170/160	—/—	6	O	—	O	O	O	O	O	O	O	✓	—	—	B,C,D,E,F,J,K,L	—	G
329/329	2/30	8	✓	—	✓	O	—	✓	O	—	O	—	—	O	B,F,J,L	—	E
—/400	—/—	10	✓	✓	O	O	O	O	O	O	O	O	✓	O	A,B,C,D,E,F,H,I,J,K,L	—	F,G,H
—/150	—/—	16	✓	O	✓	✓	O	O	O	✓	O	O	✓	O	B,C,D,E,F,H,I,J,K,L	—	D,F,G,H
—/240	—/—	16	✓	✓	✓	O	O	O	O	✓	O	O	✓	—	B,C,D,E,F,G,H,I,J,K,L	—	F,G,H,I
—/505	2/—	64	O	O	O	✓	O	O	O	O	O	—	✓	O	B,C,D,E,F,H,I,J,K,L	b	F,G

② Accepts both wired and wireless sensors. ③ Price includes installation. ④ System can identify up to 30 sensors.

RATINGS OF CHAIN SAWS

Listed by types; within types, listed in order of estimated quality. Except where separated by a bold rule, closely ranked models differed little in quality. Bracketed models were about equal in quality; listed alphabetically.

❶ Price. The manufacturer's list price and the average price paid by CU shoppers. A+ indicates shipping is extra.

❷ Engine size/motor current. As stated by the manufacturer. A bigger engine or higher amperage didn't necessarily translate into better performance.

❸ Guide-bar length. Our measurement of the effective cutting length of the bar over which the chain rides, to the nearest quarter-inch. The sizes we chose are the ones most popular with homeowners.

❹ Weight. To the nearest quarter-pound, with a full tank of chain oil and fuel.

❺ Cutting speed. We timed how long each saw needed to slice wafers from a 6×6-inch pine timber, somewhat like slicing bread. The swiftest model averaged 4 seconds a wafer; the slowest, around 14 seconds. Cutting hardwood like ash slowed down all the chain saws, but the relative speed rankings remained the same.

❻ Kickback force. Improved safeguards in recent years have dramatically reduced kickback, the potentially lethal recoil that occurs when the tip of the chain is pushed into wood. When we forced the tip of each saw into oak timber, most kicked back only a little. The *Echo* and the *Homelites* have a tip guard that eliminates kickback altogether—if it's used. But because the guard can limit the saw's usefulness, many people remove it. That's unwise, in our view, especially with the *Homelites*. Without the guard, they recoiled more than any other saw of their type.

❼ Handling and comfort. Cutting control shows how easily you can use a saw for bucking (cutting up and down to trim a log to stove-sized lengths, say) and felling (cutting horizontally through a standing tree trunk). A saw with good balance requires little effort to hold in the proper cutting position. Handle comfort judgments reflect tests with and without gloves; rear handles tend to be more uncomfortable than front ones, usually because they're too thick, too high, or too rough. Some gasoline models provide much more starting security than others; the best let you hold the saw perfectly steady while pulling the cord, while others force you to do a juggling act with your hands. The vibration level in most of the saw handles was either imperceptible or slight. Models that scored well here also tended to be less fatiguing to use. The worst shakers could lead to "white finger syndrome," a numbness and loss of feeling in the fingers.

As published in the May 1990 issue of Consumer Reports.

Better ●──◐──○──◑──● Worse

Brand and model	❶ Price, list/paid	❷ Engine, cu. in./motor current, amps	❸ Guide-bar length, in.	❹ Weight, lb.	❺ Cutting speed	❻ Kickback force	Cutting control	Balance	Handle comfort	Starting security	Vibration level	❽ Cuts per tankful	❾ Noise	Advantages	Disadvantages	Comments
Gasoline models																
✓ Stihl 024AVWB	$300/308	2.6	15½	14¼	●	○	●	●	●	●	●	●	◑	A,C,H,K,N	—	—
Husqvarna 42	360/355	2.5	15¾	14	●	◑	●	●	◑	●	◑	●	◑	E,F,H,K,N	h,l	D
Echo CS 330 EVL	300/320	2.0	15¼	12¾	○	◑①	●	●	●	●	○	○	◑	C,D,E,J	—	B
Sachs-Dolmar 102	288/265	2.4	14½	11½	◑	○	◑	◑	◑	●	○	◑	◑	A,E,F,H,J	h,n,o	—
Stihl 011AVT	220/226	2.5	15	12¼	●	◑	○	○	◑	○	◑	○	◑	A,H,N	e	—
Jonsered 380	260/260	2.3	15½	13½	◑	◑	●	◑	○	○	◑	◑	◑	N	f,g,h,l,o	C,D
Homelite 240	265/230	2.4	16	13½	◑	◑①	◑	○	◑	◑	◑	◑	◑	B,C,K	b,f,i,k	B
McCulloch Wildcat	240/235	2.3	17½	13	◑	◑	◑	●	◑	◑	◑	◑	◑	G,N	e,g,h	—
Poulan Pro 235	219/225	2.3	16	11¾	○	○	○	◑	◑	◑	◑	◑	●	F	b,m,p	—
Sears 35506	190/191	2.3	16	11¾	○	○	○	◑	◑	◑	◑	◑	●	F,J	b,m,p	G
Sears 35516	160/148	2.0	16¼	10½	○	◑	◑	○	◑	◑	●	◑	●	C,F,J	a,b,m,o,p,q	—
McCulloch Eager Beaver 2.1	②/215	2.1	15½	12¾	○	◑	●	◑	◑	◑	○	◑	◑	G,N	e,g,h	—
McCulloch Power Mac 310	220/200	2.1	15½	12¾	○	◑	●	◑	◑	◑	◑	◑	◑	G,N	e,g,h	—
Homelite Super 2	205/200	1.9	15½	10½	◑	◑①	○	○	○	◑	◑	◑	◑	C,I	a,b,f,i,m,r	A,B
Electric models																
McCulloch Electramac 16-ES	②/87	12	15½	9½	◑	◑	●	●	○	—	◑	—	●	N	c,h	E,F
McCulloch Eager Beaver 14-ES	②/74	11	13¾	9	◑	◑	●	●	○	—	◑	—	●	N	c,h	E,F
McCulloch Electramac 14-ES	②/74	11	13¾	9	◑	◑	●	●	○	—	◑	—	●	N	c,h	E,F
Sears Cat. No. 34170	75+/77+	12	15½	9½	○	○	◑	◑	○	—	●	—	◑	H,L,M	b,d,h	A
Wen Hornet Mark II 5014	70/47	12	13½	11¼	◑	◑	●	●	○	—	●	—	◑	B,C,H,L	a,b,g,m	—
Remington 75762H	②/75	9	13½	7	●	◑	◑	●	◑	—	◑	—	◑	B,H	b,c,d,h,j,k,n	—
Homelite EL-14	87/85	9	13½	7	●	○①	◑	○	●	—	◑	—	◑	B,H	b,c,d,h,j,k	B

① Tested with tip guard removed; would be judged ● with guard in place.   ② Mfr. would not provide list price.

❽ Cuts per tankful. The number of cuts the gasoline models could make on a tankful of fuel. The best lopped off about 135 wafers before running dry, about twice as many as the worst.

❾ Noise. We measured noise levels in the general area of the operator's right ear, which is closest to the engine. Even the "quietest" gasoline-powered saws could cause hearing damage if used repeatedly for just one hour a day. The electric models were quieter, though still loud enough to do damage over time. Ear protectors are a must.

Specifications and Features

All have: • Front hand guard. • Low-kickback chain and at least one other anti-kickback feature.

Except as noted, all have: • Front wraparound handle. • Chain catcher. • Automatic oiler. • Safety interlock for throttle or trigger. • 1-yr. warranty on parts and labor. • Chain brake.

All gasoline models have: • 2-cycle engine requiring gasoline/oil mixture. • Chain-oil reservoir large enough to outlast fuel supply. • Electronic ignition. • Spark-arrestor screen in muffler.

Except as noted, all gasoline models have: • Easily accessible engine kill switch that's simple to operate. • Muffler that's shielded or adequately recessed to minimize risk of burns. • Engine designed to run on regular unleaded gasoline.

All electric models: • Are double insulated, requiring only a 2-pronged extension cord.

Except as noted, all electric models have: • Oil-level sight gauge. • Electric cord no more than 12-in. long.

Key to Advantages

A— Has very effective metal bumper spike for pivoting saw around log.
B— Has fairly effective plastic bumper spike.
C— Trigger judged very comfortable.
D— No tools needed to remove air filter.
E— Rate of automatic oil flow can be adjusted.
F— Cap on fuel tank remains attached to unit when unscrewed.
G— Has both automatic and manual chain oiler.
H— Comes with hard plastic or vinyl guide-bar sheath.
I— Comes with plastic carrying case.
J— Owners manual judged very useful.
K— Started more easily than most when left outside in cold.
L— Has slip clutch, a protection against motor burnout.
M— Has chain sharpener.
N— Chain brake is automatic.

Key to Disadvantages

a— Lacks throttle or trigger lockout to prevent accidental activation of chain.
b— Lacks chain brake.
c— Front handle does not wrap around, thus providing a grip that's barely adequate for felling.
d— Has manual oiler; judged difficult to use.
e— Engine-kill switch hard to operate or poorly positioned.
f— Access to fuel filler judged poor.
g— Access to chain-oil filler judged poor.
h— Trigger judged uncomfortable; wearing gloves should lessen or eliminate the problem.
i— Fully exposed muffler: a potential burn hazard.
j— Lacks oil-level sight gauge, a big shortcoming for an electric model.
k— Owners manual judged of limited use.
l— Manual contains useful details, but it's inconvenient to use because it's printed in four languages.
m— Lacks chain catcher.
n— Comes with 90-day labor and parts warranty; much shorter than most.
o— More difficult to start than most if left outside in cold.
p— Cover must be unscrewed to reach carburetor for adjustment.
q— Narrow wraparound handle judged uncomfortable.
r— Wraparound handle has less clearance than most; user's knuckles can rub against fuel cap.

Key to Comments

A— Plastic bucking spike judged useless.
B— Has removable tip guard to prevent kickback.
C— Tilted step-through handle judged of no help to starting security.
D— Mfr. recommends minimum of 90-octane gasoline.
E— Mfr. recommends hard-to-find 10-gauge extension cord for use at 100 ft. from outlet. But saw worked fine with standard 14-gauge cord at that distance.
F— Has no cord; electric plug built into housing.
G— Discontinued, but may still be available in some Sears retail stores.

Listed in order of overall quality, based on safety, speed, results, and effort needed. Products judged approximately equal are bracketed and listed alphabetically.

❶ **Price.** Manufacturer's average or suggested retail to nearest dollar, per gallon—the amount you're likely to need for even a modest job.

❷ **Cost/sq. ft.** So you can determine the cost of an actual job. Based on the cost per ounce, with a coating about one-eighth-inch thick for the nonsolvent products, less for solvent types. You may use more or less, depending on how careful you are, how viscous the stripper is, and how many layers of paint you need to remove.

❸ **Ingredients.** The chemicals containing nonvolatile esters (E) are least hazardous to use. Products using methanol, toluene, and acetone solvents (MTA) are flammable, produce toxic vapors, and can irritate skin. Methylene chloride solvent (MC) is a possible human carcinogen and may cause heart and kidney damage. We tested one typical product of this kind.

As published in the May 1991 issue of Consumer Reports.

❹ **Safety.** Products judged less than ◐ can threaten health. The lower the score, the more serious or numerous the risks.

❺ **Speed.** The total time it took to strip a 16-square-foot door of five coats of paint. The less hazardous products took more than 10 hours; the solvent-based products, two or three.

❻ **Results.** Judged by a panel of staffers. How thoroughly the products removed paint from cracks, molding, and wood grain. Most left some paint residue.

❼ **Effort.** Removing paint by chemical means is messy at best. Some products, however, require repeated application, are difficult to scrape, leave the softened paint quite sloppy, and provide no visual clue as to when the stuff is ready to be lifted off.

Features in Common
All: • Can be applied with brush. • Are sufficiently viscous for use on vertical surfaces. • May require more than 1 application depending on finish type, condition, and thickness. • Have adequate instructions and warning labels.

All solvent-based strippers: • Come in metal container with childproof closure.
Except as noted, all: • Did not rust steel or discolor aluminum or wood.

Key to Advantages
A— Less likely to cause skin irritation or respiratory problems than solvent types.
B— Remained moister than most overnight.
C— Nonflammable.

Key to Disadvantages
a— Solvent vapors pose neurological and respiratory problems.
b— Flammable.
c— Highly alkaline; skin contact hazardous.
d— Rusted steel.
e— Stained aluminum.
f— Discolored pine and cherry wood.
g— May take overnight to soften several coats.

Key to Comments
A— Comes with plastic-coated paper to be applied over chemical; product works well even when uncovered.
B— Performance improved when covered overnight with plastic food wrap.

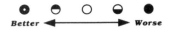

Better ◀———▶ Worse

Brand and model	Price ❶	Cost/sq. ft. ❷	Ingredients ❸	Safety ❹	Speed ❺	Results ❻	Effort ❼	Advantages	Disadvantages	Comments
Peel Away 6	$43	$2.50	E	◕	●	◕	○	A,B,C	g	A
3M Safest Stripper	20	1.20	E	◕	●	◕	◐	A,B,C	d,g	B
Easy Off Paint Stripper	25	1.50	E	◕	●	◐	●	A,C	g	B
Savogran StrypSafer	33	1.90	E	◕	●	◐	●	A,C	d,g	B
Parks No Drip Strip	20	.40	MTA	◐	◖	◐	◐	—	a,b	—
Savogran FinishOff	20	.50	MTA	◖	○	◐	◐	—	a,b	—
Bix Stripper	20	.50	MTA	●	◖	◐	◐	—	a,b,c,e,f	—
Rock Miracle Paint and Varnish Remover	24	1.10	MC	●	◖	◐	◐	—	a	—

Listed by types; within types, listed in order of estimated quality. Except where separated by bold rules, closely ranked models differed little in quality. Bracketed models performed similarly; listed alphabetically.

❶ **Brand and model.**

❷ **Price.** The manufacturer's suggested retail or approximate retail price.

❸ **Handle/grip.** Hammers with a handle made of tubular steel (TS), graphite (G), fiberglass (F), and solid steel (SS) have a rubber or synthetic-rubber (SR) or a nylon (N) grip. Wood handles (W) need no extra grip.

❹ **Weight.** The overall weight of the hammer. All the curved-claw models have a 16-ounce head. Most straight-claw hammers have a 20-ounce head.

❺ **Durability.** To find out how much punishment the hammers could take, we used lab apparatus to subject them to pulling forces that mimicked actual use. With each hammer held horizontally, fixed at its claw, we pulled at loads of 120, 200, and 250 pounds. None sustained damage at the lightest load. But at higher loads, some handles broke, bent, or pulled out from the head, and claws bent.

❻ **Nail pulling.** We pulled 2½- and 3½-inch nails driven through plywood into studs, evaluating these factors: the leverage each hammer provided, the length of nail pulled in a single stroke, any marring of the wood surface, and the ability of the claws to grip the shank of a nail.

❼ **Shock absorption.** How well each model prevents the shock of a blow from traveling to your hand and arm. We used an electronic meter with an accelerometer sensor to measure shock. Several factors combine to govern shock absorption. Among them: the hammer's overall weight, the connection between head and handle, and the handle and grip materials.

❽ **Performance notes.** Three CU staff members—varying in size and strength, yet all experienced in using hand tools—were asked to drive 3½-inch nails into panels of ¾-inch plywood attached to 2×4 studs and to note their impressions of each hammer.

Features in Common
All: • Curved-claw hammers have 16-oz. head. *Except as noted, all:* • Are between 13 and 14 in. in overall length. • Straight-claw hammers have 20-oz. head. • Have head chemically bonded to handle. • Have fairly blunt claw ends. • Wood handles are smooth and oval-shaped in cross-section. • Come with no warranty information.

Key to Advantages
A— Reinforced claws with a "third" claw, a small notch in one regular claw, for pulling nails from tight places.
B— Reinforced claws.
C— Head has no painted surfaces that can hide flaws in material or manufacture.
D— Handle taper-fitted and bonded to head; judged less likely to fly off.
E— Nylon end cap on bottom of handle; can be used for light tapping.
F— 1-piece, solid-steel construction.
G— Head attached to handle by steel wedges.
H— Head attached to handle by steel wedges as well as chemically bonded.

I— Tubular-steel shank connected at base of head.
J— Handle has metal collar at connection to head.
K— Wood plug in head; intended to absorb shock.
L— Relatively sharp claw ends.
M— Textured wood handle; intended to improve grip.
N— Wood handle is 8-sided in cross-section.
O— "Lifetime guarantee" on head and handle.
P— Striking surface flatter than most.
Q— Warranted "free of defects in materials and workmanship"; no time limitation given.
R— "Full unlimited warranty" states that if buyer is not completely satisfied, Sears will replace free of charge.

Key to Disadvantages
a—Head slightly loose on 3 of 6 samples when purchased.
b—Handle pulled out of head or bent or broke at head during durability tests.
c—Claws spread, cracked, or deformed during durability tests.
d—Handle grip ripped or tore during durability tests.
e—Head marred with rough grind marks; finish judged worse than most.
f—Hammer's ability to pull nail by shank worse than most.
g—Narrow space between claws.

Key to Comments
A—16-oz. head.
B—22-oz. head.
C—Slightly longer than others; 14⅜ in. overall.
D—Slightly shorter than most; 12½ to 12⅞ in. overall.
E—Striking area of head larger than most.

As published in the July 1991 issue of Consumer Reports.

Better ◄——————► Worse

Hammers

❶ Brand and model	❷ Price	❸ Handle/grip	❹ Weight, oz.	❺ Durability	❻ Nail pulling	❼ Shock absorption	Advantages	Disadvantages	Comments	❽ Performance notes
Curved-claw models										
Stanley Professional 51-031	$21	TS/SR	25	●	●	◑	C	—	I	Handle flat at grip.
Stanley Professional 51-041	21	G/SR	26	●	●	◑	C,D	—	—	Heavy, though driving nails was easy. Handle flat at grip.
Sears Craftsman 38045	13	W	24	●	◑	◑	A,E	—	J,L,M,R	Felt poorly balanced; adversely affected nail-driving.
Master Mechanic G16MM	21	F/SR	25	●	●	◑	—	—	—	—
Sears Craftsman 38125	17	TS/SR	25	●	◑	◑	A	—	K,R	—
Plumb Ultralite Premium 11-470	22	TS/SR	24	●	●	◑	—	—	L	Slightly light. Smooth grip.
Plumb Autograf Premium 11-436	23	W	20	●	●	◑	—	—	N	Slightly light.
Sears Craftsman 38126	18	F/SR	26	●	●	○	A	—	R	—
Vaughan Professional T016	24	TS/SR	25	●	◑	◑	—	—	H,K,L	Slightly head-heavy.
Stanley Workmaster 51-110	13	F/SR	24	●	◑	◑	D	e	—	Felt light; needed too many blows to drive nails. Handle flat at grip.
Sears Craftsman 38127	19	SS/SR	28	●	◑	○	A	—	D,F,K,R	Well balanced.
Stanley Workmaster 51-490	15	TS/SR	26	●	○	◑	—	e	I,P	Handle flat at grip.
Vaughan Professional FS 16	23	F/SR	25	●	○	○	—	—	H	—
Vaughan Professional R16	24	SS/SR	29	●	◑	○	—	—	D,F,K	Heavy.
Estwing E3-16C	25	SS/N	26	●	◑	○	—	—	F	Smooth and slippery feel to grip.
Vaughan Professional D016	20	W	23	◑	◑	○	—	—	H,N	Very well balanced.
Plumb Premium 11-402	26	F/SR	25	○	●	○	—	c,d	—	Smooth grip.
Stanley Workmaster 51-416	13	W	21	○	●	○	—	a,b,e	—	—
Stanley Professional 51-160	20	W	22	○	◑	◑	C	—	G,N	Very well balanced.
Estwing 1016C	21	W	21	○	○	○	—	b	G	Very light and easy to use.
Great Neck R16C	22	SS/SR	30	◑	○	○	—	c	D,F,K,Q	Heavy and head-heavy. Smooth grip.
Great Neck S16C	8	TS/SR	27	●	●	◑	—	b,c,d	D,I,L,Q	Very well balanced.
Alltrade 1085-S-16	15	W	23	◑	●	○	—	b,f	G,L,O	Smooth grip.
Great Neck FG16C	10	F/SR	23	●	○	◑	—	c,d	D,Q	Light. Small, smooth grip.
Great Neck W16C	8	W	23	◑	●	○	—	b,f	C,P,Q	Long handle affected balance, driving nails.
Master Mechanic Professional F16MM	18	W	23	●	◑	◑	—	b	N	Very well balanced.
Easco 81 102	22	W	22	●	○	◑	—	b,g	O,P	Light.
Alltrade 72-S-16	7	TS/SR	26	●	●	◑	—	b,c,d,f	D,I,O	Slightly head-heavy. Small grip.
Straight-claw (rip) models										
Stanley Professional 51-051	21	G/SR	29	●	○	◑	C,D	—	—	Heavy. Handle flat at grip.
Sears Craftsman 38273	19	SS/SR	36	●	◑	◑	B	—	E,F,K,R	Heavy, though driving nails was easy.
Plumb Ultralite Premium 11-472	25	TS/SR	31	●	◑	◑	—	—	B,E	Heavy and head-heavy. Smooth grip.
Stanley Professional 51-122	21	TS/SR	28	●	◑	◑	C	—	I	Slightly heavy, but driving nails was easy. Handle flat at grip.
Sears Craftsman 3821	19	F/SR	26	●	○	◑	—	—	A,R	A little heavy. Good balance.
Estwing E3-20S	28	SS/N	28	●	○	○	—	—	F	Smooth, slippery feel to grip.
Estwing E3-16S	25	SS/N	26	●	○	◑	—	—	A,F	Smooth, slippery feel to grip.
Plumb Autograf Premium 11-439	26	W	28	●	◑	○	—	—	B,E,N	Heavy and head-heavy.
Plumb Premium 11-414	29	F/SR	33	●	◑	◑	—	—	B,E	Heavy and head-heavy. Smooth grip.
Plumb Ultralite Premium 11-473	23	TS/SR	24	●	◑	○	—	—	A	Very well balanced. Driving nails was easy.
Stanley Professional 51-161	20	W	21	◑	○	◑	C	b	A,G,N	—
Stanley Professional 51-201	21	W	26	●	◑	◑	C	b	G,N	Head-heavy.

Price

184

RATINGS OF CORDLESS SCREWDRIVERS

Listed in order of estimated quality. Except where separated by bold rules, differences between closely ranked models were slight. "Professional" models are footnoted.

❶ Price. Manufacturer's suggested retail price, rounded to the nearest dollar.

❷ Shape. Pistol-shaped models (Ps) resemble an electric drill. Pencil-shaped models (Pn) look like a fat version of an ordinary screwdriver. Convertible models (C) have a movable handle that lets them take either pencil or pistol shape.

❸ Weight. To the nearest ¼ pound, not including battery charger.

❹ Bit sizes. The manufacturer's designation (or an estimate by Consumers Union noted with *, when no bit size was given) for the bits supplied. Each Phillips bit should fit either a small (number 1) or a medium (number 2) slot. Each slotted bit matches a screw of a particular diameter—a number 8 bit fits a number 8 screw, for example—or at least it's supposed to. Replacement bits are widely available.

❺ Torque. Using a precise electric brake called a dynamometer, testers at Consumers Union measured the maximum twisting motion (torque) each screwdriver could exert before stalling. The dynamometer automatically increased the load on a screwdriver at a controlled rate until stalling occurred. Then the load was reduced at the same rate and the procedure was repeated to see if the tool performed consistently. This test also gave an indication of how much power the batteries could deliver on a full charge. Screwdrivers judged 0 or better should have enough power for general work.

❻ Sustained power. Each tool was operated continuously to learn how long it could deliver 10 inch-pounds of torque. The *Skil Twist 2105* couldn't deliver that much torque; it was tested at 5 inch-pounds.

❼ Handling. A composite judgment that includes handle comfort, trigger position and response, and the presence or absence of a clutch. (A clutch stops the bit but allows the motor to keep running once the screw is driven all the way. Models with no clutch can drive a screw too far.)

❽ Bit quality. Generally mediocre. Consumers Union downgraded models supplied with bits that weren't properly finished, shaped, or sized.

❾ Charging time. How many hours each unit needs in order to take on a full charge.

As published in the August 1989 issue of Consumer Reports.

Rating symbols: ◉ ◐ ○ ◑ ● — Better ◄————► Worse

Brand and model	Price ❶	Shape ❷	Weight, lb. ❸	Phillips	Slotted	Torque ❺	Sustained power ❻	Handling ❼	Bit quality ❽	Charging time, hr. ❾	Advantages	Disadvantages	Comments
Skil 2305	$44	Ps	1½	2*	8*	◉	◉	◉	○	3	B,H,I,J	f	B
Black & Decker 9025	64	Ps	1½	1*,2*	6*,8*	◉	◐	◐	◐	16	B	c	A
Black & Decker 9034	30	Pn	1		8–10	◐	○	◐	◐	12	B,D,H	—	A,G
Wen 226	25	Ps	1¼	2,3	8,10	◐	○	○	◐	3	B,I	a,d,e,h	—
Milwaukee 6539-1①	108	C	1	1*,2*	7*	○	●	◉	◐	1	A,C,D,E,J	c	D
AEG EZ502①	108	C	1	1*,2*	7*	○	●	◉	◐	1	A,B,C,D,E,J	c	D
Skil Super Twist 2210	42	Pn	1	2*	8*	◐	◐	◐	◐	3	B,D,G,I	d	A
Stanley 75-050	50	Ps	1¾	2	8	◐	◐	◐	◐	3,12	B,C,D,F,G	a,h	D
Makita 6720DW①	72	Pn	¾	2	6*	◐	◐	◐	◉	3	—	f	B
Ryobi BD-10R①	82	Pn	¾	1*	8*	◐	◐	◐	◐	3	A,G,J	e,h	B
Black & Decker 9018	35	Pn	1	2	8–10	◐	◐	◐	◐	12	B,H	g	A
Skil Twist 2105	29	Pn	¾	2*	7*	●	●	○	◐	5	B,H	d,g,h,k	A
Sears Craftsman 11120	22	Ps	1	1,2	5,7	◐	●	◐	○	3	D,H,I	b,h,i	A,F,H
Sears Craftsman 11123	20	Pn	1	1,2	5,7	◐	●	◐	◐	3	D,H,I	b,d	A,E,H
Houseworks MES-133C	18	Ps	¾	2*	8*	◐	●	●	◐	12	D	a,f,h,i,j	B
Not Acceptable													
Sears Craftsman 11124	36	Ps	1¼	1,2	5,7	◉	○	◐	○	3	A,D,G,I	j	A,F,H
Lady's Mate 803-W-1	49	C	¾	1*,2*	5*,6*	◐	●	○	◉	12	A,D,J	j	A,C
Alltrade 794-S-1	49	C	1	1,2	6,8	●	●	○	○	12	A,C,J	f,j	B

■ *The following models were judged Not Acceptable because they broke when tested as a manual screwdriver and could no longer be used.*

① *"Professional" model.*

Key to Advantages
A— Has adjustable clutch.
B— Can be left on continuous charge.
C— Removable battery pack.
D— Has charge-indicator lamp.
E— Has full-charge indicator.
F— Has dual-speed charging.
G— Bits can be stored on screwdriver.
H— Has manual collet lock to prevent shaft from turning.
I— Trigger response judged better than most.
J— Trigger lock judged better than most.

Key to Disadvantages
a— Lacks collet lock.
b— Collet lock does not prevent shaft from turning.
c— Trigger response judged worse than most.
d— Lacks safety lock-out for trigger.
e— Screwdriver repeatedly fell out of wall-mounted charger stand.
f— No storage provision for bits.
g— Balance judged worse than most.
h— Handle design judged worse than most.
i— Trigger location judged worse than most.
j— Bit fell out of collet when screwdriver was pointed bit-down (*Sears Craftsman 11124*) or when screwdriver was inverted and shaken (*Houseworks, Lady's Mate, Alltrade*).
k— Would not sustain 10 inch-pounds of torque.

Key to Comments
A— Charging stand can be wall-mounted.
B— Has no charging stand.
C— Model tested is pink; **804-W-1** is blue.
D— Transformer at charging stand.
E— Output shaft of driver is offset from centerline of screwdriver.
F— Has wrist strap.
G— Discontinued; no longer available. According to manufacturer, model will be replaced by one with more power and other features.
H— Manufacturer provides no information on whether unit can be left on continuous charge.

Each graph lists models by size; within sizes, listed by types. Within types, listed in order of median life. Bracketed models performed about the same, overall, considering both median values and results for individual samples.

"Toy" test was designed to mimic the high-current demands imposed by motorized toys. We used a computer-controlled test rig to drain the batteries continuously, with the D cells working under a heavier load than the others. We measured the time needed for each sample's voltage to drop below 0.9 volts, which is too low to run many toys. Bars show median life for all samples of each tested model.

"Stereo" test was designed to mimic demands imposed by boom boxes, walkabout stereos, and the like—intermittent, moderate current draw. We used our test rig to draw power from AA cells for 1 hour every 12 hours; from C and D cells for 4 hours every 24 hours. The computer measured the time needed for each sample's voltage to drop below 1 volt, a level that could cause distorted sound from a cassette tape player. Bars show median life for all samples of each tested model.

As published in the November 1991 issue of Consumer Reports.

THE 'TOY' TEST

AA size

Median life, hours (0 — 8)

Brand and model	Median life, hours
Alkaline	
Duracell MN1500B	
Panasonic AM3	
Sears DieHard 93095	
Kodak Supralife KAA	
Eveready Energizer E91	
Radio Shack 23-552	
Rayovac Maximum 815	
Rechargeable	
GE Charge GC1	
Radio Shack 23-125	
Millenium B AA-BP	
Eveready CH15	
Heavy Duty	
Eveready 1215	
Mallory Long Life Plus M15SHD	
Rayovac Maximum 5AA	
Sears 993404	
Radio Shack 23-582	

C size

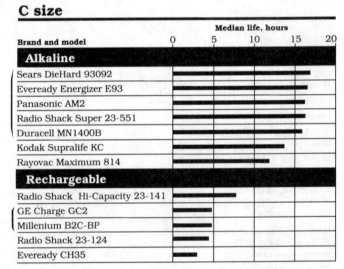

D size

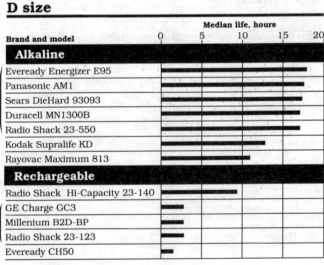

THE 'STEREO' TEST

AA size

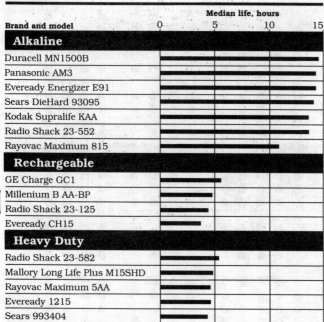

Brand and model	Median life, hours 0 5 10 15
Alkaline	
Duracell MN1500B	
Panasonic AM3	
Eveready Energizer E91	
Sears DieHard 93095	
Kodak Supralife KAA	
Radio Shack 23-552	
Rayovac Maximum 815	
Rechargeable	
GE Charge GC1	
Millenium B AA-BP	
Radio Shack 23-125	
Eveready CH15	
Heavy Duty	
Radio Shack 23-582	
Mallory Long Life Plus M15SHD	
Rayovac Maximum 5AA	
Eveready 1215	
Sears 993404	

C size

Brand and model	Median life, hours 0 5 10 15 20 25 30
Alkaline	
Duracell MN1400B	
Sears DieHard 93092	
Eveready Energizer E93	
Radio Shack 23-551	
Kodak Supralife KC	
Panasonic AM2	
Rayovac Maximum 814	
Rechargeable	
Radio Shack Hi-Capacity 23-141	
GE Charge GC2	
Millenium B2C-BP	
Radio Shack 23-124	
Eveready CH35	

D size

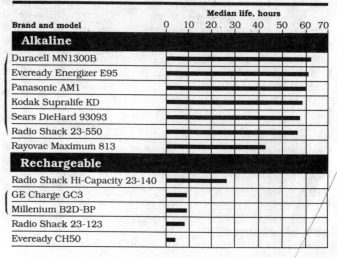

Brand and model	Median life, hours 0 10 20 30 40 50 60 70
Alkaline	
Duracell MN1300B	
Eveready Energizer E95	
Panasonic AM1	
Kodak Supralife KD	
Sears DieHard 93093	
Radio Shack 23-550	
Rayovac Maximum 813	
Rechargeable	
Radio Shack Hi-Capacity 23-140	
GE Charge GC3	
Millenium B2D-BP	
Radio Shack 23-123	
Eveready CH50	

Listed by types; within types, listed alphabetically. Brand-related properties apply to all colors tested for a brand. Color-related properties apply to a color. Dashes mean a suitable color wasn't available.

❶ Brand and model. If you can't find one of these paints, call the company.

❷ Price. In most cases, the manufacturer's approximate retail price per gallon. A * indicates the price paid.

As published in the September 1990 issue of Consumer Reports.

❸ Gloss. The descriptions here are based on Consumers Union measurements. Flat (F) is the dullest, followed by eggshell (EG), satin (S), semi-gloss (SG), gloss (G), and high gloss (HG).

❹ Brushing ease. Alkyd formulations have improved over the years, but they're still harder to apply than latex paints.

❺ Leveling. If you want a smooth finish, look to the alkyds.

❻ Sagging. How well a paint resisted the tendency to run, drip, or sag like a curtain.

❼ Adhesion. Each paint was applied to weathered panels that had been coated with a paint formulated to "chalk." When the panels had dried thoroughly, Consumers Union testers scratched them and pressed tape over the scratch to see how much paint would pull away. But any of these paints should adhere well to new surfaces or to properly prepared old paint.

Brand-related properties

❶ Brand and model	❷ Price	❸ Gloss	❹ Brushing ease	❺ Leveling	❻ Sagging	❼ Adhesion	❽ Blocking	White ❾ Hiding	❿ Color change	⓫ Chalking	⓬ Mildew	⓭ Dirt	Black ❾ Hiding	❿ Color change	⓬ Mildew	⓭ Dirt	Brown ❾ Hiding	❿ Color change	⓬ Mildew	⓭ Dirt
Alkyd (oil-based)																				
Devoe All-Weather Gloss (Series 1XX)	$32	SG																		
Devoe Velour Semi-Gloss (Series 29XX)	34	SG						—	—	—	—	—								
Dutch Boy Dirt Fighter Gloss (Series 1XX-2XX)	25	G																		
Fuller O'Brien Weather King (Series 660-XX)	28	G																		
Glidden Spred House Dura-Gloss (Series 19XX)	27*	G																		
Moore's High Gloss (130)	26	SG																		
Moore's High Gloss Enamelized (Series 110)	24	③																		
Pittsburgh Sun-Proof Gloss (1 line)	31	G						—	—	—	—	—								
Pratt & Lambert Effecto High Gloss (E31172)⑤	36	HG																		
Pratt & Lambert Permalize Gloss (C34972)⑤	31	G																		
Sears Best Weatherbeater Gloss (Series 4800)	23	SG																		
Valspar Gloss (Series 2XX)	27	HG																		
Latex (water-based)																				
Ameritone Enamelized (W2500)	25	SG																		
Benjamin Moore Moorgard (Series 103)	20	EG																		
Benjamin Moore Moorglo (Series 096)	22	S																		
Devoe Wonder Shield (Series 18XX)	28	SG																		
Devoe Regency Satin (Series 19XX)	28	F						—	—	—	—	—								
Dutch Boy Dirt Fighter Gloss (Series 19XX)	21	SG																		
Dutch Boy Super Gloss (Series 74XX)	23	SG																		
Dutch Boy Super Satin (Series 77XX)	22	EG																		
Fuller O'Brien Versaflex Gloss (Series 615-XX)	30	G						—	—	—	—	—								
Fuller O'Brien Weather King (Series 664-XX)	27	SG																		
Glidden Spred House Dura-Gloss (Series 39XX)	21*	SG																		
Glidden Spred House Dura-Satin (Series 29XX)	21*	EG																		
Lucite Enamel Gloss (Series 18XX)	18*	SG																		
Lucite Satin (Series 22XX)	17*	S						—	—	—	—	—								
Pittsburgh Manor Hall Eggshell (79 Line)	30	F																		
Pittsburgh Sun-Proof Semi-Gloss (78 Line)	26	SG																		
Pratt & Lambert Aqua Royal Satin (Z3002)⑤	29	SG																		
Sears Best Weatherbeater Satin (Series 5100)	20	EG																		
Sears House Shield (Series 2800)	10	F																		
Sears Weatherbeater Premium Satin (Series 4700)	16	EG																		
Sears Weatherbeater Premium Semi-Gloss (Series 5000)	17	SG																		
Sherwin-Williams A-100 Satin (A82 Series)	21	EG																		
Sherwin-Williams Superpaint Gloss (A84 Series)	25	SG											—	—	—	—				
Tru-Test Supreme Accent Color Semi-Gloss (AG Line)	24	SG						—	—	—	—	—								
Tru-Test Supreme Weatherall Gloss (GHP Line)	24	SG														—	—	—		
Valspar Semi-Gloss (Series 43XX)	24	S																		

① Tends to erode rapidly when exposed to the weather. ② Brighter than most yellows. ③ Gloss too variable to rate. ④ Grayer than most blues.

8 Blocking. Paint, especially latex paint, can remain tacky long after it dries. The lower the score here, the more likely the paint will stick to things that touch it.

9 Hiding. A ● means the paint should cover almost any previous color in one coat. ◒ means the paint should cover in one coat if the old color doesn't contrast sharply with the new. Paints judged ○ should cover a similar color in one coat, a darker color in two. Paints

judged ◒ or ● will require at least two coats to cover a similar color.

10 Color change. How individual colors stand up to the elements. The scores take into account fading, yellowing (for whites), and loss of gloss.

11 Chalking. White paints with the lower scores chalked the most. They might be preferable in cities or suburbs, where dirt and pollution can quickly soil white paint.

12 Mildew. How well a paint resists the buildup of mildew. No paint will eliminate existing mildew; that requires washing.

13 Dirt. The faster a paint dries, and the smoother and more tack-free its surface, the less dirt it will attract.

Names of colors tested

Alkyd paints

Devoe All-Weather Gloss: White, Black, Dark Brown, Forest Green. *Devoe Velour Semi-Gloss:* Hot Tango 2VR2A (red). Blue Saga 1BL11A, Dynamo 1BY26A (yellow). *Dutch Boy Dirt Fighter Gloss:* Gloss White, Black, Cocoa Brown. Triple Blue. *Fuller O'Brien Weather King:* White, Black, Sealskin (brown). Meadow Green, Sunray (yellow). *Glidden Spread House Dura-Gloss:* White, Black, Stratford Brown. Crylight Green. *Moore's High Gloss:* Brilliant White. *Moore's High Gloss Enamelized:* Outside White, Black, Tudor Brown, Chrome Green *Pittsburg Sun-Proof Gloss:* White, Bahama Brown, Colonial Red. Kentucky Green Blue Mood, French Lacquer (yellow). *Pratt & Lambert Effecto:* High Hiding White, Black-Gloss. Leather Brown, Grenadier Red, Dublin Green, Postal Blue, Canary Yellow. *Pratt & Lambert Permalize:* High Hiding White, Black, London Brown, Glen Green. *Sears Best Weatherbeater:* White, Barcelona Brown. *Valspar:* Non-Chalking White, Black, Chocolate Brown, Cranberry (red). Forest Green, Blue (custom-mixed). Yellow (custom-mixed).

Latex paints

Ameritone: White, Black, Spanish Brown, Lustre Glos 1D39C (yellow). *Benjamin Moore Moorgard:* Brilliant White, Black, Tudor Brown, Blue 791, Yellow 321. *Benjamin Moore Moorglo:* White, black, Tudor Brown, Tartan Red. Chrome Green, Blue 791, Yellow 321. *Devoe Wonder Shield:* White, Black, Dark Brown, Forest Green. *Devoe Regency Satin:* Hot Tango 2VR2A (red). Blue Saga 1BL11A. Dynamo 1BY26A (yellow). *Dutch Boy Dirt Fighter:* White, Cocoa Brown. Triple Blue, Pawnee (yellow). *Dutch Boy Super Glose:* White, Gloss Black, Cocoa Brown, Triple Blue. *Dutch Boy Super Satin:* White, Blkack, Cocoa Brown. Triple Blue, Pawnee (yellow). *Fuller O'Brien Versaflex Glose:* Bright Red, National Blue, Sunshine (yellow). *Fuller O'Brien Weather King:* White, Black, Seal Skin (Brown). Meadow Green, Sunray (yellow). Glidden Spread House Dura-Glose: White, Black, Stratford Brown. Crylight Green. Victorian Yellow. *Glidden Spred House Dura-Satin:* White, Stratford Brown. Crylight Green. Victorian Yellow. *Lucite Enamel Glose:* White, Black, Bark Brown. *Lucite Stain:* White, *Pittsburgh Manor Hall:* Super White, Ebony Black. Bahama Brown. Kentucky Green, Blue Mood, French Lacqure (yellow). *Pittsburg Sun-Proof:* White, Black, Bahama Brown. Kentucky Green Blue Mood, French Lacquer (yellow). *Pratt & Lambert:* White Black, London Brown, Glen Green. *Sears Best Weatherbeater:* White, Molten Black, Barcelona Brown. Mowbray Hunt Green, Tiber River Blue. *Sears House Shield:* White, Molten Black, Barcelona Brown, Desert Palm (green), Daring indigo (blue). *Sears Weatherbeater Premium Satin:* White, Molten Black, Barcelona Brown, Azalea Leaf (green), Daring Indigo (blue). *Sears Weatherbeater Premium Semi-Gloss:* White, Molten Black, Barcelona Brown, Azalea Leaf (green), Daring Indigo (blue). *Sherwin-Williams A-100:* White, Tricorn Black, Chateau Brown, Mown Grass (green). Yellow Corn. *Sherwin-Williams Superpaint:* Super White. Chateau Brown, Mown Grass (green). Yellow Corn. *Tru-Test Supreme:* Tru-Brown, Tru-Red, Tru-Green, Tru-Blue, Tru-Yellow. *Tru-Test Supreme Weatherall:* White, Black, Valspar:* White, Black, Chocolate Brown, Cranberry (red). Forest Green, Dominion Blue, Oleo Yellow.

Color-related properties

⑤ *Product number of white only.*

189

RATINGS OF ELECTRIC AIR PUMPS

Listed by types; within types, listed in order of estimated quality. Bracketed models, judged equal, are listed alphabetically.

❶ **Brand and model.**

❷ **Price.** The manufacturer's suggested retail price. A + indicates shipping is extra; an * indicates an approximate price.

❸ **Power source.** The 120v models run on house current. The 12v batt models draw power from a 12-volt car or boat battery, typically via a cord plugged into a cigarette-lighter socket.

❹ **High-pressure performance.** To fill a P225/75R 15-inch radial car tire to 35 psi, the fastest pumps averaged a little more than 3½ minutes; the slowest, about 16 minutes. To fill a 27×1⅛-inch bicycle tire to 100 psi, the fastest averaged 24 seconds; the slowest, 1 minute, 42 seconds. Basketball inflation times ranged from 8 seconds to 1 minute, 31 seconds.

❺ **Low-pressure performance.** The relative time needed to fill a 90×49×16-inch vinyl boat and a set of pool devices (a surfboard, air mattresses, and the like). The fastest low-pressure pump filled the boat in about 3½ minutes; the slowest, in 9½ minutes. The pressures achieved by those pumps in our tests ranged from a low of 0.3 psi to a high of 0.7 psi. (The best high-pressure pumps needed about 10 minutes to inflate the boat; the others labored for nearly 30 minutes.)

❻ **Maximum working pressure.** A relative indication of the highest pressure that we could get each high-pressure pump to deliver. Some failed to meet their claimed pressures or broke down in the effort.

❼ **Noise.** Measured with a sound-level meter at the operator's ear. The higher the score, the quieter the pump. We recommend using ear protection with the noisiest.

❽ **Hose and cord lengths.** The longer the better. Three low-pressure pumps have no air hose; they fit directly into whatever is being inflated.

Specifications and Features
All have: • On/off switch. • Adapters for various sizes of inflator valve.
All high-pressure models have: • Clamp-on chuck. • Universal inflator nozzle. • Needle inflator nozzle.
All low-pressure models have: • Inflator and deflator adapters.
Except as noted, all battery-powered models have: • Cigarette-lighter plug.

As published in the October 1990 issue of Consumer Reports.

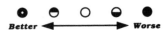

⊙ ◓ ○ ◒ ●
Better ◄——► Worse

❶ Brand and model	❷ Price	❸ Power source	Weight	❹ High-pressure performance: Car tire	Bicycle tire	Basketball	❺ Low-pressure performance: Vinyl boat	Pool devices	❻ Max. working pressure	❼ Noise	❽ Hose length	❽ Cord length	Advantages	Disadvantages	Comments
High-pressure pumps															
Black & Decker Air Station 9527	$92	120v	5 lb.	⊙	⊙	⊙	○	○	⊙	◒	6½ ft.	6ft.	A,C,D,E,I	b,c,d	*A,C,J*
Sears Cat. No. 15025	50+	120v	5	⊙	⊙	⊙	○	○	⊙	◒	8½	6	A,C,D,E,I	b,c,d	*A,C,H,I*
Intercompressor 9-8275	56*	12v batt	6	◓	○	○	●	●	○	◓	2¾	16	C,D,F,G,H	a,b,f,g,h	*K*
Interdynamics Laser 250	53*	12v batt	3½	◒	◒	●	●	●	○	◓	2	10¼	B,D,F,G,J	a,b,g,h	*D,J*
Black & Decker 9512	35	12v batt	2¾	●	●	○	●	●	●	◓	2½	12½	C,H	a,b,e,g,h	*I,N*
Low-pressure pumps															
AWL Infl-1	30	12v batt	1¼	—	—	—	⊙	⊙	—	○	—	9¾	—	—	*G,M*
Coleman 2211-718	30	12v batt	1¾	—	—	—	◓	◓	—	○	—	13	—	—	*E,H,L*
Coleman 2212-718	22	12v batt	½	—	—	—	◓	○	—	⊙	—	13	—	—	*B,E,H,L*
Intercompressor 9-8280	16*	12v batt	1½	—	—	—	○	◒	—	⊙	2¼	8	—	h	*F*

Key to Advantages
A— Attained relatively high pressure (130 psi) in CU's tests.
B— You can preset pump for desired pressure between 12 and 160 psi; shuts off automatically at preset pressure. Light on end of cigarette-lighter plug indicates when circuit is complete and when unit is shut off.
C— Has easy-to-read pressure gauge.
D— Metal clamp-on chuck; judged more durable than plastic chuck on others.
E— Clamp-on chuck proved able to hold plastic as well as metal valve extensions.
F— Detachable work light.
G— Power-cord storage provision.
H— Storage carrying case.
I— Convenient carrying handle.
J— Mounts in car trunk with bracket and holding strap provided.

Key to Disadvantages
a— Failed to reach maximum pressure cited by manufacturer, and broke down in CU's severe test.
b— Got quite hot at hose and pump housing after continuous running.
c— Not as mobile as other pumps because it must be plugged into electrical outlet.
d— Relatively short power cord.
e— Pressure gauge read 5 psi low.
f— Pressure gauge read 15 psi low.
g— Clamp-on chuck tended to slip off plastic valve extensions.
h— Relatively short air hose.

Key to Comments
A— Double insulated.
B— Smallest pump tested; could fit in handbag or jacket pocket.
C— Comes with air tube for blowing dirt from hard-to-reach places.
D— Requires 4 "C" batteries for detachable work light.
E— 15-ft. power cord available as option.
F— No warranty.
G— 90-day warranty.
H— 1-yr. warranty.
I— 2-yr. warranty.
J— 5-yr. warranty.
K— Lifetime warranty.
L— On/off switch on power cord.
M— No cigarette-lighter plug. Instead, battery clips must be attached to battery terminals.
N— Discontinued; replaced by essentially identical 9515.

RATINGS OF HEAT GUNS

Listed in order of estimated quality, based on safety, comfort, and number of heat settings. Products judged approximately equal are bracketed and listed alphabetically.

❶ Price. Manufacturer's suggested retail.

❷ Watts. As drawn in tests at the lowest and highest heat settings. Higher-wattage models consume more power but don't necessarily perform more vigorously. All models can be used with a common 15-amp household electrical circuit. If you need an extension cord, use one rated for the wattage the gun can draw.

❸ Heat settings. Guns with a continuous (Cont.) setting allow a wide range of adjustments. But some models have only an On/Off switch; others offer two settings, High and Low.

❹ Maximum air temperature. In degrees Fahrenheit, measured one inch from nozzle tip after running for several minutes. Machines that blow out hotter air don't nec-

essarily remove paint faster. Stripping speed also depends on fan speed and air flow.

❺ Safety. Heat guns are inherently hazardous. They can start a fire and burn skin. In addition, they can leave scrapings that can dry out and find their way into the air as dust. That's a serious danger if the paint contains lead (see story). Some models lost points because they lack a rapid cool-down setting.

❻ Speed. Based on stripping tests on old paint. The models were about equally fast, and all were much faster than any chemical paint remover.

❼ Handling. How comfortable each model was to use and how balanced it felt in our testers' hands.

❽ Results. Judged by a panel of staffers. All guns removed paint thoroughly from cracks, moldings, and wood grain.

Features in Common
All: • Reach dangerously high temperature at

nozzle tip. • Can be rested without tipping over. • Can be hung on a hook when not in use. • Have 6-ft., heat-resistant cord. • Have convenient, lockable On/Off switch in "trigger" position on handle.
Except as noted, all: • Have plastic body.

Key to Advantages
A—Has fan-only setting for rapid cool-down.
B—Has very low setting for cool-down.
C—Fan air volume adjusted with louvered inlet.
D—Switch guard prevents accidental start-up.
E—Comes with shaped auxiliary nozzle tips.
F—Has continuous rotary heat adjustment.
G—Bracket keeps gun upright when not in use.

Key to Disadvantages
a—Lacks setting for accelerated cool-down.
b—Slightly noisier than others.

Key to Comments
A—Has double-insulated housing and 2-pronged plug.
B—Has metal housing.
C—Has 3-pronged grounded plug.

As published in the May 1991 issue of Consumer Reports.

Better ◀——————▶ Worse

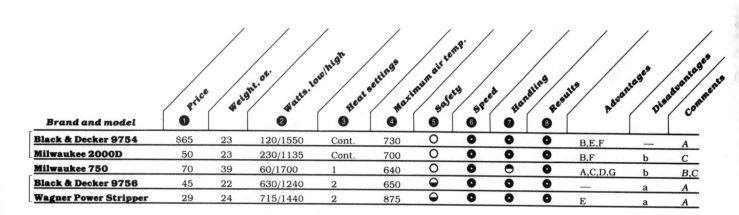

Brand and model	Price ❶	Weight, oz.	Watts, low/high ❷	Heat settings ❸	Maximum air temp. ❹	Safety ❺	Speed ❻	Handling ❼	Results ❽	Advantages	Disadvantages	Comments
Black & Decker 9754	$65	23	120/1550	Cont.	730	○	●	●	●	B,E,F	—	A
Milwaukee 2000D	50	23	230/1135	Cont.	700	○	●	●	●	B,F	b	C
Milwaukee 750	70	39	60/1700	1	640	○	●	◗	●	A,C,D,G	b	B,C
Black & Decker 9756	45	22	630/1240	2	650	◗	●	●	●	—	a	A
Wagner Power Stripper	29	24	715/1440	2	875	◗	●	●	●	E	a	A

RATINGS OF FINISHING SANDERS

Listed in order of estimated quality. Except where separated by a bold rule, closely ranked models differed little in quality.

❶ Brand and model. Moderately priced models for occasional use and more expensive professional models were tested. If you can't find a model, call the company.

❷ Price. The manufacturer's suggested retail price. Discounts are common.

❸ Type. The palm sanders, designed to be guided with one hand, are better suited for experienced users. The two-handled models are better for novices because they are less likely to sand depressions into the wood.

❹ Sheet size. The part of a standard 9 × 11-inch sheet of sandpaper each sander holds: quarter-sheet, about 4½ × 5½ inches; one-third-sheet, about 3½ × 9 inches; half-sheet, about 4½ × 11 inches. The one-sixth-sheet model takes a sheet about 3½ × 4½ inches. One-third-sheet models are a good in-between size for all-around work; larger models may not perform well in tight quarters, while the smaller ones have to be moved continuously to sand uniformly.

❺ Weight. In ounces, including the cord. Weight only matters when you're working overhead or on a vertical surface; you have to support the sander and hold it against the work.

❻ Sanding speed. Shows how rapidly each sander removed wood from pine boards using 100-grit paper. (Sanders that can be switched between orbital and back-and-forth motion were tested in their orbital mode.) The best sander was nearly three times faster than the slowest.

❼ Clamp quality. A major point of convenience with any finishing sander. The best clamps open and close easily, have a wide opening, and keep the paper taut and flat against the sander's base.

❽ Handling. How easy it was to guide the sander across a board. In tests, some sanders hopped, rotated, or resisted changes in direction.

❾ Evenness. It's difficult to sand wood with a wide grain, such as fir. The light parts of the wood are softer than the dark parts and wear away faster. The better models sanded fir plywood without leaving valleys in the softer parts. Sanders with lower scores left noticeable valleys.

❿ Noise. The better the score, the quieter the sander. The loudest exceeded 90 decibels, a level that Consumers Union testers believe requires hearing protection.

⓫ Vibration. The assessment of each sander's ability to minimize the vibration you'll feel when you use the tool. The worst will leave your hands tingling.

⓬ Pad contact. How evenly each sander's pad contacted the surface being sanded. A low score means that a large part of the pad did not touch the surface, increasing the possibility of sanding unevenly. In actual practice, if the sandpaper is tight and the sander kept in constant motion, pad contact won't matter much.

⓭ Cord length. The longer the power cord the better, provided the cord isn't so stiff it impedes your ability to move the sander across the wood. Models with particularly good or bad cords are noted in the Advantages and Disadvantages.

As published in the September 1990 issue of Consumer Reports.

Better ◄──── ────► Worse

❶ Brand and model	❷ Price	❸ Type	❹ Sheet size	❺ Weight	❻ Sanding speed	❼ Clamp quality	❽ Handling	❾ Evenness	❿ Noise	⓫ Vibration	⓬ Pad contact	⓭ Cord length	Advantages	Disadvantages	Comments
Black & Decker 4011	$79	Palm	¼	47 oz.	◐	⊙	◐	◐	○	⊙	◐	96 in.	A,B,D,G,I,J,K	—	A,D
Black & Decker 7458	122	2-handled	½	64	◐	⊙	○	◐	○	○	●	72	A,D,E,F,K	c,q,t,v	B,F
Hitachi SV12SA	80	Palm	¼	47	◑	⊙	○	○	○	⊙	◐	100	F,J	—	A
Makita B04550	86	Palm	¼	37	◑	◐	⊙	○	○	◐	◐	74	A,B,D,F,J	—	B,H
Sears Craftsman 11602	33	Palm	¼	40	◐	◐	○	○	○	◐	●	96	F,H	i	A,B
Skil 7582	121	2-handled	⅓	71	⊙	○	◐	◐	◐	◐	◐	96	J	a,g,j,v	B,C
Black & Decker 7448	47	2-handled	⅓	37	◐	◐	◐	◐	◐	○	◐	72	I	a,v,w	B,F
Ryobi S500A	79	Palm	⅙	42	◑	◐	◐	◑	◐	◐	○	79	F,J	a,n	—
Makita 9035	112	2-handled	⅓	56	◑	◐	◐	○	◐	◐	◐	82	I,J	a,m,v,w	B,H
Skil 7382	69	2-handled	⅓	55	◐	◑	◐	○	○	◐	◑	60	C,D	a,l,m,r,s,t,w	B
Milwaukee 6016	84	Palm	¼	46	○	◐	○	●	◑	○	●	105	F,H	o,t,w	B,E
Skil 7575	70	Palm	¼	43	◑	◑	○	◑	○	◐	⊙	96	F,I,J	d,v	B
Skil 7576	78	Palm	¼	43	◑	◑	○	◑	○	◑	◐	96	A,B,D,I,J	b,d,v	B
Ryobi S600	90	Palm	¼	46	●	○	⊙	●	◑	○	⊙	80	J	k,v	G
Sears Craftsman 11611	23	2-handled	⅓	50	○	●	○	○	○	○	●	72	F,H	a,e,n,s	B,I
Ryobi LS35	98	2-handled	⅓	54	◑	●	○	○	◑	◐	●	80	J	a,g,m,p,w	—
Sears Craftsman 11616	67	2-handled	½	83	○	●	◐	⊙	●	●	○	122	C,D,H,L	e,i,k,l,n,s,t,u	B,D
Porter-Cable 330	97	Palm	¼	61	●	◑	◐	◐	◑	⊙	⊙	82	I,J	d,f,i,k,v	B
Sears Craftsman 11613	55	2-handled	⅓	67	◑	●	◐	●	●	●	●	72	C,D,F,H,L	a,e,i,l,n,p,s,t,u	B,D
Wen 300	50	2-handled	⅓	54	◑	●	◐	◑	○	◑	◑	71	J,L	a,d,h,i,j,k,v,x	B,I

Specifications and Features

All: Run on 120 volts and are double-insulated.

Except as noted, all: • Use only orbital motion. • Lack provision for dust collection. • Can sand to within ⅛-in. of perpendicular edge on at least one side. • Have rocker or toggle On/Off switch that's easy to operate but poorly marked. • Have easily used finger-operated clamps to hold paper; clamps tend to pull paper taut as they close. • Come with good instruction manual. • Have reasonably limp power cord, which doesn't interfere with work. • Judged suitable for use with self-adhesive sandpaper. • Can be used on wood, metal, and plastics, or to remove paint. • Have one-yr. warranty against defects in noncommercial use.

Key to Advantages

A— Has through-the-paper dust collection; requires punching holes in paper with tool provided.
B— Paper punch cuts all holes at once, with paper on sander.
C— Has dust-collecting skirt around base.
D— Has dust-collecting bag.
E— Variable speed.
F— Sands to within less than ⅛-inch of perpendicular edge on front and sides.
G— User can replace motor brushes without disassembling sander.
H— On/Off switch has better markings than most.
I— Power cord limper than most; less likely to interfere with sander's motion across work.
J— Judged more suitable than most for repairs by user.

Key to Disadvantages

a— Uses ⅓ or ⅙ of standard sandpaper sheet; often requires measuring to cut sheet to proper size.
b— Punch for dust-collecting system doesn't perforate paper cleanly.
c— Punch cuts only one hole at a time in sandpaper.
d— Harder to load paper than most.
e— Clamps do not tend to tighten paper.
f— Clamps require tool to operate easily.
g— Clamps require strong fingers to operate.
h— Sandpaper must be folded to fit into clamps.
i— Clamps protrude from base far enough to scratch adjacent vertical edge of work.
j— Instructions worse than most.
k— Sanded no closer than ⅛ to ⅜ in. from adjacent perpendicular edge.
l— Dust-collecting skirt must be removed to get sander close to adjacent perpendicular edge.
m— On/Off trigger switch requires two operations to lock sander on. Judged hard for left-handed persons to use.
n— On/Off switch harder to operate than most.
o— On/Off switch more likely than most to be operated by accident.
p— Front handle judged too small for people with large hands to control easily.
q— Front handle judged too large for people with small hands to control easily.

K— Instructions better than most.
L— Has switch to convert sander from orbital to straight-line motion.

r— Front handle judged too low for good control when using sander at arm's length.
s— Main handle judged too low for good control when using sander at arm's length.
t— Power cord stiffer than most; could interfere with sander's motion.
u— Dust-collecting bag not securely fastened to sander.
v— Judged unsuitable for use with self-adhesive paper.
w— Instructions judged only fair.
x— Levers to switch from orbital to straight-line sanding confusingly marked.

Key to Comments

A— Round base available as option (not tested).
B— Instructions don't recommend users replace motor brushes.
C— Instructions cover more than one sander.
D— Optional dust-collecting system allows sander to be connected to vacuum cleaner; can be useful for people sensitive to wood dust, but may make sander awkward to use.
E— Has unlimited warranty against defects in noncommercial use.
F— Has two-yr. warranty against defects.
G— Instructions say to use sander on wood only.
H— According to instructions, motor brushes are self-limiting; when brushes wear out, the motor won't run, preventing major damage to motor.
I— Discontinued. (*Wen 300* may still be available in some stores.)

Listed by groups in order of estimated quality, based on brand- and color-related properties. Within groups, listed alphabetically. Note that not all colors in a given brand line performed similarly. Dashes mean a suitable shade of that color wasn't available.

❶ Brand and model. Generally, we chose paints at or near the top of each manufacturer's line, but we included lower-priced products for comparison.

As published in the July 1991 issue of Consumer Reports.

❷ Price. Manufacturer's suggested retail, per gallon, rounded to the nearest dollar. Prices marked with asterisk (*) are average CU paid. Two asterisks (**) indicate price for white only; price of colors varies. Substantial discounts are often available.

❸ Gloss. Based on our measurements. Flat (F) is the least shiny, followed by low-luster (LL), which looks flat when viewed head-on but shows a slight sheen from an angle. Satin (S) is noticeably glossier than flat from any perspective.

❹ Stain removal. How thoroughly we could remove a greasy black stain from painted panels, using a sponge and an all-purpose cleaner.

❶ Brand and model	❷ Price	❸ Gloss	Water resistance	White Hiding, 1 coat ❾	White Hiding, 2 coats ❾	White Fading ❿	Gold color	Gold Hiding, 1 coat ❾	Gold Hiding, 2 coats ❾	Gold Fading ❿
✓ Pratt & Lambert Accolade	$31	LL	One Coat White	2	5		Sunshade	6	6	
Benjamin Moore Regal Aquapearl	23**	S	White	1	4		Golden Glow	2	6	
Benjamin Moore Regal Aquavelvet	23**	LL	White ①	1	3		Golden Glow	3	6	
Pittsburgh Manor Hall Eggshell	29	LL	White	2	6		Bamboo Shoot	5	6	
Sears Best Easy Living Flat 9500, A Best Buy	19	F	Pure White ①	2	5		Golden Harvest	3	6	
Devoe Regency 25XX	27*	F	White ②	1	2		Gold	3	6	
Devoe Wonder-Tones Eggshell 34XX	23*	LL	White	1	3		Gold	3	6	
Dutch Boy Super Satin	22	F	White ①	1	3		Tanella	2	6	
Enterprise One & Only Low Lustre	22	F	White	2	5		Safari III	3	6	
Fuller O'Brien Liquid Lustre Eggshell 604	27	F	White	1	4		Grass Cloth	2	5	
Glidden Spred Lo-Lustre 3100	17	S	White	0	1		Harvest	2	5	
Glidden Spred Ultra Eggshell 4100	22	LL	White ②	1	3		Colonial Brass ③	1	4	
Glidden Spred Ultra Flat 4000	20	F	White ②	1	2		Colonial Brass ③	2	6	
Kelly Moore Acry-Plex Flat 555	23	F	White ②	1	2		Muse	5	6	
Kelly Moore Sat-N-Sheen Flat 1610	21	LL	White ②	1	2		Muse	3	6	
Pittsburgh Wallhide Flat	22	F	White	1	3		Bamboo Shoot	2	6	
Pratt & Lambert Aqua Satin	30	S	One Coat White ①	2	5		Sunshade	6	6	
Pratt & Lambert Vapex Flat	30	F	One Coat White ①	2	6		Sunshade	6	6	
Sears Best Easy Living Satin 9300	20	LL	Pure Pure White ①	2	6		Golden Harvest	2	6	
Sears Easy Living Flat 9700	12	F	White ①	2	5		Golden Harvest	2	6	
Sherwin-Williams Superpaint Flat	18*	F	Pure White	2	6		Gold	4	6	
Sherwin-Williams Superpaint Satin	19*	F	Pure White	2	6		Gold	5	6	
Tru-Test Supreme E-Z Kare Flat EZ	21	LL	White	2	4		Parchment	4	6	
Tru-Test Supreme E-Z Kare Flat EZF	16	F	White	2	5		Parchment	3	6	
Tru-Test Ultra Satin ⑥	27	S	Ultra White	2	5		—	—	—	—
Devoe Wonder-Tones Flat 36XX	22*	F	White	1	3		Gold	3	6	
Dutch Boy Dirt Fighter Flat	20	F	White	2	5		Champagne	2	6	
Fuller O'Brien Liquid Velvet Flat 602	22	F	White	1	4		Grass Cloth ③	2	6	
Glidden Spred Satin 3400	17	F	White ②	1	2		Burnished Gold	3	6	
Sears Easy Living Satin 9600	16	LL	Non Yellow. W. ①	1	3		Golden Harvest	1	4	
Sherwin-Williams Classic 99	13*	F	Pure White	1	3		Gold	2	6	
Standard Brands Decade Flat	13	F	White ②	2	4		Mink	6	6	
Standard Brands Premium Flat	17	LL	White ②	3	6		Praline	5	6	
Standard Brands Satin	13	S	White ②	1	3		Mink	3	6	
Valspar Our Best Quality Acrylic Flat 914	20	F	White	1	4		Glori	2	6	
Wards Great Coat 15 Flat	14	F	White ①	1	4		Light Coin Gold ③	3	6	
Colony Flat	13	F	White	2	5		Warm Sand	1	4	
Dutch Boy Super Kem-Tone Flat	13	F	White	1	4		Wheat Grain	2	6	
Glidden Spred Wall Flat 3200	12	F	White ②	1	2		Harvest	3	6	
Wards Great Coat Satin 10	13	LL	White ①	1	4		Light Coin Gold ③	1	3	

Brand related properties: Price ❷, Gloss ❸, Stain removal ❹, Scrubbing ❺, Spatter ❻, Blocking ❼, Water resistance ❽

① *Grayer than most whites.* ② *Whiter than most whites.* ③ *Tended to change color when scrubbed with scouring powder.*

⑤ **Scrubbing.** Paint should last. We counted the scrubs needed to remove a standard thickness of paint.

⑥ **Spatter.** The better the score, the less likely that paint will fly off the roller.

⑦ **Blocking.** This tendency of paint to remain tacky even after it's dry makes windows stick to windowsills. It can be a problem among the glossier products.

⑧ **Water resistance.** All latex paints can be tender when wet. Avoid using any product judged lower than ⊖ where paint could come in contact with water.

⑨ **Hiding.** The numbers here correspond to paint concealment (based on a Consumers Union test of rolled-out paints). On a scale of light-to-dark—or worst to best coverage—1 is light and 6 is dark. The two columns indicate these results after the first and second coats of paint, respectively. Very few paints scored 5 or 6 after one coat.

⑩ **Fading.** Exposure to even indirect sunlight can age some colored paints prematurely. If you use a product that scored low, the walls are likely to show color differences if you rearrange pictures a few years after you've painted.

Color-related properties

Pink	Hiding, 1 coat ⑨	Hiding, 2 coats ⑨	Fading ⑩	Green	Hiding, 1 coat ⑨	Hiding, 2 coats ⑨	Fading ⑩	Blue	Hiding, 1 coat ⑨	Hiding, 2 coats ⑨	Fading ⑩	Yellow	Hiding, 1 coat ⑨	Hiding, 2 coats ⑨	Fading ⑩
Rose Mist	2	6	●	Silver Leaf	4	6	●	Azure Foam	4	6	●	Celestial Yellow	2	6	⊖
Heathermist	2	6	●	Green (436)	5	6	●	Blue (715)	3	6	⊖	Yellow (276) ③	2	6	⊖
Heathermist	2	6	●	Green (436)	4	6	●	Blue (715)	3	6	●	Yellow (276) ③	2	6	⊖
Stick Candy	3	6	●	Frosted Mint	5	6	●	Blue Bell	5	6	●	Candlelight	3	6	⊖
Peppermint Ice	2	5	●	Aspen Meadow	5	6	●	Crystal Blue	2	6	●	Chiffon Yellow	2	6	⊖
Pink	1	4	●	Green	2	6	○	Blue	2	6	●	Yellow	1	4	⊖
Pink	1	3	●	Green	2	6	○	Blue	2	6	●	Yellow	1	3	⊖
Light Tint	1	4	●	Aurora Green ⑤	1	4	⊖	Jawyn Blue	2	6	●	Macaroon Yellow	2	6	○
Peppermint	2	6	⊖	Glacial Green	2	6	⊖	Blue Chiffon	1	5	●	Corn Silk	2	5	○
Boutique	0	2	●	Green Breath	1	5	●	Whisper Blue	1	4	●	Arctic Sun ③	1	4	⊖
Peach Tree	0	2	●	Green Cove	0	2	⊖	Blue Bow	1	3	●	Froth	0	1	⊖
Lotus	2	6	●	Vagabond	1	5	●	Opaline	3	6	●	May Yellow	1	3	○
Lotus	2	5	●	Vagabond	1	5	⊖	Opaline	3	6	●	May Yellow	1	3	○
Peppermint	2	5	●	Fresh Lime	3	6	⊖	Aqua Crystal	5	6	●	Pond Lily ③	0	2	⊖
Peppermint	2	5	●	Fresh Lime ③	3	6	○	Aqua Crystal	3	6	●	Pond Lily ③	0	2	⊖
Stick Candy	1	3	●	Frosted Mint	2	6	⊖	Blue Bell	2	6	●	Candlelight	1	3	⊖
Rose Mist	2	5	●	Silver Leaf	2	6	●	Azure Foam	3	6	●	Celestial Yellow ③	2	6	⊖
Rose Mist	2	6	●	Silver Leaf	4	6	●	Azure Foam	3	6	●	Celestial Yellow ③	2	6	⊖
Peppermint Ice	1	3	○	Aspen Meadow	5	6	●	Crystal Blue	2	6	●	Chiffon Yellow	2	6	⊖
Peppermint Ice	1	4	○	Aspen Meadow	4	6	●	Crystal Blue	2	6	●	Chiffon Yellow	1	4	⊖
Pink	2	6	●	Green	2	6	●	Blue	3	6	●	Yellow	2	6	○
Pink	2	6	●	Green	2	6	●	Blue	3	6	●	Yellow	2	6	○
Tender Pink	2	6	●	Gossamer	2	6	●	Country Mist	3	6	●	Lemon Chiffon ③	2	6	⊖
Tender Pink	2	6	●	Gossamer	2	6	●	Country Mist	2	6	●	Lemon Chiffon ③	2	6	●
Pink Hibiscus	2	6	●	Tropic Mist	3	6	●	Suave	2	6	●	Celestial Yellow	2	6	●
Pink	1	4	●	Green	2	6	○	Blue	2	6	●	Yellow	1	3	⊖
Blush Pink	2	6	⊖	Mint Frost	1	4	○	Crystal Blue	2	6	●	Sunlight	2	6	○
Boutique	1	3	●	Green Breath	1	5	●	Whisper Blue	1	5	●	Arctic Sun	2	6	⊖
Sweet Pea	1	3	●	Green Ice	1	3	○	Blue Bow	2	6	●	Gin Fizz ③	1	3	●
Peppermint Ice	0	2	●	Aspen Meadow	2	6	●	Crystal Blue	1	3	●	Chiffon Yellow	0	2	⊖
Pink	1	3	●	Green	1	5	●	Blue	2	5	●	Yellow	1	4	○
Pink Dream	2	6	●	Mae Mist	4	6	●	Clear Blue Sky	3	6	●	Sunny Yellow	2	6	●
Flamingo	2	6	●	Celedon Green	6	6	●	Desert Sky	5	6	●	Yellow	1	4	●
Pink Dream	1	3	●	Whisper Green	1	3	●	Clear Blue	3	6	●	Sunny Yellow	1	3	⊖
Blush	1	4	⊖	Green Haze	2	6	●	Chalk Blue	3	6	●	Pond Lily	0	3	⊖
Pink Cloud	1	3	●	Dew Drop	2	5	●	Blue Diamond	2	6	●	Lemon Dew ③	1	3	⊖
Winsome	1	3	●	My Lover	2	6	●	Baltic	2	6	●	Jonquil	0	3	⊖
—	—	—	—	—	—	—	—	Hazy Blue	3	6	●	Lemon Yellow	2	5	●
Peach Tree	2	5	●	Green Cove	2	6	○	Blue Bow	3	6	●	Froth	1	5	⊖
Pink Cloud	0	2	●	Dew Drop	0	2	●	Blue Diamond	1	4	●	Lemon Dew ③	0	2	○

④ *Too variable to rate.*   ⑤ *Not a current color.*   ⑥ *New formulation now in stores.*

195

Ratings of Interior Semigloss Paints

Listed by types. Within types, listed alphabetically. Brand-performance judgments apply to all colors within a brand. Dashes indicate that a suitable color wasn't available. Prices are the manufacturer's suggested retail price per gallon, rounded to the nearest dollar.

❶ Gloss. Some "semiglosses" were shinier than others. Observed judgments of gloss are divided into three categories. Low (L) appeared merely satiny. High (H) approached the shininess of a glossy enamel. Medium (M) was in between, and is probably the best choice if you're looking for a clear-cut semigloss finish.

❷ Brushing ease. Alkyd paints are stickier and thus not as easy to brush on as the latexes.

❸ Leveling. A paint that scored well shows a minimum of brush marks when it is dry.

❹ Sagging. A judgment of how much a paint may run or "curtain" when applied with a brush.

❺ Spattering. Paints that scored well here resisted the tendency to spin paint mist off a roller.

❻ Scrubbing. The tougher a paint's dried surface, the more it can resist repeated cleanings.

As published in the May 1989 issue of Consumer Reports.

Brand and model	Price ❶	Gloss ❶	Brushing ❷	Leveling ❸	Sagging ❹	Spattering ❺	Scrubbing ❻	Water ❼	Blocking ❽	WHITE Color name	One-coat hiding ❾	Two-coat hiding ❾	Fading ❿	GOLD Color name	One-coat hiding ❾	Two-coat hiding ❾	Fading ❿
Alkyd (oil-based)																
Benjamin Moore Satin Impervo Series 235	$25	L	○	◐	○	◐	◐	●	●	White	1	4	○	Golden Glow	3	6	◐
Devoe Velour Series 26XX	27	M	◐	○	○	◐	◐	●	●	White	1	4	○	Swirl	5	6	◐
Dutch Boy Dirt Fighter Series 555XX	18	M	○	○	○	●	◐	●	●	Diamond White	2	5	◐	Champagne	3	6	◐
Glidden Spred Lustre Series 4600	27	H	○	○	○	◐	◐	●	●	White	1	3	◐	Buttered Rum	2	6	◐
Glidden Spred Ultra Series 4200	30	L	○	◐	○	◐	◐	●	●	Bright White	2	5	○	Buttered Rum	2	6	◐
Pittsburgh Wallhide Series 27	26	H	○	◐	○	●	◐	●	●	White	1	4	◐	Cactus Flower	2	3	◐
Pratt & Lambert Pro-Hide Plus E3800	21	M	○	◐	○	●	◐	●	●	White	2	5	○	Wind Song	5	6	◐
✓ Pratt & Lambert Cellu-Tone Series C30572	30	L	○	◐	◐	◐	◐	●	●	One Coat White	2	6	○	Wind Song	5	6	◐
Sherwin-Williams Classic 99	26	L	○	○	◐	◐	◐	●	●	Pure White	2	5	◐	Caramel Corn	3	6	●
Tru-Test Supreme Satin W-Line	22	L	○	◐	◐	○	◐	●	●	White	2	5	◐	Sunny Mesa	2	6	○
Valspar Semi-Gloss Enamel Series 614	25	M	○	◐	○	◐	◐	●	●	Super White	2	6	●	Javelin	5	6	●
Latex (water-based)																
Benjamin Moore Regal Aquaglo Series 333	23	L	●	◐	◐	○	◐	◐	○	Non-Yellowing White	2	5	●	Golden Glow	3	6	○
Devoe Wonder-Tones Interior Series 38XXN	26	H	●	◐	◐	●	◐	◐	○	White	2	4	◐	Swirl	2	6	○
Dutch Boy Super Kem-Tone	18	L	●	◐	◐	◐	◐	◐	●	White	1	2	●	Wheat Grain	4	6	●
Dutch Boy Dirt Fighter Series 73XX	18	L	●	◐	◐	◐	◐	●	●	White	1	2	●	Champagne	3	6	●
Dutch Boy (K Mart) Fashion Fresh	14	L	●	◐	◐	○	○	◐	●	White White	1	2	●	Honeycomb	2	5	●
Dutch Boy (K Mart) The Fresh Look	18	L	●	◐	○	①	◐	◐	●	White White	1	3	●	Honeycomb	3	6	●
Fuller-O'Brien Double AA Series 214XX	21	M	●	○	◐	◐	◐	●	◐	White	1	4	●	Perfect Gold	6	6	◐
Fuller-O'Brien Ful-Flo Series 614XX	25	M	●	○	○	◐	◐	◐	●	White	2	4	◐	Perfect Gold	2	6	◐
Glidden Spred Enamel Series 3700	21	L	●	◐	◐	◐	◐	○	●	High Hiding White	1	3	●	Buttered Rum	2	6	○
Kelly-Moore Acry-Plex Series 1650	24	M	●	◐	◐	○	◐	○	●	White	1	3	●	Gold	4	6	●
Lucite Wall & Trim Enamel Series 1699	19	L	●	◐	●	◐	◐	○	●	White	1	3	●	Natural Beige	2	6	●
Magicolor Luster Plus Series 4211	18	L	●	◐	◐	◐	◐	○	●	Non-Yellowing White	2	4	●	Spice Beige	5	6	●
Montgomery Ward Ultra Coat Series 3696②	22	L	●	○	●	◐	◐	◐	○	White	2	5	●	Light Coin Gold	2	5	●
Pittsburgh Satinhide Series 88-00	21	L	●	○	◐	①	○	○	●	White	1	4	●	Cactus Flower	1	2	●
Pratt & Lambert Aqua Satin Series Z32372	26	L	●	◐	○	◐	◐	○	●	One Coat White	2	4	◐	Wind Song	3	6	◐
Sears Easy Living Semi-Gloss Series 7100	15	L	●	◐	◐	◐	◐	○	●	Non-Yellowing White	2	5	●	Golden Harvest	2	6	●
Sears Easy Living for a Lifetime Series 7700	20	L	●	◐	◐	◐	◐	●	◐	Pure White	3	6	●	Golden Harvest	4	6	●
Sherwin-Williams Classic 99	21	L	●	◐	◐	◐	◐	◐	◐	Pure White	1	3	●	Caramel Corn	2	6	●
✓ Sherwin-Williams Superpaint	24	L	●	◐	◐	●	◐	●	◐	Pure White	2	6	●	Caramel Corn	4	6	●
Tru-Test Supreme E-Z Kare Series EZS	22	L	●	○	◐	◐	◐	○	●	White	1	4	●	Sunny Mesa	2	6	●
Valspar Acrylic Series 42214	22	L	●	◐	◐	●	◐	○	●	White	2	5	●	Javelin	3	6	◐

① *Too variable, sample to sample, to spatter.*   ② *This brand discontinued in the colors tested.*

7 Water-resistance. This measures how impervious to standing water a paint was. Important for surfaces likely to be wetted, such as tabletops, bathroom walls, and plant shelves.

8 Blocking. Blocking is a tendency for paint to stay tacky even after it has dried. More of a problem with latex paints, blocking makes some brands unsuitable for use on working surfaces such as bookshelves and tables.

9 Hiding power. The numbers here correspond to paint concealment (based on a Consumers Union test of rolled-out paints). On a scale of light to dark—or worst to best coverage—1 is light and 6 is dark. The two columns indicate these coverage results after the first and second coats of paint, respectively. Very few paints scored a "6" after only one coat.

10 Fading. How well the individual colors hold up to the bleaching effects of sunlight. The lowest-scoring paints can fade even in indirect sun.

Properties specific to individual colors

PINK	One-coat hiding ⑨	Two-coat hiding ⑨	Fading ⑩	GREEN	One-coat hiding ⑨	Two-coat hiding ⑨	Fading ⑩	BLUE	One-coat hiding ⑨	Two-coat hiding ⑨	Fading ⑩	YELLOW	One-coat hiding ⑨	Two-coat hiding ⑨	Fading ⑩
Heathermist	2	6	◐	Green Whisper	2	6	◐	Country Blue	6	6	◐	Chrysanthemum	1	4	●
Pixie Pink	2	5	◐	Pistachio	2	6	◐	Blue Magic	4	6	◐	Spring Tint	1	3	○
—	—	—	—	Mint Frost	2	6	◐	Crystal Blue	3	6	◐	Sunlight	2	4	◐
Sweet Clover	2	5	◐	Green Ice	2	5	○	Biscayne Blue	3	6	◐	Gin Fizz	1	3	○
Sweet Clover	2	6	○	Green Ice	2	6	◒	Biscayne Blue	5	6	◐	Gin Fizz	2	3	○
Stick Candy	1	5	●	Frosted Mint	4	6	●	Danish Blue	3	6	●	Sugar Cookie	2	4	◐
Rose Mist	2	5	◐	Cool Eve	3	6	◐	Azure Foam	3	6	◐	Celestial Yellow	2	5	◐
Rose Mist	2	5	◐	Cool Eve	4	6	◐	Azure Foam	3	6	◐	Celestial Yellow	2	5	◐
Cotton Candy Pink	2	5	●	Iceberg Lettuce	3	6	●	Clearly Blue	4	6	●	Yellow Primrose	1	2	◐
Orange Blossom	1	3	○	Gossamer Green	2	6	○	Skyline Blue	4	6	○	Lemon Cream	1	2	○
Blush	2	6	●	Green Haze	4	6	◐	Sky	4	6	●	Sunshine Yellow	2	4	●
Heathermist	1	3	●	Green Whisper	2	6	●	Country Blue	4	6	●	Chrysanthemum	2	3	◐
Pixie Pink	2	6	◐	Pistachio	4	6	◐	Blue Magic	5	6	◐	Spring Tint	2	4	○
—	—	—	—	Orient Green	2	5	●	Hazy Blue	3	6	●	Lemon Yellow	2	5	◐
—	—	—	—	Mint Frost	1	4	●	Crystal Blue	4	6	●	Sunlight	1	3	○
—	—	—	—	Mint Frost	1	3	◐	Bellflower	2	6	●	Corn Yellow	1	2	◐
Pink Whisper	2	6	●	Mimosaceae	1	5	●	Bellflower	3	6	●	Yellow Bud	1	3	●
Pink Ruff	1	2	●	Marsh	5	6	●	Heidi	4	6	●	Marguerite	1	2	●
Pink Ruff	1	2	◐	Marsh	5	6	◐	Heidi	3	6	◐	Marguerite	1	2	◐
Sweet Clover	1	3	●	Green Ice	1	3	●	Biscayne Blue	2	5	●	Gin Fizz	1	2	◐
Pink	2	6	●	Green	3	6	●	Blue	3	6	●	Yellow	1	3	◐
Rose Pearl	1	3	●	Spring Green	2	6	◐	Dove Blue	2	6	●	—	—	—	—
—	—	—	—	Mint Cooler	2	4	◐	Blue Horizon	2	6	●	Daffodil Yellow	1	4	◐
Pink Cloud	2	6	●	Light Mint	2	6	◐	Blue Diamond	4	6	●	Sunflower	1	2	◒
Stick Candy	1	2	●	Frosted Mint	2	5	◐	Danish Blue	2	6	●	Sugar Cookie	1	2	◐
Rose Mist	2	5	◐	Cool Eve	3	6	◐	Azure Foam	2	6	◐	Celestial Yellow	2	4	○
Apple Blossom	2	6	◒	Huckleberry Green	4	6	●	Federal Slate	3	6	●	Sunflower Yellow	2	4	◐
Apple Blossom	3	6	◒	Huckleberry Green	6	6	●	Federal Slate	5	6	●	Sunflower Yellow	2	6	●
Cotton Candy Pink	1	3	●	Iceberg Lettuce	2	6	●	Clearly Blue	3	6	●	Yellow Primrose	1	3	◐
Cotton Candy Pink	1	3	●	Iceberg Lettuce	4	6	●	Clearly Blue	3	6	●	Yellow Primrose	2	3	◐
Rose Quartz	1	4	●	Gossamer Green	2	6	●	Skyline Blue	1	4	●	Lemon Chiffon	1	2	○
Blush	2	5	◒	Green Haze	2	6	●	Sky	3	6	●	Sunshine Yellow	1	4	◐

RATINGS OF LIGHT BULBS

Listed by types. Within types, listed in order of overall quality based on measurements of life and light output.

① Product. Energy-saving bulbs run on 5 watts less power than the other bulbs in their group.

② Price. Average price paid. Bulb prices often are discounted, and rebates and coupons are common.

③ Labeled lumens. The manufacturer's claim of light output, from the packages. Long-life bulbs sacrifice some light to gain extra life.

④ Light output. An assessment of relative brightness when the bulbs were new and after 500 hours of testing (1,500 hours for the

Duro-Lites). The tests included 36 bulbs per brand (18 for the Duro-Lites); to simulate home use, lights were turned off for 12 minutes every four hours. The tests showed that the manufacturers' estimates of lumen output are accurate, for the most part. The exceptions: the Philips Econo-Miser bulbs and the 60-watt Duro-Lite, which when new delivered 8 to 10 percent less light than promised. Light bulbs can be expected to dim somewhat over time, but some dim more than others.

⑤ Life. What the manufacturer says on the label and on estimate of median life, in hours. The median is the number at which half the bulbs lasted longer and half burned out sooner. However, the lifetimes of individual bulbs can vary a lot.

⑥ Percent exceeded labeled life. The percentage of test samples that outlived their labeled lifetime. Another way of looking at longevity, this shows your chances of getting a long-lasting bulb, given the variability in the lifetimes of individual bulbs. (The relation of this number to the median lifetime depends on how tightly the lifetimes were clustered around the median.)

⑦ Cost per 1,000 hours. Typically, a bulb is used 1,000 hours a year. This figure was arrived at by dividing the cost of a bulb by its hours of life.

⑧ Efficiency. The average over the bulb's lifetime, measured in lumens per watt. The higher the number, the more efficient the bulb.

As published in the January 1990 issue of Consumer Reports.

Better ◄────► Worse

① Product	② Price	③ Labeled lumens	④ Light output	⑤ Life, hours	⑥ % exceeded labeled life	⑦ Cost per 1,000 hours	⑧ Efficiency, lumens per watt
60-watt bulbs							
Philips Soft White	$ .70	860	●/◖	1000/1380	92%	$ .51	13.0
General Electric Miser	.89	855	●/○	1000/984	44	.90	13.9
Sylvania Soft White	.70	870	●/◖	1000/949	31	.74	13.1
General Electric Soft White	.77	855	●/◖	1000/1018	53	.76	13.1
Sylvania Soft Energy Pincher	.87	870	●/○	1000/855	17	1.02	13.8
Philips Econo-Miser	.95	860	◖/○	1000/1013	53	.94	13.4
Duro-Lite X2500 (long life)	1.70	780	◖/●	2500/4500+	83	.34	10.5
100-watt bulbs							
Philips Soft White	.67	1710	●/○	750/820	72	.82	15.2
General Electric Soft White	.77	1710	●/○	750/717	25	1.07	15.3
General Electric Miser	.90	1710	●/◖	750/716	39	1.26	15.6
Sylvania Soft Energy Pincher	.93	1710	●/◖	750/646	31	1.44	15.7
Sylvania Soft White	.70	1710	●/◖	788/728	36	.96	14.5
Philips Econo-Miser	.90	1670	○/◖	750/856	75	1.05	14.7
Duro-Lite X2500 (long life)	1.61	1490	○/●	2500/2912	72	.55	13.1

Listed by type. Within types, listed by height in order of estimated quality, based primarily on safety and on convenience as judged by a panel of users.

❶ **Brand and model.** The fiberglass/aluminum models are popular with contractors. The others are sold primarily to do-it-yourselfers. Fiberglass/aluminum and wood ladders can safely be used anywhere. Aluminum ladders should not be used outdoors with electric tools because the ladders can conduct electricity. If you can't find a model, call the company.

❷ **Price.** The average price paid. A + indicates that shipping was extra.

❸ **Working load.** Manufacturers' claims for the maximum weight a ladder should bear, as determined in standard industry tests. These figures correspond to the weight limits in the duty rating displayed on each ladder. For safety's sake, your weight plus that of the materials you bring onto the ladder with you should never exceed the working load. A 200- or 225-pound working load is enough for most people.

❹ **Resistance to swaying.** A key judgment from panelists. It shows the stability of a ladder as you climb, shifting your weight from step to step, or perch on the highest step you can safely occupy.

❺ **Resistance to "walking."** This panel test judgment shows which ladders are most likely to chatter along the floor as you shift your weight from step to step. A ladder that "walks" too much can scuff the floor, upset a can of paint, or even make you fall.

As published in the September 1990 issue of Consumer Reports.

❶ Brand and model	❷ Price	Weight	❸ Working load	❹ Swaying	❺ "Walking"	❻ Tipping	❼ Opening & closing	❽ Carrying	❾ Moving	Advantages	Disadvantages	Comments
Fiberglass/aluminum, 6-ft.												
Keller 976	$92	21 lb.	300 lb.							A,B	—	A,E
Werner 7206	168	23	300							A,E	h	A,E
Aluminum, 6-ft.												
Werner 376	120	14	250							A,B,C,D,E,F	—	A,C
Keller 916	63	17	250							B,C,D	—	A
Keller Greenline 926	53	12	225							B,C,D	—	A
Keller 936	48	11	200							B,C,D	—	A
Sears Craftsman 42386	58+	14	225							A,D	c,h	A,G,H
White Metal Wonderlight 21006	67	11	225							D	c,h	G
Werner 366	74	12	225							A,B,C,F	—	A
Sears Craftsman 42156	40	11	200							D	f,h	H
White Metal Easylight 31106	42	10	200							D	f,h	—
Werner 356	60	12	200							B,F	—	A
Aluminum, 8-ft.												
Keller Greenline 928	93	17	225							C,D	h	A
White Metal Heartsaver 22008	81	17	225							A,D	c,h	A,G
Sears Craftsman 42388	79	18	225							A,D	h	A,G,H
Wood, 6-ft.												
Werner W356	29	20	200							A,B,D	d	—
Werner W366	58	22	225							A,B,D,F	—	A
Putnam Peerless	59	22	225							A,D	h	D
Sears 40116	20	17	200							A,D	b	B,H
Lynn No. 76 Supertred SUS06	58	21	225							A,B,D	a,g	—
Werner W336	38	17	200							A,B,D,F	d,g	—
Lynn No. 75 Patriot PA506	46	19	200							A,B	a,g	D
Archbold 16006	38	21	225							A,B,D	b,d,g	—
Keller W2-6	27	21	225							A,B,D	g	—
Keller W-6	32	18	200							A,B,D	a,d,g	—
Putnam Durable	48	20	200							A,D	h	D
Archbold 14006	28	19	200							A,B,D	a,b,g	F
Wood, 8-ft.												
Werner W368	78	30	225							A,B,D	i	A
Keller W2-8	56	30	225							A,B,D	d,e	—

⑥ **Resistance to tipping.** Panelists gauged tippiness by putting one foot on the ladder's lowest step and grabbing the ladder with one hand while carrying a small but bulky load in the other. The wider the angle between an open ladder's front and back legs, the less likely the ladder is to tip.

⑦ **Ease of opening and closing.** The panelists opened and closed each ladder several times. Balky hinges, sticky pivots, and such lowered a ladder's score.

⑧ **Ease of carrying.** A difference of a pound or two didn't seem to matter to panelists, who carried the ladders closed.

⑨ **Ease of moving.** How easily you can pick up an opened ladder and move it a few feet. Light weight, a comfortable handhold, and proper balance were assets panelists looked for.

Specifications and Features
All 6-ft. models: Let you safely stand no more than 3 ft. 7 in. to 3 ft. 10 in. from ground.
All 8-ft. models: Let you safely stand no more than 5 ft. 3 in. to 5 ft. 9 in. from ground.

Except as noted, all models have: Grooves or traction treads on steps to deter slipping.
All wood models have: Steel tie rods under steps for structural integrity.
All aluminum and fiberglass/aluminum models have: Pad at bottom of each leg to protect floors and deter slipping.

Key to Advantages
A— Space between side rails reduces pinching hazard.
B— Spreaders, which hold ladder open, unlikely to pinch fingers
C— Pail shelf has rounded corners. For 6-ft. models, that design judged less hazardous than sharp corners on others; for 8-ft. models, rounded corners matter less, since shelf is 6½ ft. from floor.
D— Pail shelf folds automatically when ladder closes.
E— Spreaders are protected from damage because they are inside side rails.
F— Has clips to keep folded ladder closed (but clips are easily lost).

Key to Disadvantages
a— Wobbled noticeably without load.
b— Leg bottoms were not horizontal to floor and could damage it.
c— Failed American National Standards Institute test for step-bending.

d— Tested samples had splinters as received.
e— Pail shelf broke when ladder was closing.
f— Pail shelf judged likely to strike you in the face when folding ladder.
g— Pail shelf could strike you in the face when folding ladder, a slight hazard.
h— Spreaders could pinch or squeeze fingers when you're closing the ladder.
i— Truss block, which supports steps, fell out when we tested ladder's ability to withstand severe load.

Key to Comments
A— Top plate or pail shelf accommodates tools.
B— Lacks spreaders; pail shelf keeps ladder open.
C— Has "H"-shaped spreaders with handle; allows ladder to be opened and closed with one hand.
D— Has smooth (not grooved) step surfaces, judged comfortable for standing.
E— Lacks pail shelf.
F— The rods under steps judged likely to need tightening more often than on most wood models.
G— Has 5-yr. warranty.
H— Discontinued but may still be available in some Sears retail stores. Replacements as follows: 40116 by 40306, $20; 42386 by 42176, $50; 42156 by 42216, $40; 42388 by 42178, $80.

Listed in order of estimated quality, based on water resistance.

❶ Brand and model. Most are available only in white; footnotes list the exceptions. If more than one color was available, both white and beige were tested.

❷ Type. The oil-based epoxy liquids (OEL) have to be mixed with the catalyst provided and applied within 30 minutes or they become too thick to use. The oil-based liquids (OL) come ready to use but should only be applied to dry walls because oil does not adhere to water. Cementlike powders (P) have to be mixed with water; if you mix more than you can apply in about 4 hours, the paint hardens in the pail. The powders are best applied to a wet wall. Water-based liquids (WL) are the easiest to use; they are ready-mixed and can be brushed onto damp or dry walls. Water-based epoxy (WEL), like the other epoxies, must be mixed with a catalyst.

❸ Price. The manufacturer's suggested retail price, rounded to the nearest dollar.

These paints are rarely on sale. + means shipping is extra.

❹ Size. Only the weight of the powders is listed. It's hard to say how many gallons of paint they can make because the amount of water to be added varies with each brand.

❺ Cost for sample basement. An estimate, rounded to the nearest $25, of what it costs to apply two coats to 1120 square feet of concrete wall. These paints are generally comparable in price to interior wall paint, but a gallon doesn't go as far since it has to cover a rough, pitted surface.

❻ Water resistance. The bars in the graph show how waterproof these paints were. To measure water resistance, testers at Consumers Union put two coats of paint on concrete blocks, sealed the openings in each block, then suspended a water tank 8 feet overhead; tubing from the tank let water flow into the cavities, to simulate the water pressure exerted at the bottom of a typical basement wall. The condition of the blocks was checked periodically, and the water tank was weighed to find out how much water was seeping through the paint. Statisticians analyzed the leakage-rate data to produce the index of water resistance shown here.

❼ Ease of application. How easy it was to apply each paint, using a short, stiff-bristled brush. Waterproofing paints are much harder to work with than wall paints because you must apply them with a stabbing or scrubbing motion to seal all the pin-sized holes in concrete blocks.

❽ Stain removal. How easily a grease stain could be removed from a painted block, using a soft brush and an all-purpose household cleaner.

❾ Surface smoothness. The smoothest felt like standard wall paint; the roughest, like a concrete driveway. Rough walls may not matter if you use your basement for storage only, but you may want a nicer finish if the basement serves as a living space.

As published in the February 1990 issue of Consumer Reports.

Better ◄———► Worse

❶ Brand and model	❷ Type	❸ Price	❹ Size	❺ Cost of sample basement	❻ Water resistance	❼ Ease of application	❽ Stain removal	❾ Surface smoothness
✓ Barrier System Cat. No. 502 Epoxy Resin①②	OEL	$41+	5 qt.③	$500	100	○	◕	●
✓ Atlas Epoxybond Epoxy Waterproof Sealant①	OEL	54	3 qt.③	825		◕	●	●
Glidden Spred Waterproof Basement Paint④	OL	15	1 gal.	350		○	●	●
Bondex Waterproof Cement Paint④	OL	21	1 gal.	475		◕	◕	◕
Tru-Test Supreme						◕	◕	◕
Tru-Seal Waterproofing Masonry Paint④	OL	18	1 gal.	400		◕	●	●
UGL Drylok Masonry Waterproofer	OL	18	1 gal.	400		◕	◕	◕
Moore's Waterproofing Masonry Paint⑤	OL	18	1 gal.	400		◕	◕	◕
Thoro Super Thoroseal Redi-Mix Liquid④	OL	57	2 gal.	625		◕	◕	●
Thoro Super Thoroseal④	P	29	20 lb.	675		◕	◕	●
Quikrete Heavy Duty Masonry Coating	P	12	40 lb.	150		●	●	●
Bondex Waterproof Cement Paint	P	19	25 lb.	100		◕	●	○
UGL Drylok Double Duty Sealer④	P	26	35 lb.	350		◕	●	●
Quikrete Waterproofing Masonry Coating	P	10	20 lb.	225		◕	●	●
Muralo Tite Vinyl Latex Waterproofing Paint	WL	15	1 gal.	350		●	●	●
Sears Basement Waterproofing Latex Wall Paint (Series 5640)	WL	11+	1 gal.	250		⊙	⊙	●
Not Acceptable								
■ *The following product was judged Not Acceptable because of extremely poor water resistance.*								
Sears Dry Living Aqua Poxy (Series 5616)	WEL	27+	1 gal.⑥	550		⊙	○	⊙

Water resistance scale: 0 20 40 60 80 100

① Available only as clear sealer. Manufacturer of **Atlas** says product can be tinted slightly.
② Available from Defender Indo, P.O. Box 820, New Rochelle, N.Y. 10801-0820.
③ Includes catalyst.
④ Available in white only.
⑤ Available in white only. Manufacturer says product can be tinted.
⑥ Includes catalyst and filler.

INDEX